The Hidden Meaning of Birthdays .

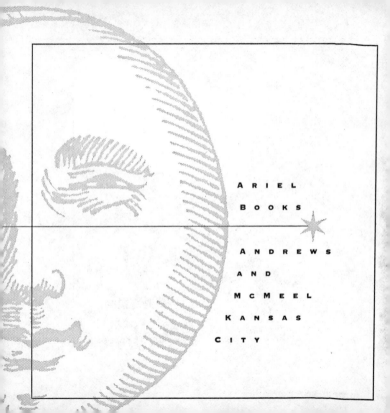

ARIEL BOOKS

ANDREWS AND McMEEL KANSAS CITY

The
Hidden
Meaning
of Birthdays

NANCY ARNOTT

Back Design by JUDITH STAGNITTO ASBATE
Typesetting by NINA GASKIN

ISBN: 0-8362-1516-8

Library of Congress Catalog Card Number:
96-83360

First Printing, August 1996
Third Printing, June 1997

Introduction

ARE YOU A TRAILBLAZER?
A true romantic? A behind-the-scenes negotiator?
Is your mate—or your best friend—supportive
and affectionate? Idealistic? Creative and
impetuous? What makes you who you
are? What makes you (and everyone you
know) tick?

Birthdays—the "launching pads"
of our lives—play a bigger role than
we realize in shaping our character.
They speak a mysterious but powerful language, carrying a secret for-

mula that defines the very essence of personality and human nature.

On your birthday, many invisible influences conspired to create *you,* with all the traits, quirks, and tendencies that mark you as an individual. Milestones in history, new inventions, famous people, and astrological events round out your personal portrait. Look up your birthday, your mate's, or your friends' as you explore the fascinating mystery of personality, destiny, and romance.

Discover the hidden meaning of birthdays!

The
Hidden
Meaning
of Birthdays .

January 1

ASTROLOGICAL SIGN: Capricorn

PEOPLE BORN TODAY: J. D. Salinger, Ellen DeGeneres, Paul Revere, Grandmaster Flash, Idi Amin Dada, Frank Langella, Alfred Stieglitz, Rocky Graziano, J. Edgar Hoover, Barry Goldwater, Betsy Ross, E. M. Forster

FAMOUS EVENTS: Emancipation Proclamation signed by President Abraham Lincoln (1863); first Rose Bowl game (1902); first female Episcopal priest ordained (1977)

LUCKY NUMBER: 2

BIRTHSTONE: Garnet

POSITIVE TRAITS: Honest, responsible, committed

NEGATIVE TRAITS: Conventional, impatient, oversensitive

You were born to be boss. Both at home and at work, you are most comfortable charting the course for others and steering them along. You set ambitious goals for yourself and more often than not, you meet them. With your diligence and fortitude, the inevitable setbacks you encounter along the way will hardly break your stride. Your patience and leadership abilities can make you a great parent and teacher. To find fulfillment in love, give your striving, competitive spirit a breather. Let your partner see frequent glimpses of your romantic, emotional nature that you are so good at concealing. Team sports can help you relax—particularly if you tone down your desire to be coach, captain, and star player all at once.

January 2

ASTROLOGICAL SIGN: Capricorn

PEOPLE BORN TODAY: Isaac Asimov, David Bailey, Nathaniel Bacon, Jim Bakker, Tia Carrere, Roger Miller, Ferdinand I

FAMOUS EVENTS: First gramophone records manufactured (1900); *Luna I* becomes first spacecraft to orbit the Sun (1959); Joe Namath signed by New York Jets (1965)

LUCKY NUMBER: 3

BIRTHSTONE: Garnet

POSITIVE TRAITS: Industrious, exacting, realistic

NEGATIVE TRAITS: Insecure, workaholic, self-critical

You are a classic "self-starter" whom everyone can count on to carry out responsibilities like clockwork. You enjoy duties and deadlines, but your physical and mental health will benefit if you make room in your life for pleasure and fun. No matter how busy you are, take the time to get together with friends and loved ones. They will keep you in touch with the lighter side of life and ease the worries that tend to overwhelm you. Your love life will improve greatly if you make an effort to put aside your projects and let your emotions flow. Escape from your structured routine with leisure activities that bring out the child in you such as roller skating, finger painting, or playing the kazoo.

January 3

ASTROLOGICAL SIGN: Capricorn

PEOPLE BORN TODAY: Mel Gibson, Stephen Stills, Victoria Principal, Danica McKellar, George Martin, Bobby Hull, Osip Mandelstam, Father Damien

FAMOUS EVENTS: Yerba Buena, California, renamed San Francisco (1847); oleomargarine patented (1871); New York Yankees bought by George Steinbrenner (1973)

LUCKY NUMBER: 4

BIRTHSTONE: Garnet

POSITIVE TRAITS: Persuasive, charming, dedicated

NEGATIVE TRAITS: Stubborn, willful, manipulative

You are single-minded and unstoppable: Whenever there's a job to be done, you give it your all and use whatever it takes—charm, guile, or pressure—to ensure that others do the same. Although you're a consummate team player, you have to be careful not to let your natural reserve keep you from voicing your own individual needs and desires. Your conversational gifts make you a delightful companion and your sense of honor and love of sensual pleasures makes you a loyal and satisfying partner. Your craving for success applies to romantic relationships as well: You want to make them work. An early-to-bed, early-to-rise routine, a varied diet, and adequate vitamin intake will keep you moving full steam ahead.

January 4

ASTROLOGICAL SIGN: Capricorn
PEOPLE BORN TODAY: Dyan Cannon, Don Shula, Michael Stipe, Patty Loveless, Jane Wyman, Floyd Patterson, George Washington Carver
FAMOUS EVENTS: First U.S. presidential address delivered (1790); first appendectomy performed (1885); Utah becomes the 45th state (1896);
LUCKY NUMBER: 5
BIRTHSTONE: Garnet
POSITIVE TRAITS: Analytical, independent, imaginative
NEGATIVE TRAITS: Controlling, unemotional, intolerant

You are quick-witted, well-organized, pragmatic, and creative. Your ideas and solutions get better results than those proposed by others. Patience is a virtue you have in spades: Despite the fact that your imagination and verve are magnets for potential mates, your wait for the perfect partner will cause you no pain and, more often than not, result in a lifelong pairing. In addition, you approach romantic possibilities with logic rather than with emotion. A structured hobby, such as tending to a collection, will satisfy your passion for organization and let you goof off without feeling guilty. Try to accept that everyone isn't as organized as you are; this will keep both your temper and your blood pressure from going through the roof.

ASTROLOGICAL SIGN: Capricorn

PEOPLE BORN TODAY: Alvin Ailey, Diane Keaton, Robert Duvall, Raisa Gorbachev, Walter Mondale, John Delorean, King Juan Carlos, Chuck Null

FAMOUS EVENTS: Nellie Ross becomes first female governor in U.S. (1925); "Heartbreak Hotel" recorded by Elvis Presley (1956); bill signed to create the Space Shuttle (1972)

LUCKY NUMBER: 6

BIRTHSTONE: Garnet

POSITIVE TRAITS: Hardy, confident, resourceful

NEGATIVE TRAITS: Complacent, inflexible, overoptimistic

You climb on toward your goal no matter how often you lose your footing—and when you set your cap for someone, you're unwavering in your quest to win your valentine's heart. Once you do so, you share your winning outlook with your mate and provide comfort and stability in challenging times. In fact, challenges are what you like best: They give you an opportunity to test your perseverance and creativity. Setbacks don't faze you; they simply offer opportunities to do what you do best: rebound. "If at first you don't succeed, try, try again" is your motto, and you teach it to others by example. Though your health is strong and your recuperative powers exceptional, try not to push your luck.

January 6

ASTROLOGICAL SIGN: Capricorn

PEOPLE BORN TODAY: E. L. Doctorow, Nancy Lopez, Howie Long, Lou Holtz, Earl Scruggs, Sun Myung Moon, Kahlil Gibran, Carl Sandburg, John Singleton

FAMOUS EVENTS: Telegraph demonstrated by Samuel Morse (1838); New Mexico becomes 47th state (1912); Nancy Kerrigan attacked by assailant linked to skating rival Tonya Harding (1994)

LUCKY NUMBER: 7

BIRTHSTONE: Garnet

POSITIVE TRAITS: High-minded, philosophical, courageous

NEGATIVE TRAITS: Naive, eccentric, unrealistic

You constantly look beneath the surface, seeking a spark of divinity in people and profound meaning in events. Your focus on the sublime may lead opponents to underestimate you, though your refusal to dwell on the negative and mundane may propel you to lofty heights. You fall in love easily, but beware turning a blind eye to your partner's faults. You relate to children on their own level, sharing their spontaneity and wide-eyed wonder at the world. Intellectual stimulation is a must for you and your quick wit makes you a favorite at parties and around dinner tables. Don't let your passion for mankind make you neglect your own well-being: Eat regularly and get plenty of sleep so you can energetically tackle new challenges.

January 7

ASTROLOGICAL SIGN: Capricorn

PEOPLE BORN TODAY: Kenny Loggins, Katie Couric, Nicolas Cage, Jean-Pierre Rampal, Jann Wenner, Vincent Gardenia, Zora Neale Hurston, Millard Fillmore

FAMOUS EVENTS: First balloon crossing of English Channel (1785); first U.S. presidential election held (1789); first game played by Harlem Globetrotters (1927)

LUCKY NUMBER: 8

BIRTHSTONE: Garnet

POSITIVE TRAITS: Curious, penetrating, broad-minded

NEGATIVE TRAITS: High-strung, isolated, intense

You are drawn to anything different, even strange, though most of your walks on the wild side take place in your imagination. You can best appreciate the passing parade from a stable base at home and at work, where you can be a successful mediator for divergent views and help to create a harmonious environment. Your generous nature allows you to encourage others to fulfill their creative urges and you delight in their successes and spontaneity, just as you accept their eccentricities. Unusual physical outlets like *tai chi* appeal to you and your avid curiosity may lead you to experiment with exotic or esoteric diets, though your basic common sense will keep you from going off the deep end in any venture.

January 8

ASTROLOGICAL SIGN: Capricorn

PEOPLE BORN TODAY: Elvis Presley, David Bowie, Stephen Hawking, Charles Osgood, Nolan Miller, Yvette Mimieux

FAMOUS EVENTS: British defeated at Battle of New Orleans (1815); French president Charles de Gaulle inaugurated (1959); Elvis Presley stamp issued (1993)

LUCKY NUMBER: 9

BIRTHSTONE: Garnet

POSITIVE TRAITS: Impressive, forceful, gifted

NEGATIVE TRAITS: Self-important, disdainful, relentless

Whether as scene-stealing showman or quiet authority, you make your presence felt. Because you have complete confidence in the rightness of your ideas and expect others to acknowledge your wisdom, you are bound to dominate most situations, acting as arbiter of behavior and trends. Your priorities may sometimes hinder your ability to recognize the contributions of others, but when they are brought to your attention, you are lavish with praise. Let go the reins in love and years of bliss can be yours. Though you enjoy playing games that test your knowledge, particularly those where there is only one right answer, spend some time playing cooperative games like team charades, which give you a chance to laugh—at yourself.

January 9

ASTROLOGICAL SIGN: Capricorn

PEOPLE BORN TODAY: Richard Nixon, Simone de Beauvoir, Joan Baez, Crystal Gayle, Judith Krantz, Jimmy Page, Gypsy Rose Lee, Pope Gregory XV

FAMOUS EVENTS: First successful balloon flight in U.S. (1793); first income tax imposed, in England (1799); first women's golf tournament (1811); ocean liner *Queen Elizabeth* gutted by fire (1972)

LUCKY NUMBER: 1

BIRTHSTONE: Garnet

POSITIVE TRAITS: Striving, dynamic, unstoppable

NEGATIVE TRAITS: Ruthless, self-centered, opportunistic

You want nothing but the best and you will do whatever it takes to achieve it. Whether you are climbing the career ladder, striving for a picture-perfect family life, or both, you keep your eye on the ball and shrug off any setbacks. You will be happiest with a mate who shares your high ideals and seriousness of purpose, and who will not feel neglected living with an ambitious, driven go-getter like yourself. Don't put your health on the line with your hard-driving habits. You may be reluctant to "waste" time on sports, hobbies, or travel, but daily workouts and frequent getaways may be just what the doctor ordered to restore balance and perspective to your life—and intimacy to your relationship.

January 10

ASTROLOGICAL SIGN: Capricorn

PEOPLE BORN TODAY: Rod Stewart, Donald Fagen, Sherrill Milnes, Ray Bolger, George Foreman, Pat Benatar, Max Roach, Robinson Jeffers, Jesse James

FAMOUS EVENTS: First correspondence course offered (1840); first-ever subway system opened, in London (1863); first meeting of the United Nations General Assembly (1946)

LUCKY NUMBER: 2

BIRTHSTONE: Garnet

POSITIVE TRAITS: Truthful, uncompromising, realistic

NEGATIVE TRAITS: Guarded, tactless, judgmental

You are a straight shooter who tells it as it is, a quality that may take you far—or land you in trouble. You may not advance as quickly as those more diplomatic, but you will ultimately earn respect. Romantic partners find your unpretentiousness refreshing, but you may find yourself in the doghouse more often than not if you do not take care to soften your typically blunt words. Your clearsighted and realistic approach to life makes it easy for you to cope with ups and downs, but the same qualities often make it hard for you to sympathize with those who find the vicissitudes of life more problematic. Find a physical outlet that will temper your strength with judgment and grace.

January 11

ASTROLOGICAL SIGN: Capricorn

PEOPLE BORN TODAY: Clarence Clemons, Grant Tinker, Naomi Judd, Daryl Dawkins, Rod Taylor, Tex Ritter, Eva Le Gallienne, Alexander Hamilton

FAMOUS EVENTS: Insulin first administered to diabetic patient (1922); Amelia Earhart becomes first woman to fly solo from Hawaii to mainland United States (1935); smoking cigarettes declared hazardous to health by U.S. surgeon general (1964)

LUCKY NUMBER: 3

BIRTHSTONE: Garnet

POSITIVE TRAITS: Incisive, even-tempered, analytical

NEGATIVE TRAITS: Stubborn, inflexible, judgmental

You carry an invisible yardstick with which you measure everyone you meet; you see to the core of people and situations and evaluate them according to your own high and unyielding standards. If anything, you place even higher standards on yourself and have the boldness and courage to live up to them. In love, once you find a partner who measures up you are loyal and devoted and take great pleasure in cultivating intimacy. In fact, you are most at ease in an intimate relationship where you can let go of your inhibitions and allow your romantic nature free expression. Though you don't wear your heart on your sleeve, close friends know you as tender and compassionate—a friend indeed.

January 12

ASTROLOGICAL SIGN: Capricorn

PEOPLE BORN TODAY: Jack London, Kirstie Alley, Howard Stern, Rush Limbaugh, the Amazing Kreskin, Joe Frazier, John Singer Sargent

FAMOUS EVENTS: First American public museum opens in Charleston, South Carolina (1773); first woman elected to U.S. Senate (1932); *All in the Family* premieres on TV (1971)

LUCKY NUMBER: 4

BIRTHSTONE: Garnet

POSITIVE TRAITS: Ambitious, aspiring, dedicated

NEGATIVE TRAITS: Obsessive, self-absorbed, unbalanced

Whatever you consider your destiny, whether it is directing a multinational corporation, feeding the starving millions, or raising a family, it becomes your single purpose in life. You cultivate friendships with those who share your dedication, and it matters little whether you have anything else in common with them. You admire and desire people who mirror your intensity, but a less obsessive partner will complement you better and provide the fun you might otherwise miss out on. You are constantly on the go, gathering information or following leads that will allow you to pursue your goals more creatively and efficiently. Though eating properly and exercising regularly may not be high on your "to do" list, do it anyway: Your energy is remarkable but not infinite.

January 13

ASTROLOGICAL SIGN: Capricorn

PEOPLE BORN TODAY: Robert Stack, Gwen Verdon, Julia Louis-Dreyfus, Charles Nelson Reilly, Brandon Tartikoff, Horatio Alger, Sophie Tucker

FAMOUS EVENTS: Accordion patented (1854); first opera broadcast over the radio (1910); Robert Weaver becomes first African-American cabinet member (1966); Hank Aaron elected to Baseball Hall of Fame (1982)

LUCKY NUMBER: 5

BIRTHSTONE: Garnet

POSITIVE TRAITS: Discriminating, exacting, accomplished

NEGATIVE TRAITS: Snobbish, egotistical, stubborn

You are an achiever; you make it all look easy. You coolly calculate what it will take to reach your goals, and effortlessly hurdle every obstacle in your path. High expectations of others makes you a tough taskmaster at work and at home. Holding back is not your style: If you deem people sloppy or lazy, you let them know. You seek a mate who is your social equal, or even a step up on the ladder, and although you share the fruits of your success with friends and family, wanting them to go far, this is partly because it will reflect well on you. You come closest to relaxing when making connections on the golf course or tennis court or networking at a social function.

ASTROLOGICAL SIGN: Capricorn

PEOPLE BORN TODAY: Andy Rooney, Faye Dunaway, Lawrence Kasdan, L. L. Cool J., Julian Bond, Jack Jones, John Dos Passos, Benedict Arnold, Albert Schweitzer, Berthe Morisot

FAMOUS EVENTS: First successful cesarean delivery (1794); *The Today Show* premieres on TV (1952); Marilyn Monroe and Joe DiMaggio wed (1954)

LUCKY NUMBER: 6

BIRTHSTONE: Garnet

POSITIVE TRAITS: Honest, observant, mediating

NEGATIVE TRAITS: Critical, unfeeling, undemonstrative

You see the world through a wide-angle lens, easily assimilating the details of the vast panoply under observation. Your keen eye and cool head let you play peacemaker, finding solutions that can bring together rival colleagues, estranged friends, or squabbling siblings; your good humor and good manners make you sought-after company. Your affections are deep and uncomplicated by jealousy; your ideal partner will be one who does not equate passion with possessiveness. Luckily, you are seldom tempted into bad habits such as smoking or excessive drinking, and your calm disposition has a protective effect on both your physical and mental health. Photography and journal writing will supply natural outlets for your powers of observation and your untapped well of creativity.

ASTROLOGICAL SIGN: Capricorn

PEOPLE BORN TODAY: Martin Luther King Jr., Aristotle Onassis, Lloyd Bridges, Gene Krupa, Chad Lowe, Lisa Lisa, Molière

FAMOUS EVENTS: First Super Bowl game (1915); Pentagon completed (1948); Sara Jane Moore sentenced for assassination attempt on President Gerald Ford (1976)

LUCKY NUMBER: 7

BIRTHSTONE: Garnet

POSITIVE TRAITS: Idealistic, sensual, kind

NEGATIVE TRAITS: Vain, self-indulgent, controlling

You possess both high ideals and a desire to wear the hero's crown; you would rather lead a splashy fund-raising campaign than toil anonymously in the local soup kitchen. As long as you get the credit, you are happy to contribute your innovative ideas to any cause. A mate who shares your big heart and caters to your appetite for attention will fit the bill perfectly. Though you are a loving partner and an affectionate friend, you often find yourself wishing that others would praise you more readily for your good deeds—or just for being you. Watch your calories: Your pleasure-loving side can lead you to excess. Work off extra pounds at a busy health club, where you can strive for perfection while others admire your form.

January 16

ASTROLOGICAL SIGN: Capricorn

PEOPLE BORN TODAY: Debbie Allen, Sade, Kate Moss, Marilyn Horne, Francesco Scavullo, Ronnie Milsap, Susan Sontag, Dizzy Dean, Ethel Merman

FAMOUS EVENTS: Prohibition begins (1920); first jazz concert at Carnegie Hall by Benny Goodman and band (1938); Whitey Ford and Mickey Mantle elected to Baseball Hall of Fame (1977)

LUCKY NUMBER: 8

BIRTHSTONE: Garnet

POSITIVE TRAITS: Professional, dedicated, industrious

NEGATIVE TRAITS: Overworking, bossy, demanding

You are the consummate professional, applying yourself diligently until your projects are successfully completed. Your organizing ability is an asset, but don't let it blind you to the talents and contributions of those around you. Although perfection is your goal, learn to support those with whom you are involved, even when results are less than perfect. Avoid becoming obsessed with your work; dedicate plenty of time to your family and friends, who, when you are not telling them what to do, sincerely enjoy your invigorating company. Resist your tendency to boss your mate around and try not to approach every romantic rendezvous as a scene to be directed by you. Have plenty of high-energy snacks around to keep you going at your preferred speed—full tilt.

January 17

ASTROLOGICAL SIGN: Capricorn

PEOPLE BORN TODAY: Muhammad Ali, Jim Carrey, Shari Lewis, Maury Povich, David Caruso, Paul Young, Betty White, James Earl Jones, Moira Shearer, Al Capone, Benjamin Franklin

FAMOUS EVENTS: Cable car system patented (1871); first United Nations Security Council meeting (1948); Gulf War (Desert Storm) begins (1991); major Los Angeles earthquake (1994)

LUCKY NUMBER: 9

BIRTHSTONE: Garnet

POSITIVE TRAITS: Tough-minded, disciplined, purposeful

NEGATIVE TRAITS: Antagonistic, argumentative, guarded

Defending your turf comes naturally to you, but you must learn that often more can be gained through cooperation and goodwill than through force. You are slow to trust, but longtime friends know you as loyal, affectionate, and supportive. If you feel insecure in love you may feign unhappiness to test your partner, yet when you find a mate who makes you feel safe, your devotion will last a lifetime. You find it difficult to watch loved ones take a fall and you're frequently the first one there to offer a helping hand—or a battle plan. Volunteer work will let you fight for worthy causes and at the same time help you to form cooperative relationships. Work out your aggressions in sports that require toughness and teamwork.

January 18

ASTROLOGICAL SIGN: Capricorn

PEOPLE BORN TODAY: Danny Kaye, Cary Grant, Kevin Costner, Bobby Goldsboro, John Boorman, Oliver Hardy, A. A. Milne, Daniel Webster

FAMOUS EVENTS: Hawaiian Islands discovered (1778); first aircraft landing on an aircraft carrier (1911); Bill Haley's *Rock Around the Clock* becomes the first rock and roll album to appear on the charts (1956)

LUCKY NUMBER: 1

BIRTHSTONE: Garnet

POSITIVE TRAITS: Creative, visionary, generous

NEGATIVE TRAITS: Unrealistic, childish, impractical

Your combination of canniness and imagination can lead to heights undreamed-of by less-visionary souls. Your flights of fancy and gentle good humor make you a much sought-after guest and a favorite with your friends, family, and business associates. Plenty of people will want to hitch their wagon to your star; your visionary ideas and unlimited potential draw people toward you like a magnet. If you pad your dreams with a little practicality and take the time to look around, one of those people could be the love of your life. Though you enjoy the thrills of skydiving or expert skiing, don't disdain the calmer pleasures; hiking a nature trail will keep you grounded and teach you to reach your goals one steady step at a time.

January 19

ASTROLOGICAL SIGN: Capricorn

PEOPLE BORN TODAY: Janis Joplin, Dolly Parton, Michael Crawford, Stefan Edberg, Desi Arnaz Jr., Robert Palmer, Paul Cézanne, Edgar Allan Poe, Robert E. Lee

FAMOUS EVENTS: Antarctica discovered (1840); Verdi's opera *Il Trovatore* premieres (1853); speed record for transcontinental air travel set by Howard Hughes (1937)

LUCKY NUMBER: 2

BIRTHSTONE: Garnet

POSITIVE TRAITS: Intense, deep, individualistic

NEGATIVE TRAITS: Excessive, exhibitionistic, obsessive

You experience life on a deep and powerful level. The depth of your reactions may confound others, since you sense what they often miss. Though your perceptual abilities are a major asset, your best friends are likely to be level-headed types who provide you with a needed reality check. Love partners are awed—in fact, some may even be scared off—by your ardor, but the partner you choose for life will find that your intensity makes life with you exciting and pleasantly unpredictable, particularly in the bedroom. Avoid letting your obsessive tendencies draw you into destructive patterns; instead, join your work ethic to your vast creative potential, and you will experience success in just about any field that interests you.

January 20

ASTROLOGICAL SIGN: Aquarius

PEOPLE BORN TODAY: George Burns, Patricia Neal, David Lynch, Lorenzo Lamas, Paul Stanley, Arte Johnson, Federico Fellini, DeForest Kelley

FAMOUS EVENTS: First basketball game played (1892); Franklin Delano Roosevelt becomes first president sworn in on this date (1937); American hostages in Iran released (1981)

LUCKY NUMBER: 3

BIRTHSTONE: Amethyst

POSITIVE TRAITS: Adventurous, whimsical, trailblazing

NEGATIVE TRAITS: Confused, dreamy, oversensitive

You aren't always sure where you are headed, but you have no doubt that you will get there. Others may regard you as scatterbrained or disorganized, yet all the important details are neatly filed away in your head. When faced with a professional setback or a personal crisis, you marshal your resources and clear even the highest hurdles with great good humor. In love, your mate can rely on you for both sturdy moral support and lighthearted fun. You take a child's pleasure in tall tales and have a gift for telling stories. Though your health is only average, your recuperative powers are exceptional. In your leisure time you enjoy discovering new places—whether reading about them in books or exploring them in the real world.

January 21

ASTROLOGICAL SIGN: Aquarius

PEOPLE BORN TODAY: Placido Domingo, Geena Davis, Hakeem Olajuwon, Robby Benson, Billy Ocean, Jack Nicklaus, Christian Dior, Leadbelly, Mac Davis

FAMOUS EVENTS: King Louis XVI of France guillotined (1793); Lenin dies (1924); microwave oven invented (1967)

LUCKY NUMBER: 4

BIRTHSTONE: Amethyst

POSITIVE TRAITS: Likable, charismatic, fun

NEGATIVE TRAITS: Scattered, permissive, needy

Your dazzling charm and soaring ambition guarantee you a place at the top. Although you are a star performer, your eagerness to be liked may limit your effectiveness somewhat. Your outer radiance and inner warmth attract potential partners in droves, but your ideal mate will mirror your kind and gentle nature and not exploit it. Though you tend to give in to others rather than risk their disapproval, you draw the line at anything that offends your inherent sense of right and wrong. Activities that are half sport and half social, like golf, bowling, or sailing appeal to you, but the perfect way to spend your leisure time is regaling your friends over a leisurely meal; the pleasure will be as much theirs as yours.

January 22

ASTROLOGICAL SIGN: Aquarius

PEOPLE BORN TODAY: George Balanchine, Bill Bixby, Michael Hutchence, Rasputin, Steve Perry, Sam Cooke, Lord Byron, George Foreman, D. W. Griffith, Mike Bossy

FAMOUS EVENTS: Death of Queen Victoria (1901); *Roe v. Wade* decision by U.S. Supreme Court legalizes abortion (1972); George Foreman beats Joe Frazier for heavyweight title (1973)

LUCKY NUMBER: 5

BIRTHSTONE: Amethyst

POSITIVE TRAITS: Electrifying, imaginative, passionate

NEGATIVE TRAITS: Impatient, short-tempered, headstrong

You are driven by a clear and highly original vision in your life and work. Just as you chafe at having to follow orders from those you regard as less inspired, so you demand dedication to your ideals from those you supervise, whether they are your children or your coworkers. In love, you attract admiring followers more readily than equal partners, since few can match your imagination and willfulness. Make an effort to appreciate others' virtues even if they differ drastically from your own; this will fuel your creativity and lessen any resentments resulting from your bullish tendencies. Watch your blood pressure; take an aerobics class, which will allow you to focus your electric energy and blow off steam at the same time.

January 23

ASTROLOGICAL SIGN: Aquarius

PEOPLE BORN TODAY: Humphrey Bogart, Chita Rivera, Princess Caroline of Monaco, Richard Dean Anderson, Jeanne Moreau, Tiffani-Amber Thiessen, Derek Walcott, Django Reinhardt, Sergey Eisenstein, Edouard Manet, Stendhal

FAMOUS EVENTS: Elizabeth Blackwell becomes first American woman to receive a medical degree (1849); *Casablanca* premieres (1943); Chuck Berry, Elvis Presley, and Fats Domino inducted into new Rock and Roll Hall of Fame (1986)

LUCKY NUMBER: 6

BIRTHSTONE: Amethyst

POSITIVE TRAITS: Strong, principled, self-reliant

NEGATIVE TRAITS: Rebellious, heedless, isolated

You are a rebel; rarely, if ever, do you seek advice from others. You adhere strictly to your own personal code of behavior. Though you may be penalized for not playing by the rules, it is more likely that you will be in situations in which you are making the rules—not following them. Your can-do attitude may lead some potential partners to think you don't need anybody but yourself; but when you do settle down your mate will appreciate your loyalty as well as your originality in the kitchen and the bedroom. Despite your resentment, heed your health advisers when they tell you to quit smoking or lose weight. At least you can live to thumb your nose at society another day!

January 24

ASTROLOGICAL SIGN: Aquarius

PEOPLE BORN TODAY: Neil Diamond, John Belushi, Anita Baker, Mary Lou Retton, Nastassja Kinski, Aaron Neville, Robert Motherwell, Edith Wharton, Hadrian

FAMOUS EVENTS: Gold discovered at Sutter's Mill in California (1848); first heart transplant operation performed (1964); death of Sir Winston Churchill (1965); Moog synthesizer introduced (1970)

LUCKY NUMBER: 7

BIRTHSTONE: Amethyst

POSITIVE TRAITS: Glamorous, exciting, popular

NEGATIVE TRAITS: Vain, wary, shallow

You appear larger than life, with all the glamour of a Las Vegas headliner. At work and home, you play your appointed role to the hilt and never fail to win rave reviews. Friends clamor for your company and put you first on their party lists, yet few get close enough to call you a bosom friend. Your challenge in love is to let your partner see the insecure, imperfect you behind the shiny, happy façade. You're a natural with children—making them laugh is especially easy for you. In-line skating could be good for your character, alternately ego-gratifying and constructively humbling. Help your body find balance by alternating your favored lobster-and-champagne suppers with home-cooked meals heavy on the steamed vegetables.

January 25

ASTROLOGICAL SIGN: Aquarius
PEOPLE BORN TODAY: Virginia Woolf, Etta James, Corazon Aquino, Edwin Newman, Somerset Maugham, Robert Burns
FAMOUS EVENTS: Transcontinental telephone service begins (1915); death of Al "Scarface" Capone (1947); first live-televised presidential news conference (1961)
LUCKY NUMBER: 8
BIRTHSTONE: Amethyst
POSITIVE TRAITS: Altruistic, centered, idealistic
NEGATIVE TRAITS: Frustrated, frenzied, nervous

You are a do-gooder with a strong sense of purpose. You believe you were put on earth to accomplish something, and you won't be satisfied until you do. Without direction you may drift from job to job or from project to project; with it, you will become a bold and effective leader. In love, you prefer partners who share your views, though this isn't a prerequisite; and because of your generous and trusting nature, any partner you choose will enjoy plenty of freedom within your relationship. Your idealism makes you a cheerful and upbeat companion and you are on everyone's invitation list. Take time out from your busy schedule and accept these invitations—your friends and you will both benefit.

January 26

ASTROLOGICAL SIGN: Aquarius

PEOPLE BORN TODAY: Paul Newman, Gene Siskel, Wayne Gretzky, Roger Vadim, Eartha Kitt, Eddie Van Halen, Angela Davis, Jules Feiffer, Douglas MacArthur

FAMOUS EVENTS: Michigan becomes the 26th state (1837); filming begins on *Gone with the Wind* (1939); *Phantom of the Opera* opens on Broadway (1988)

LUCKY NUMBER: 9

BIRTHSTONE: Amethyst

POSITIVE TRAITS: Commanding, certain, dynamic

NEGATIVE TRAITS: Opinionated, disdainful, unbending

You possess an air of authority and an unshakable confidence and you excel at marshaling people onto teams or committees. Your tendency to make snap judgments about people can limit your effectiveness: Keep an open mind and let them win your good opinion gradually. Others naturally defer to you when decisions are necessary and you are happy and assured making them. It's when your decisions are questioned that problems arise, especially in personal relationships where compromise is called for. Learn to listen: Your partner *may* have a good idea! Blast out of your normal patterns occasionally to spice up your love life; early to bed, early to rise is fine, but be careful not to let a routine become a rut.

January 27

ASTROLOGICAL SIGN: Aquarius

PEOPLE BORN TODAY: Wolfgang Amadeus Mozart, Donna Reed, Bridget Fonda, Jerome Kern, Lewis Carroll, William Randolph Hearst Jr., Learned Hand

FAMOUS EVENTS: Electric light patented by Thomas Edison (1880); television first demonstrated (1926); Vietnam Peace Treaty signed (1973)

LUCKY NUMBER: 1

BIRTHSTONE: Amethyst

POSITIVE TRAITS: Gifted, exuberant, quick-witted

NEGATIVE TRAITS: Self-indulgent, petty, immature

Your impressive intellectual and artistic gifts were evident at an early age and you have been attempting to bring them to full flower ever since. Develop a work ethic that matches your innate abilities and you will reach your chosen pinnacle. In personal relationships, you must learn to give as well as receive affection and attention; this shouldn't be hard for someone as thoughtful and good-natured as you. Though you are likely to be the doted-on darling of your mate, to whom you look for security and comfort, your tendency toward self-absorption may cause rifts that could easily be avoided if you would learn to turn outward. Eat your vegetables to keep your high spirits and quick wit finely tuned.

January 28

ASTROLOGICAL SIGN: Aquarius

PEOPLE BORN TODAY: Alan Alda, Mikhail Baryshnikov, Arthur Rubinstein, Elijah Wood, Acker Bilk, Colette, Jackson Pollock, Henry VII

FAMOUS EVENTS: First telephone switchboard operated (1878); first Emmy Awards given (1948); *Challenger* space shuttle explodes (1986)

LUCKY NUMBER: 2

BIRTHSTONE: Amethyst

POSITIVE TRAITS: Curious, intelligent, determined

NEGATIVE TRAITS: Conceited, showy, attention-seeking

Your creative potential is as great as your desire to display your gifts for all the world to see; you're a star performer. The applause of the crowd means as much to you as your achievements, which are nonetheless substantial. Your chosen mate will recognize you as a truly special individual—which indeed you are—and be willing to spend a large amount of time reiterating just how special that is. You have probably mastered a musical instrument to show off your talents. Regular physical examinations will serve as a reliable barometer of your well-being; don't let your yen to stand out tempt you to dismiss mundane health complaints or to inflate the minor ones you have into exotic afflictions.

January 29

ASTROLOGICAL SIGN: Aquarius

PEOPLE BORN TODAY: Tom Selleck, Oprah Winfrey, Greg Louganis, Sara Gilbert, Ann Jillian, John Forsythe, Germaine Greer, Barnett Newman, W. C. Fields, Anton Chekhov, William McKinley

FAMOUS EVENTS: First Librarian of Congress appointed (1802); gasoline-powered automobile patented by Karl Benz (1886); Baseball Hall of Fame established (1936)

LUCKY NUMBER: 3

BIRTHSTONE: Amethyst

POSITIVE TRAITS: Diplomatic, articulate, even-tempered

NEGATIVE TRAITS: Reticent, inhibited, unassertive

You can rise to any occasion, although you'd rather not. When you do speak up, especially for others, you can be forceful without being offensive or tactless. This skill serves you well in social and business situations. In love, your tendency is to shrink from confrontations with your mate. Don't be afraid to clear the air when it's called for; your sensitive communication style will guard against hurt feelings. Whether in a classroom, at the office, or at home, your empathy and patience make you a good instructor, though your self-effacing style often results in others taking credit for your accomplishments. Curling up with a crossword puzzle or a good book brings you pleasure, and so does time spent catching up with close friends.

January 30

ASTROLOGICAL SIGN: Aquarius

PEOPLE BORN TODAY: Brett Butler, Christian Bale, Jody Watley, Vanessa Redgrave, Gene Hackman, Louis Rukeyser, Harold Prince, Boris Spassky, Franklin D. Roosevelt, Ernie Banks

FAMOUS EVENTS: First radio episode of *The Lone Ranger* (1933); Mohandas Gandhi assassinated (1948); last public performance by the Beatles (1969)

LUCKY NUMBER: 4

BIRTHSTONE: Amethyst

POSITIVE TRAITS: Caring, involved, outspoken

NEGATIVE TRAITS: Driven, manipulative, untruthful

Everyone knows where you stand on an issue; you don't hesitate to broadcast your beliefs and put them into action. Though you may sometimes fudge the truth if you think your ends justify the means, in most situations your decisions are straightforward and rational. You are materially generous and emotionally honest, although at times you appear a bit cool. Get involved in community affairs; they provide a natural outlet for your social concerns and leadership skills— and a perfect way to meet the partner who is just right for you. Once you do, there will be no end to the activities necessary to keep you two revved up. Though constantly on the go, your fire isn't limited to social crusades: You're a passionate lover—with boundless energy.

January 31

ASTROLOGICAL SIGN: Aquarius

PEOPLE BORN TODAY: Nolan Ryan, Philip Glass, Phil Collins, Jackie Robinson, Suzanne Pleshette, Norman Mailer, Oe Kenzaburo, Anna Pavlova, Zane Grey

FAMOUS EVENTS: Evaporated milk invented (1851); first TV soap opera broadcast (1949); twist-off bottle cap invented (1956)

LUCKY NUMBER: 5

BIRTHSTONE: Amethyst

POSITIVE TRAITS: Pleasing, entertaining, appealing

NEGATIVE TRAITS: Unrevealing, groveling, fragile

Being liked is your chief goal, and you achieve it with ease. You are a giving coworker and a delightful companion, though your need for approval may lead you to behave in ways that belie your more genuine feelings. Your entertaining personality makes you very popular socially, but demonstrating your serious side will help you build real rapport with a mate. People listen to you; your ideas are imaginative and because your approach is nonthreatening, you can get things accomplished where others only meet roadblocks. Don't struggle to conform to others' expectations of you and run the risk of losing your considerable charm. A challenging physical workout will help you develop some needed toughness—both physical and mental.

February 1

ASTROLOGICAL SIGN: Aquarius

PEOPLE BORN TODAY: Garrett Morris, Sherilyn Fenn, Lisa Marie Presley, Laura Dern, Boris Yeltsin, Clark Gable, Langston Hughes, John Ford, Princess Stephanie of Monaco

FAMOUS EVENTS: First session of the U.S. Supreme Court (1790); "Battle Hymn of the Republic" published (1862); first auto insurance policy issued (1898); first single record released (1949)

LUCKY NUMBER: 3

BIRTHSTONE: Amethyst

POSITIVE TRAITS: Inventive, clever, inspiring

NEGATIVE TRAITS: Headstrong, fickle, confused

You are an inspiring, if sometimes dizzying, leader. Others admire your cleverness and are swayed by your convictions, though it is not uncommon for you to make a complete turnaround only a few days later. You are zealous in your pursuit of romantic partners, but think nothing of making a detour when a more attractive prospect beckons. Once committed to a mate, however, your impulsiveness may become more benign: frequent changes of dinner menus, vacation destinations, remodeling plans. Being steered by momentary passions can wear you out emotionally and physically, so you should ground yourself by adhering religiously to a sensible diet and exercise routine. Put your one- and five-year plans in writing and post them prominently to remind yourself what really matters.

February 2

ASTROLOGICAL SIGN: Aquarius

PEOPLE BORN TODAY: Liz Smith, Farrah Fawcett, James Joyce, Christie Brinkley, Graham Nash, Holly Hunter, Stan Getz

FAMOUS EVENTS: First lie detector test given (1935); singing debut made by Frank Sinatra (1940); death by heroin overdose of Sex Pistol Sid Vicious (1979)

LUCKY NUMBER: 4

BIRTHSTONE: Amethyst

POSITIVE TRAITS: Tasteful, stylish, smooth

NEGATIVE TRAITS: Uncooperative, distant, detached

Although you never impose your methods on coworkers or friends, you have a pleasingly distinct way of thinking, working, and dressing, and you fiercely resist every attempt to make you adopt any particular style of dress or mode of behavior. By going your own way, and steadfastly polishing your style, you effortlessly attract admirers, though you tend to leave loved ones at arm's length. Look up from your own concerns from time to time, and reach out with the human warmth that makes you more than just an attractive mannequin. Trading massages with your partner will bolster your health while keeping you "in touch." Making your own jewelry or furniture are hobbies that play up your exquisite taste and let you embellish your image.

February 3

ASTROLOGICAL SIGN: Aquarius

PEOPLE BORN TODAY: Fran Tarkenton, Morgan Fairchild, Dave Davies, Gertrude Stein, James Michener, Norman Rockwell

FAMOUS EVENTS: Massachusetts issues first paper money in the U.S. (1690); sporting goods company founded by Albert Spalding (1876); Buddy Holly, Richie Valens, and the Big Bopper killed in plane crash (1959)

LUCKY NUMBER: 5

BIRTHSTONE: Amethyst

POSITIVE TRAITS: Proficient, adaptable, persistent

NEGATIVE TRAITS: Calculating, irresponsible, unstable

You switch gears effortlessly, which can be a boon when you are stymied. But beware the flip side: You could spend a lifetime experimenting with various techniques and never attain your goals. Persistence often pays off better than novelty, so limit your dilettantish tendencies and temper your adaptability with a strong dose of perseverance. You may be tempted to bail out of relationships at the first hint of trouble—but why do this when flexibility is your strong point? In fact, there will be very few problems or situations that your yielding nature cannot resolve. You are a favorite among your family and friends who find your broad interests and quick wit particularly agreeable. Curb your desire for fad diets and good health is yours.

February 4

ASTROLOGICAL SIGN: Aquarius

PEOPLE BORN TODAY: Charles Lindbergh, Rosa Parks, Lawrence Taylor, Dan Quayle, Betty Friedan, David Brenner, Hank Aaron, Roger Staubach

FAMOUS EVENTS: George Washington elected president (1789); Yalta Conference held (1945); Patty Hearst kidnapped by Symbionese Liberation Army (1974)

LUCKY NUMBER: 6

BIRTHSTONE: Amethyst

POSITIVE TRAITS: Unconventional, ingenious, imaginative

NEGATIVE TRAITS: Baffling, bumbling, wacky

You stand out with little effort—and sometimes in spite of your attempts to fit in. Though everyone admires your hard work and dedication, the logic behind your actions is frequently incomprehensible—even to you. Don't try to win hearts by curbing your originality; the right partner will find your skewed worldview and wacky approach uniquely appealing. Your methods may be unorthodox, but most people will find your problem-solving techniques original and effective. Alternative medicine and holistic health practices probably appeal to you, but be careful to distinguish between innovation and quackery. Keep your video camera within easy reach; home movies are the perfect outlet for expressing your singular spin on life.

February 5

ASTROLOGICAL SIGN: Aquarius

PEOPLE BORN TODAY: Hank Aaron, Adlai Stevenson, Red Buttons, Christopher Guest, Jennifer Jason Leigh, Bobby Brown

FAMOUS EVENTS: Adding machine patented (1850); *Apollo XIV* astronauts land on Moon (1971); Governor Evan Mecham of Arizona impeached (1988)

LUCKY NUMBER: 7

BIRTHSTONE: Amethyst

POSITIVE TRAITS: Perceptive, articulate, reliable

NEGATIVE TRAITS: Condescending, glib, repressed

You have the gift of gab. You can sum up a situation with a few well-chosen words, which makes you an outstanding communicator and negotiator. But if you decide that others do not deserve the benefit of your insights, you may choose to keep your opinions to yourself, even if this means continued friction and hard feelings. Once you find that rare person who measures up to your high standards, your buried charm rises to the surface and romance isn't far behind. Few people can tell a story or a joke with your confidence and wit; don't hold back if you want to make a lasting impression. In fact, resist your natural tendency to keep things inside since repressed emotions can undermine your physical and mental health.

February 6

ASTROLOGICAL SIGN: Aquarius
PEOPLE BORN TODAY: Babe Ruth, Ronald Reagan, Natalie Cole, Axl Rose, Tom Brokaw, Bob Marley, Rip Torn, François Truffaut
FAMOUS EVENTS: Death of King George VI, father of Queen Elizabeth II (1952); first performance by Elvis Presley (1955); Senator Hubert Humphrey's seat filled by wife Muriel following his death (1978)
LUCKY NUMBER: 8
BIRTHSTONE: Amethyst
POSITIVE TRAITS: Accessible, popular, likable
NEGATIVE TRAITS: Approval-seeking, needy, unsure

Positive feedback from others is as important to you as air and water. You're a determined people pleaser, happy to perform tasks and do favors in order to earn approval. You are a generous, giving partner in love and life, and win high marks for your enthusiastic and optimistic approach to everything. Just make sure that your own needs and desires are not completely sublimated while you cater to the whims of others. People like you—and not just because you're accommodating. Your compassion, good nature, quick wit, and unpretentiousness all contribute to your popularity and make you a desirable friend and lover. Aerobics classes let you stay fit while earning the instructor's kudos, and interactive computer games provide fun with feedback.

February 7

ASTROLOGICAL SIGN: Aquarius

PEOPLE BORN TODAY: Garth Brooks, Chris Rock, Jason Gedrick, Charles Dickens, Eubie Blake, James Dean, Lana Turner

FAMOUS EVENTS: Beatles land at Kennedy Airport for first U.S. concert tour (1964); Elizabeth Dole sworn in as first female secretary of transportation (1983); first untethered space walk (1984)

LUCKY NUMBER: 9

BIRTHSTONE: Amethyst

POSITIVE TRAITS: Visionary, reforming, free-thinking

NEGATIVE TRAITS: Critical, meddling, disobedient

You are liberal-minded and yet intolerant, refusing to witness cruelty or injustice without speaking or acting out. You have little patience for the enforced conformity of the typical workplace and may be happiest working at home as an entrepreneur or consultant, ideally in a business related to improving social conditions or the environment. Your partner will share your rarefied values and activist disposition, and your social circle will be composed of like-minded individuals who share your strong sense of responsibility to their fellow human beings. Weekend retreats to the woods or beach will provide respite from your heavy cares and renew your spirit. A physical fitness program that is part of a philosophical or spiritual belief system, such as yoga, is the way for you.

February 8

ASTROLOGICAL SIGN: Aquarius

PEOPLE BORN TODAY: James Dean, John Williams, Mary Steenburgen, Audrey Meadows, Jack Lemmon, Ted Koppel, Nick Nolte, John Grisham

FAMOUS EVENTS: Mary, Queen of Scots, beheaded (1587); fountain pen invented by Louis Waterman (1883); first gas-chamber execution (1924)

LUCKY NUMBER: 1

BIRTHSTONE: Amethyst

POSITIVE TRAITS: Sensitive, intellectual, gentle

NEGATIVE TRAITS: Unassertive, unstable, fearful of conflict

You are more of a dreamer than a doer, yet many of your dreams come true. This amazes onlookers whose more obvious efforts yield fewer rewards. Your ability to intuit others' true meanings and intentions makes you a confidant treasured by your friends. Though your mate finds you tender and responsive, you frequently need prompting to be more assertive. You are naturally nurturing and encouraging; friends and family rely on you to see them through all kinds of situations. Curb your desire to sleep late and dream away your weekends; too much sleep plays havoc with your internal clock. Try ballroom dancing with your partner: It will add beauty and harmony to your life and burnish your ability to anticipate the next move.

February 9

ASTROLOGICAL SIGN: Aquarius
PEOPLE BORN TODAY: Alice Walker, Carole King, Joe Pesci, Mia Farrow, Travis Tritt, Judith Light
FAMOUS EVENTS: Jefferson Davis elected president of the Confederacy (1861); Beatles appear on *The Ed Sullivan Show* (1964); debut of Paul McCartney's band Wings (1972)
LUCKY NUMBER: 2
BIRTHSTONE: Amethyst
POSITIVE TRAITS: Cheerful, hardy, positive
NEGATIVE TRAITS: Combative, unrestrained, inconsistent

You take repeated knocks—not because you're a pushover but because you set your goals high—and keep bouncing back. Such resiliency can lead to great achievements, so long as you merely cope with trouble and don't actively seek it. You're a natural teacher, showing others by example how to rise to life's challenges and the effectiveness of a winning attitude. Romantic partners are attracted to your relentless optimism and zest for life, and those same qualities, together with your grace and good humor, will serve you well through the inevitable storms of a long-term union. Comfort foods like mashed potatoes and rice pudding warm your embattled soul, and your unstinting energy keeps the potatoes from turning into pounds.

February 10

ASTROLOGICAL SIGN: Aquarius
PEOPLE BORN TODAY: Roberta Flack, Mark Spitz, George Stephanopoulos, Robert Wagner, Greg Norman, Peter Allen
FAMOUS EVENTS: Queen Victoria and Prince Albert wed (1840); first gold record awarded, for Glenn Miller's *Chattanooga Choo Choo* (1942); *Death of a Salesman* opens on Broadway (1949)
LUCKY NUMBER: 3
BIRTHSTONE: Amethyst
POSITIVE TRAITS: Directed, self-assured, masterful
NEGATIVE TRAITS: Grandiose, impersonal, detached

Because your inner voice speaks loud and clear, you always know where you are going and the fastest way to get there. Though the pursuit of your goals usually takes precedence over everything else in your life, you can be a caring friend when you look outside yourself, which you should do more often. Your professional achievements will undoubtedly garner you a fan club, but remember that admiration is no substitute for affection. In love, you follow the same straight path: intuitively knowing just the right steps to your valentine's heart. Once you have won that heart, don't neglect it. If you can show your partner that your passions are not limited to pursuing your goals, success in love will be yours.

February 11

ASTROLOGICAL SIGN: Aquarius

PEOPLE BORN TODAY: Leslie Nielsen, Burt Reynolds, Tina Louise, Eva Gabor, Virginia Johnson-Masters, Thomas Edison, Jennifer Aniston

FAMOUS EVENTS: Vermont becomes first state to outlaw slavery (1777); casket of King Tutankhamen opened (1927); Margaret Thatcher elected first female leader of Britain's Conservative Party (1975)

LUCKY NUMBER: 4

BIRTHSTONE: Amethyst

POSITIVE TRAITS: Ingenious, modest, sensual

NEGATIVE TRAITS: Rebellious, self-indulgent, childish

You are often the first to put yourself down, but in such a charmingly humorous way that it enhances rather than detracts from your appeal. Your knack for making others feel good about themselves secures you many loyal friends who are willing and anxious to do things for you. Your original style and self-deprecating wit prove irresistible to romantic partners, but when it's time to settle down, you may need to curb your attraction to the high life—or find a mate who shares it. You are likely to be more playmate than parent to your children and can dismay loved ones with occasional tantrums of your own. Soothe your frayed nerves with a long soak in a hot tub—not with alcohol.

February 12

ASTROLOGICAL SIGN: Aquarius

PEOPLE BORN TODAY: Arsenio Hall, Scott Turow, Chynna Phillips, Joanna Kerns, Judy Blume, Charles Darwin

FAMOUS EVENTS: Queen of England Lady Jane Grey and husband Lord Guildford Dudley beheaded (1554); toothpick machine patented (1872); first public performance of *Rhapsody in Blue* by George Gershwin (1924)

LUCKY NUMBER: 5

BIRTHSTONE: Amethyst

POSITIVE TRAITS: Conservative, unequivocal, imaginative

NEGATIVE TRAITS: Inflexible, moody, pugnacious

You are a bold defender of the status quo—provided it meets your moral and ethical standards. If not, you will work within the system to change it, which makes you a valued and sought-after employee. In both your personal and professional life, you tend to stick to the tried and true; once you and your mate have worked out your respective roles in your relationship, you stay cast in those parts for years. Although change of any sort is difficult for you, you are not completely predictable: You often surprise family and friends with your flights of imagination and unusally creative, even offbeat, approaches to problem solving. Don't put habit before health; if your doctor isn't responsive to your needs, make a switch.

February 13

ASTROLOGICAL SIGN: Aquarius

PEOPLE BORN TODAY: Chuck Yeager, Stockard Channing, Peter Gabriel, George Segal, Kim Novak, Tennessee Ernie Ford

FAMOUS EVENTS: First American public school opens (1635); first American magazine published, *The American Magazine* (1741); Bruno Hauptmann convicted of first-degree murder in kidnapping of Lindbergh baby (1935)

LUCKY NUMBER: 6

BIRTHSTONE: Amethyst

POSITIVE TRAITS: Visionary, fun, creative

NEGATIVE TRAITS: Remote, eccentric, shy

Whether you're on an assembly line, a space shuttle, or your own front porch, you look around and see a world of possibilities. Your ideas sometimes seem far-fetched to colleagues, but you are determined to share your vision with the world. Because you are incapable of seeing suffering and not trying to do something to alleviate it, you are often active in community or church organizations that reach out to the less fortunate. Your address book bulges with numbers, but you find it easier to be befriend everyone than to let any one person get too close to you. When you can overcome your natural shyness, you can be a fun and intellectually stimulating companion who keeps your partner young in spirit.

February 14

ASTROLOGICAL SIGN: Aquarius

PEOPLE BORN TODAY: Carl Bernstein, Gregory Hines, Molly Ringwald, Florence Henderson, Meg Tilly, Jack Benny

FAMOUS EVENTS: St. Valentine's Day massacre (1929); White House tour hosted by Jacqueline Kennedy televised (1962); Dan Rather chosen to anchor *CBS Evening News* (1980)

LUCKY NUMBER: 7

BIRTHSTONE: Amethyst

POSITIVE TRAITS: Astute, amusing, observant

NEGATIVE TRAITS: Acerbic, insensitive, demanding

Your unimposing appearance belies the arrows hidden in your quiver: a shrewd eye and a sharp tongue. These weapons make you a strong ally and a formidable foe in the workplace, but can cause trouble in personal relationships. Though you may amuse others with your witty but cutting observations on the passing parade, your barbs will be less appreciated when they are directed at your loved ones. Talk is often a way for you to camouflage your emotions, which you have difficulty controlling once you let your guard down: You cry at movies and visibly suffer over others' misfortunes. This emotional vulnerability may confound your acquaintances, who expect you to be tougher, but your mate knows the real you is a lamb, not a lion.

February 15

ASTROLOGICAL SIGN: Aquarius
PEOPLE BORN TODAY: Melissa Manchester, Jane Seymour, Matt Groening, Harvey Korman, Marisa Berenson, Cesar Romero, Susan B. Anthony, Galileo
FAMOUS EVENTS: Bill signed permitting women attorneys to argue cases before U.S. Supreme Court (1879); Union Jack retired and maple leaf flag becomes official in Canada (1956)
LUCKY NUMBER: 8
BIRTHSTONE: Amethyst
POSITIVE TRAITS: Curious, artistic, self-motivated
NEGATIVE TRAITS: Pushy, dissatisfied, fault-finding

You are a human elevator who can raise a craft or skill to undreamed-of heights. Both at home and on the job, you quickly master all the basics and then refine them to a point that few others have even imagined. It is impossible for you to sit on the sidelines and watch others at work: You can't help but jump in and show them a better way—your way. In love, you can help your partner attain his or her fullest potential, but you have to fight against regarding your mate as one of your projects. You love the great outdoors; camping especially excites you, because it is another venue for you to demonstrate your skills, your adaptability, and your artistry.

February 16

ASTROLOGICAL SIGN: Aquarius
PEOPLE BORN TODAY: Edgar Bergen, Sonny Bono, John McEnroe, James Ingram, Patty Andrews, Andy Taylor
FAMOUS EVENTS: *Ladies Home Journal* premieres (1883); nylon, first synthetic fiber, patented (1937); Fidel Castro appoints himself premier of Cuba (1959)
LUCKY NUMBER: 9
BIRTHSTONE: Amethyst
POSITIVE TRAITS: Impassioned, self-assured, knowledgeable
NEGATIVE TRAITS: Overbearing, arrogant, unreasonable

You think you know it all, and sometimes you *do*. When it comes to your chosen specialty, you are quick to tell others exactly what to do and how to do it. They may bridle at your imperious manner, but usually end up admitting you were right and admiring your cleverness. Your bossy attitude may turn off potential partners, especially if you routinely ridicule or override their decisions, but your exceedingly affectionate nature—and your basic willingness to please—can do a lot to compensate for your pushiness. Your flair for making money won't draw any complaints, nor will your generosity in dispersing it. Try to strike a balance between your inner and outer worlds by becoming more conscious of your feelings—and expressing them.

February 17

ASTROLOGICAL SIGN: Aquarius

PEOPLE BORN TODAY: Michael Jordan, Lou Diamond Phillips, Hal Holbrook, Mary Ann Mobley, Gene Pitney

FAMOUS EVENTS: Thomas Jefferson elected president (1801); National Congress of Mothers, forerunner of PTA, founded (1897); death of Geronimo (1909)

LUCKY NUMBER: 1

BIRTHSTONE: Amethyst

POSITIVE TRAITS: Disciplined, ambitious, appealing

NEGATIVE TRAITS: Sheltered, puzzling, sober

Self-discipline is your ticket to success. You carefully channel your talents and plot your path, blind to the distractions around you. Romance may have to take a backseat until you attain a certain measure of success, but once you set your cap for someone, your seductive charms will be impossible to resist. Tolerance and sympathy come naturally to you, and though you are often repelled by those who don't share these traits, you usually find something to admire in everyone you meet. Fun and games seldom lure you from your responsibilities, but you're no stick-in-the-mud. To soothe and refresh both body and soul, make it a goal to do nothing for at least twenty minutes a day.

February 18

ASTROLOGICAL SIGN: Aquarius
PEOPLE BORN TODAY: John Travolta, Cybill Shepherd, Yoko Ono, Helen Gurley Brown, Matt Dillon, Vanna White
FAMOUS EVENTS: *The Adventures of Huckleberry Finn* published (1885); planet Pluto discovered (1930); first 3-D movie premieres (1953)
LUCKY NUMBER: 2
BIRTHSTONE: Amethyst
POSITIVE TRAITS: Youthful, energetic, forward-looking
NEGATIVE TRAITS: Challenging, childish, impetuous

You radiate the boundless energy and optimism of a five-year-old, regardless of your age. At work, you're the first to propose a bold plan and the last to say, "It can't be done." At home, you excite your family with ambitious party plans, redecorating schemes, and exotic travel itineraries. Even if your mate isn't as thrilled about a project as you are, you can usually entice him or her along for the ride. Your friends are happy coconspirators eager to cheer you on should others pooh-pooh your ideas. You relax—a little—by poring over self-help books of the positive-thinking variety, and your relentlessly upbeat attitude is your body's best friend, fending off illness and aging better than any wonder drug.

February 19

ASTROLOGICAL SIGN: Aquarius

PEOPLE BORN TODAY: Andrew Shue, Smokey Robinson, Amy Tan, Prince Andrew, Jeff Daniels, Hana Mandlikova

FAMOUS EVENTS: Former vice president Aaron Burr arrested (1807); phonograph patented by Thomas Edison (1878); third consecutive Olympic speed skating championship won by Bonnie Blair (1994)

LUCKY NUMBER: 3

BIRTHSTONE: Amethyst

POSITIVE TRAITS: Adventurous, daring, wholehearted

NEGATIVE TRAITS: Excessive, risky, foolhardy

You have a hearty appetite for life. Your challenge is to satisfy it with healthy food rather than forbidden fruit. You quickly make a name for yourself wherever you go, but whether you're pegged as a leader or a loser depends on your ability to carry your share of the load. The sedentary life is not for you: You have the wanderlust and thrive on new situations and new people. Your appetite for love is also huge; you won't settle down until you have sown your wild oats. In your youth, you gravitated toward partners your parents rightly regarded as bad influences; with maturity, you are likelier to share your time with those who share your adventurous spirit without being detrimental to your well-being.

February 20

ASTROLOGICAL SIGN: Pisces

PEOPLE BORN TODAY: Charles Barkley, Cindy Crawford, Kelsey Grammer, Kurt Cobain, Sidney Poitier, Robert Altman, Patty Hearst

FAMOUS EVENTS: Federal Postal System created by President George Washington (1792); Earth orbited three times by Col. John Glenn aboard *Friendship 7* spacecraft (1962); presidential candidacy announced by Ross Perot (1992)

LUCKY NUMBER: 4

BIRTHSTONE: Aquamarine

POSITIVE TRAITS: Cerebral, attractive, well-rounded

NEGATIVE TRAITS: Oversensitive, indecisive, compromising

You are that rare hybrid of brawn and brain. Your face and form may be your fortune, but your intellect makes you a standout in your career, at home, and on the social scene. Be sure to pick a partner who can appreciate your smarts; a union based on physical attraction alone will not hold your interest for long. You teach those around you not to rely on looks or charm, but to back up their natural assets with a solid education. You are a great reader and enjoy spirited discussions with all and sundry, but you're also physically active, staying in shape through aerobics or sports. Schedule your yearly checkups on time: You are too smart to take chances with your health.

February 21

ASTROLOGICAL SIGN: Pisces

PEOPLE BORN TODAY: Tyne Daly, Hubert de Givenchy, Barbara Jordan, Erma Bombeck, Rue McClanahan, Jerry Harrison, W. H. Auden

FAMOUS EVENTS: First woman to graduate from dental school (1866); Polaroid Land camera demonstrated (1947); Richard Nixon becomes first American president to visit China (1972)

LUCKY NUMBER: 5

BIRTHSTONE: Aquamarine

POSITIVE TRAITS: Imposing, forceful, influential

NEGATIVE TRAITS: Overpowering, awkward, thin-skinned

You were born to lead, not to follow. Though you may spend years trying to fit into boxes made for smaller and more timid souls, you will only reach your full potential when you decide to be yourself and take your rightful place at the helm. Don't play the shrinking violet; you will do better seeking a partner who admires your dominating presence and is secure enough to encourage and support you. You are a tower of strength for your family and friends and teach them how to withstand peer pressure by respecting their own judgment. Learn to pay more attention to the ideas of others; your leadership skills will become more effective and your circle of friends will grow too.

February 22

ASTROLOGICAL SIGN: Pisces

PEOPLE BORN TODAY: Kyle MacLachlan, Julius Erving, Michael Chang, Drew Barrymore, Ted Kennedy, George Washington

FAMOUS EVENTS: First F. W. Woolworth store opens (1879); battle of Verdun begins (1916); Harold Washington elected Chicago's first African-American mayor (1983)

LUCKY NUMBER: 6

BIRTHSTONE: Aquamarine

POSITIVE TRAITS: Gifted, precocious, captivating

NEGATIVE TRAITS: Imprudent, immature, wasteful

You glowed with promise early in life and, for the most part, you have lived up to it. Because your natural talents and complete self-confidence often lead you to take on responsibilities you aren't quite prepared to handle, whether at home or on the job, you suffer setbacks—but you rarely find them insurmountable. A well-chosen mate will treasure you for your special gifts and encourage you to put them to good and profitable use. He or she will also become the family disciplinarian, and help to keep your extravagant nature in check. Your need to be naughty may lure you toward bad habits, like smoking or spending too much, but you will eventually find your way back from every false turn.

February 23

ASTROLOGICAL SIGN: Pisces

PEOPLE BORN TODAY: Peter Fonda, Johnny Winter, Ed "Too Tall" Jones, Bobby Bonilla, Sylvia Chase, Helena Sukova

FAMOUS EVENTS: Assassination plot against President Abraham Lincoln foiled (1861); Rotary Club founded (1905); Federal Radio Commission, forerunner of FCC, created (1927)

LUCKY NUMBER: 7

BIRTHSTONE: Aquamarine

POSITIVE TRAITS: Competent, self-starting, physically fit

NEGATIVE TRAITS: Stolid, steady, self-effacing

You take care of business both at work and at home with confident efficiency. You may often finish a close second to showier types, but that doesn't trouble you, since you truly believe that your accomplishments are their own reward. Romantically, you are not attracted to the flashier types; you want a mate you can count on and one who will, like you, be there when the going gets tough. Because you always want to do everything well, you ceaselessly fine-tune your environment and everything in it, turning your home and office into welcoming and desirable places to be. Because you want to stay young, you eat carefully; because you want to stay sexy, you exercise a lot to maintain your impressive physique.

February 24

ASTROLOGICAL SIGN: Pisces
PEOPLE BORN TODAY: Paula Zahn, Edward James Olmos, Sally Jessy Raphael, James Farentino, Abe Vigoda, Renata Scotto
FAMOUS EVENTS: First Nazi Party meeting held (1920); first rocket launched (1949); Jean Harris convicted of murdering diet guru Dr. Herman Tarnower (1981)
LUCKY NUMBER: 8
BIRTHSTONE: Aquamarine
POSITIVE TRAITS: Popular, entertaining, easily understood
NEGATIVE TRAITS: Manipulative, uninspired, shallow

Your intuitive powers are highly developed. You sense what others want, and you know how to deliver it, which makes you a highly sought-after friend, collaborator, or mate. The danger lies in paying too much attention to the wishes of others and neglecting your own. Take the time to crystallize your aims and desires and then act on them. Unless you demand equal time in romantic relationships, your partners may come to regard you as their personal genie, standing ready to grant their wishes, but useless for anything else. Use your people-pleasing skills judiciously so that everyone, including you, benefits. Others will take you more seriously when they see that you are committed to pursuing goals of your own.

February 25

ASTROLOGICAL SIGN: Pisces

PEOPLE BORN TODAY: George Harrison, Tom Courtenay, Bobby Riggs, Karen Grassle, Enrico Caruso, Zeppo Marx

FAMOUS EVENTS: First Cabinet meeting held (1793); Hiram Revels elected first African-American U.S. Senator (1870); resignation of Philippine president Ferdinand Marcos (1986)

LUCKY NUMBER: 9

BIRTHSTONE: Aquamarine

POSITIVE TRAITS: Optimistic, supportive, ambitious

NEGATIVE TRAITS: Frustrated, wary, obsessive

Success comes to you through collective efforts. Talented though you may be, you shine most brightly when surrounded by even more glittering stars. If you can make peace with your fate, you will be the perfect team player both in career matters and in personal relationships, willing to hitch your wagon to those destined to go far. You will probably choose love partners who have a sparkling personality and a bright future, hoping to contribute to and share in the excitement they generate. Conversely, these same types will be drawn to you because of your optimism and unfailing energy. You are not without your own personal agenda, however, and your team-player mentality only applies to positive situations—you're out to win.

February 26

ASTROLOGICAL SIGN: Pisces

PEOPLE BORN TODAY: Johnny Cash, Fats Domino, Jackie Gleason, Betty Hutton, Tony Randall, Robert Alda

FAMOUS EVENTS: Glass-blowing machine patented in U.S. (1895); Tower Commission report on Iran-Contra affair issued (1987); World Trade Center bombed by terrorists (1993)

LUCKY NUMBER: 1

BIRTHSTONE: Aquamarine

POSITIVE TRAITS: Honest, uncompromising, appreciative

NEGATIVE TRAITS: Stubborn, myopic, testy

Although you never attempt to be anyone but yourself, your appeal cuts across all boundaries. Even business contacts and social acquaintances whose backgrounds and styles differ drastically from your own are forcibly impressed by your integrity, self-assurance, and genuineness. Love partners admire, and perhaps envy, your ease in your own skin, and the simple and unaffected way you have of showing affection. You usually find something to like in everybody and, like a restorer of fine antiques, you labor patiently to expose the underlying character and value of everything around you. Spiritual exercises are probably more appealing to you than physical ones, so watch your calories—or find a regime that will keep you fit body and soul.

February 27

ASTROLOGICAL SIGN: Pisces

PEOPLE BORN TODAY: Michael Bolton, Chelsea Clinton, Elizabeth Taylor, Joanne Woodward, James Worthy, Ralph Nader

FAMOUS EVENTS: Cigar-rolling machine patented by grandfather of lyricist Oscar Hammerstein II (1883); highest scoring game in basketball history played (1959); record $100,000 contract signed by Mickey Mantle (1963)

LUCKY NUMBER: 2

BIRTHSTONE: Aquamarine

POSITIVE TRAITS: Altruistic, ambitious, involved

NEGATIVE TRAITS: Sensuous, acquisitive, social-climbing

You aim to acquire wealth and clout for the sake of others as well as yourself; as soon as you gain real influence, you will use your power to help those less fortunate. If promoted at work, you will place the concerns of your former peers at the top of your agenda; in your personal life, you are more likely to be working to improve your community than you are to be making luxurious improvements to your home. Learn to say "no" or you risk overcommitment, which can cause guilt and conflicts. In love, you will be happiest with a spouse who shares your altruism and your ambitions, and who, like you, can get as fired up in the bedroom as in the boardroom.

February 28

ASTROLOGICAL SIGN: Pisces

PEOPLE BORN TODAY: Bernadette Peters, Tommy Tune, Vincente Minnelli, Bubba Smith, Bugsy Siegel, Greta Scacchi, Mario Andretti

FAMOUS EVENTS: Republican Party formed to oppose slavery (1854); Frances Perkins, first female Cabinet member, appointed secretary of labor (1933); last episode of *M*A*S*H* airs, drawing largest TV audience ever (1983)

LUCKY NUMBER: 3

BIRTHSTONE: Aquamarine

POSITIVE TRAITS: Radiant, lively, exuberant

NEGATIVE TRAITS: Melodramatic, overenthusiastic, thrill-seeking

Your natural ebullience lights up the lives of your family and friends and your hundred-watt energy fires up coworkers with enthusiasm. You are often center stage at social gatherings, where you love to ham it up and entertain others. Though your mate will enjoy basking in your warm glow, you would be wise to dim your light occasionally and let your partner shine. Though you crave the admiration of the crowd, you are also adept at one-on-one encounters, leaving others with the impression that you have their interests at heart—which you do. Life in the fast lane can take its toll on your health, so be sure to work in occasional days of quiet and solitude to keep your light from burning out.

February 29

ASTROLOGICAL SIGN: Pisces

PEOPLE BORN TODAY: Dinah Shore, Jimmy Dorsey, James Mitchell, Henri Richard, William Wellman, Joss Ackland

FAMOUS EVENTS: First leap year (46 B.C.); law passed in Scotland making it a crime for a man to refuse a woman's marriage proposal tendered on this day (1288); Morocco struck by earthquake, fire, and tidal wave (1960)

LUCKY NUMBER: 4

BIRTHSTONE: Aquamarine

POSITIVE TRAITS: Youthful, vivacious, offbeat

NEGATIVE TRAITS: Immature, eccentric, frivolous

You are so irrepressibly youthful (only one birthday every four years) that you may not be taken seriously enough in your early years, especially in the workplace. As time goes on, however, your ageless vivacity will become a tremendous asset. You tend to be drawn to considerably younger partners, finding them a better match than your contemporaries in terms of physical energy and mental outlook. When your children are small, they may be embarrassed by the contrast between you and their friends' parents, but as they mature, they will admire your vigor and hope to inherit it. You find skateboarding and other kids' stuff a cool sort of exercise, but be sure your grown-up bones are well padded in case of spills.

March 1

ASTROLOGICAL SIGN: Pisces
PEOPLE BORN TODAY: Ron Howard, Harry Belafonte, Timothy Daly, Roger Daltrey, Glenn Miller, David Niven
FAMOUS EVENTS: Yellowstone becomes first national park established by Congress (1872); first American hydrogen bomb detonated at Bikini Atoll (1954); Jim Morrison arrested for lewd and lascivious behavior (1969)
LUCKY NUMBER: 4
BIRTHSTONE: Aquamarine
POSITIVE TRAITS: Aesthetic, refined, managerial
NEGATIVE TRAITS: Controlling, dictatorial, inactive

You've got the soul of an artist and the mind of a manager. Both at home and at work, you excel at transforming concepts into achievements. Coworkers and family members look to you to mediate their disputes dispassionately and with an equal respect for the position of both sides. Your personal life runs smoothly and when you are in love, you don't hold back, expressing your affection with daily endearments and charming and whimsical love notes. You are the creative director par excellence, channeling the imaginative impulses and ideas of your friends and loved ones into constructive projects. Be sure to get enough exercise: Resist the temptation to stand on the sidelines telling others how to improve their form and get out there yourself.

March 2

ASTROLOGICAL SIGN: Pisces
PEOPLE BORN TODAY: Mikhail Gorbachev, John Irving, Lou Reed, Kurt Weill, Desi Arnaz, Karen Carpenter, Dr. Seuss
FAMOUS EVENTS: Rutherford B. Hayes elected president (1877); inaugural flight of the Concorde supersonic jet (1969); compact disc system introduced (1983)
LUCKY NUMBER: 5
BIRTHSTONE: Aquamarine
POSITIVE TRAITS: Purposeful, directed, profound
NEGATIVE TRAITS: Isolated, shy, reclusive

You have your own personal vision, which you pursue with little regard for changing fashions or outside influences. Although you may find yourself in difficulties when the political climate changes at work, or be subjected to supermarket snickers for your independent style of dress, none of this fazes you. Your mate might not be everyone's idea of a great catch, but more than likely your relationship will last a lifetime; and that lifetime will be sexually, mentally, and spiritually fulfilling. Your self-reliance and independence can cause you to become too isolated; force yourself out into the world and the world will be a better place for it. You have a lot to offer: Don't keep it all to yourself.

March 3

ASTROLOGICAL SIGN: Pisces
PEOPLE BORN TODAY: Jackie Joyner-Kersee, James Doohan, Miranda Richardson, Herschel Walker, Jean Harlow, Alexander Graham Bell
FAMOUS EVENTS: Florida becomes the 27th state (1845); Bizet's opera *Carmen* premieres to audience jeers (1875); "The Star-Spangled Banner" adopted as official national anthem (1931)
LUCKY NUMBER: 6
BIRTHSTONE: Aquamarine
POSITIVE TRAITS: Pragmatic, realistic, determined
NEGATIVE TRAITS: Limited, moody, earthbound

You are unfailingly practical without being pessimistic; you are quick to recognize the limitations of any situation and know how to work within them. Though you see the big picture, you also have an acute and penetrating eye for the details. Friends and lovers find your company relaxing since you never expect the impossible, but you should make sure that you are granted the same consideration. Practicality doesn't negate passion and your moods can be extremely volatile. Though you have a short fuse, your recovery period is equally short; you're not the type to hold grudges and resent those who do. You're happiest when everyone around you is happy, and you don't mind going out of your way to create a congenial atmosphere.

March 4

ASTROLOGICAL SIGN: Pisces
PEOPLE BORN TODAY: Emilio Estefan, Catherine O'Hara, Kevin Johnson, Jane Goodall, Charles Goren, Knute Rockne
FAMOUS EVENTS: President Andrew Jackson inaugurated (1829); Jeannette Rankin becomes first woman elected to House of Representatives (1917); *People* magazine premieres (1974)
LUCKY NUMBER: 7
BIRTHSTONE: Aquamarine
POSITIVE TRAITS: Strategic, scientific, ingenious
NEGATIVE TRAITS: Scheming, impersonal, bossy

Rarely do you take a misstep; even more rarely do you make a move you haven't planned well in advance. Given enough time and concentration, you can untangle even the knottiest professional challenge or domestic problem. However, your habit of retreating from the world to plot your schemes in solitude can make it difficult for you to connect with people or to keep the spark alive in romantic relationships. Allow others to set their own goals and then work *with* them to create optimum efficiency; this way they will appreciate your ingenuity and not resent it. Taking a brisk walk once a day will lessen your isolation and stretch your tension-cramped muscles. Playing a few lighthearted games (but *not* chess) might also help.

March 5

PEOPLE BORN TODAY: Niki Taylor, Dean Stockwell, Marsha Warfield, Rex Harrison, Andy Gibb, Jack Cassidy

FAMOUS EVENTS: Louisiana Territory passed from French to Spanish possession (1766); phrase "the Iron Curtain" coined by Winston Churchill (1946); death of John Belushi from drug overdose (1982)

LUCKY NUMBER: 8

BIRTHSTONE: Aquamarine

POSITIVE TRAITS: Smooth, charming, intelligent

NEGATIVE TRAITS: Troubled, depressive, insecure

Though your surface is as smooth as glass, troubled waters churn below. Your easy manners conceal a complex nature that is as fascinating as it is conflicted. Your frustrations are often a result of your large ambitions, which, because they cannot all be realized at once, make you feel thwarted. Your self-image would improve greatly if you would just focus on how much you have attained and not on what is still to be done. Though you are neither malicious nor manipulative, you never hesitate to put your considerable charms to work for you in social or romantic situations. Because you tend to overdo things, stay out of harm's way by declaring tobacco, alcohol, and even unhealthy foods off limits.

March 6

ASTROLOGICAL SIGN: Pisces

PEOPLE BORN TODAY: Shaquille O'Neal, Gabriel García Márquez, Kiri Te Kanawa, Rob Reiner, Mary Wilson, Michelangelo, Ed McMahon, Tom Arnold

FAMOUS EVENTS: Fall of the Alamo (1836); Congress creates the Census Bureau (1902); frozen food first sold in stores (1930)

LUCKY NUMBER: 9

BIRTHSTONE: Aquamarine

POSITIVE TRAITS: Inspired, sensual, romantic

NEGATIVE TRAITS: Wishful, naive, lazy

The lure of the lovely is your driving force in life. You are happiest when ensconced in pleasant surroundings, accompanied by pretty people, and creating objects of beauty as tangible as a fresco or as evanescent as a song. Whatever their deeper qualities, your partners are certain to be sensual, sexual, and physically attractive, though their good looks may be more exotic than conventional. You have the ability to open the eyes of all your loved ones to the beauty around them, and to teach them to appreciate every flower and snowflake. Your home is likely to be a lush cocoon filled with rich colors, soothing textures, and sweet fragrances—a lovely place to indulge your sybaritic nature and display your natural style sense.

March 7

ASTROLOGICAL SIGN: Pisces

PEOPLE BORN TODAY: Michael Eisner, Janet Guthrie, Lord Snowdon, Willard Scott, John Heard, Tammy Faye Bakker

FAMOUS EVENTS: King Henry VIII declares himself head of the Church of England (1530); telephone patented by Alexander Graham Bell (1876); nutrition-labeling system proposed for all packaged foods (1990)

LUCKY NUMBER: 1

BIRTHSTONE: Aquamarine

POSITIVE TRAITS: Warmhearted, generous, approachable

NEGATIVE TRAITS: Nonconfrontational, sentimental, vulnerable

Though you take your work and family duties seriously, being liked is at least as important to you as being successful. On the job, you work at establishing friendly rapport with your colleagues, taking care to remember personal details like birthdays and children's names. At home, you give even the youngest family members a vote when deciding what to make for dinner, and you feel dejected if the dog doesn't like his new food. Because a spat with your partner can give you the blues for days, you try hard to avoid conflict, which in turn makes you feel resentful and leaves your mate wondering what the problem is. Learn to assert yourself: Once you get the hang of it, everyone will be better off.

March 8

ASTROLOGICAL SIGN: Pisces

PEOPLE BORN TODAY: Aidan Quinn, Lynn Redgrave, Mickey Dolenz, Carole Bayer Sager, Jim Rice, Jamie Lyn Bauer

FAMOUS EVENTS: First woman granted airplane pilot license in France (1910); Babe Ruth signs $80,000 per year contract (1930); record for kissing more than four thousand women in eight hours set by John McPherson (1985)

LUCKY NUMBER: 2

BIRTHSTONE: Aquamarine

POSITIVE TRAITS: Nonconformist, crusading, tenacious

NEGATIVE TRAITS: Demanding, perverse, disrespectful

You may appear agreeable enough to the casual observer, but anyone who probes deeper will find you are surprisingly tough, uncompromising, and filled with the courage of your convictions. You're feisty and chafe at being told what to do, which presents an attractive challenge to suitors, but it can also wear them out. You help others by teaching them to think for themselves, though you frequently communicate your lack of respect for authority in doing so. A vigorous regular workout will help you keep toned without locking you into a stifling routine. Your assertiveness serves you well in health matters: You're not afraid to pepper your doctor with questions and you insist on healthy foods at restaurants prepared exactly the way you want.

March 9

ASTROLOGICAL SIGN: Pisces
PEOPLE BORN TODAY: Faith Daniels, Raul Julia, Bobby Fischer, Jackie Wilson, Danny Sullivan, Jeffrey Osborne
FAMOUS EVENTS: Napoléon and Josephine wed (1796); first run for political office announced by Abraham Lincoln (1832); first Ford Mustang produced (1964)
LUCKY NUMBER: 3
BIRTHSTONE: Aquamarine
POSITIVE TRAITS: Colorful, bold, innovative
NEGATIVE TRAITS: Rash, restless, imprudent

You are a bold explorer willing to venture into unknown territory, an innovator always eager to test your new ideas both at the office and at home. Your dashing style draws numerous admirers, though others more conservative may urge you to apply the brakes when they see you rushing headlong into uncharted lands. You rarely pay attention to such precautionary advice, however, because you never act as rashly as some people think. Friends often follow your lead, learning to trust themselves and their instincts, and taking risks they might not have without your guidance. Your bent for the new and dramatic makes you an exciting romantic partner, whether it's a passionate fling or a lifelong love affair. And children adore you.

March 10

ASTROLOGICAL SIGN: Pisces
PEOPLE BORN TODAY: Sharon Stone, David Rabe, Edie Brickell, Jasmine Guy, Chuck Norris, Bix Beiderbecke
FAMOUS EVENTS: First royal wedding at Windsor Castle (1863); first telephone message transmitted (1876); Great Long Beach earthquake registers 6.3 on Richter scale (1933)
LUCKY NUMBER: 4
BIRTHSTONE: Aquamarine
POSITIVE TRAITS: Introspective, focused, empathetic
NEGATIVE TRAITS: Fragile, vulnerable, overprotective

You have a clear sense of who you are and what you want in life and love. If you can steel yourself against critics and competitors, your self-knowledge and perceptiveness will take you far. Because you are constantly tuned in to your own feelings and those of the people around you, you are an extraordinarily sensitive and giving partner. A mate who respects your tender feelings and appreciates your emotional responsiveness is your ticket to a balanced and healthy partnership. Identifying too strongly with the problems of others can bring on undue emotional stress; learn to empathize from a healthy distance and your caring will be much more effective and constructive. Push yourself out into the world more; people like you are in constant demand.

ASTROLOGICAL SIGN: Pisces

PEOPLE BORN TODAY: Bobby McFerrin, Rupert Murdoch, Dorothy Schiff, Sam Donaldson, Cheryl Lynn, Lawrence Welk

FAMOUS EVENTS: Paper invented in China (A.D. 105); the real Romeo and Juliet wed (1302); *MTV Unplugged* premieres (1992)

LUCKY NUMBER: 5

BIRTHSTONE: Aquamarine

POSITIVE TRAITS: Imaginative, current, progressive

NEGATIVE TRAITS: Trendy, gossipy, messy

You keep one foot planted in the here and now, and the other pointed toward the future. Whether you start trends or spread them, you are the source others rely on to keep them abreast of the next big thing in business, fashion, or the arts. An enthusiastic amateur inventor, you can spend hours fashioning new gadgets or reconfiguring old ones. Your imagination and energy are equally apparent in your personal life; romance is just another avenue for your ingenuity and playfulness. Though life with you is lively and fun, discipline and routine are not part of your repertoire. This won't bother friends—and children will love you for it—but your partner may have to make some adjustments if there is to be domestic harmony.

March 12

ASTROLOGICAL SIGN: Pisces

PEOPLE BORN TODAY: Liza Minnelli, Al Jarreau, James Taylor, Darryl Strawberry, Johnny Rutherford, Edward Albee

FAMOUS EVENTS: The Girl Guides, which became the Girl Scouts of America, founded (1912); Russian Revolution begins (1917); Paul McCartney and Linda Eastman married (1969)

LUCKY NUMBER: 6

BIRTHSTONE: Aquamarine

POSITIVE TRAITS: Daring, exciting, dramatic

NEGATIVE TRAITS: Impulsive, irresponsible, tempestuous

You play for high stakes in business and in love, because risk-taking exhilarates you and makes you feel alive. Professionally, you think nothing of passing up a secure position for one that promises more money, freedom, or opportunity. Romantically, you may be attracted to illicit affairs or partners with an air of danger about them; but when Cupid strikes, you'll go for the whole kit and kaboodle—love, marriage, children—willing to risk everything for lasting happiness. Your mate will most likely share your sense of adventure. In fact, it is not unlikely that the two of you will be joint venturers in business as well as love. Though you keep your emotions well under control, you are not emotionally repressed.

March 13

ASTROLOGICAL SIGN: Pisces
PEOPLE BORN TODAY: Dana Delany, Adam Clayton, Glenne Headly, Neil Sedaka, Deborah Raffin, Walter Annenberg
FAMOUS EVENTS: Harvard University named (1639); planet Uranus discovered (1781); First National Bank of Iowa robbed by John Dillinger and gang (1934)
LUCKY NUMBER: 7
BIRTHSTONE: Aquamarine
POSITIVE TRAITS: Authoritative, farsighted, wise
NEGATIVE TRAITS: Cynical, meddling, smug

Your propensity for public discourse sets you apart; it could lead you to a career as a politician, journalist, or diplomat, or simply gain you respect as the voice of your community or neighborhood. Friends and coworkers value your insights and confide their plans to you, and you are not shy about urging them on or warning them off accordingly. Because you tend toward cynicism, you may be tempted to write off a romance before it has had a chance to take root. Let your partners get to know the private, intuitive, and sensual you and resist your temptation to scuttle relationships just to prove your predictions right. Predict that you will lose those extra pounds or quit smoking, then make it come true.

March 14

ASTROLOGICAL SIGN: Pisces
PEOPLE BORN TODAY: Billy Crystal, Kirby Puckett, Michael Caine, Quincy Jones, Prince Albert of Monaco, Albert Einstein
FAMOUS EVENTS: Cotton gin patented by Eli Whitney (1794); Jack Ruby convicted of murdering Lee Harvey Oswald (1964); Burt Reynolds appears nude in *Cosmopolitan* centerfold (1972)
LUCKY NUMBER: 8
BIRTHSTONE: Aquamarine
POSITIVE TRAITS: Inventive, open-minded, gentle
NEGATIVE TRAITS: Distant, preoccupied, ambivalent

Your dazzling inventiveness and mental dexterity let you hopscotch from one concept to another without losing track of your logic. Whether in the boardroom or the kitchen, you can take familiar ingredients and make them seem new by combining them in unexpected ways. Your gentle spirit attracts a wide variety of romantic partners, though you are happiest with a mate who can keep up with your wide-ranging intellectual interests. Your friends and family delight in your imaginative storytelling and impromptu game playing, and you are drawn to hobbies or pastimes that engage your wits. Because you cannot abide the boring or the mundane, to stay in shape you must seek the kind of physical activity that lets you forget you are exercising.

ASTROLOGICAL SIGN: Pisces

PEOPLE BORN TODAY: Ruth Bader Ginsburg, Judd Hirsch, Terence Trent D'Arby, Jimmy Swaggart, Fabio, Sly Stone

FAMOUS EVENTS: Julius Caesar assassinated (44 B.C.); Elvis Presley drafted into army (1958); Elizabeth Taylor and Richard Burton wed first time (1964)

LUCKY NUMBER: 9

BIRTHSTONE: Aquamarine

POSITIVE TRAITS: Charismatic, stirring, larger-than-life

NEGATIVE TRAITS: Egotistical, arrogant, excessive

You are gutsy and determined, and sure to attain a position of leadership in whatever area you pursue. Once you reach the pinnacle, however, you are a shrewd and benevolent leader, keeping your arrogance and egotism well in check. This is especially important, as others tend to regard you as a role model. In your push to the top, you are wise enough not to neglect your friendships or allow your romance to sputter and fizzle: You know that your achievements will mean nothing to you without the people you care about around you. You love the outdoors, preferring a campsite to a hotel room and never pass up an opportunity to travel, even if it's just a Sunday outing to a country fair.

March 16

PEOPLE BORN TODAY: Kate Nelligan, Isabelle Huppert, Jerry Lewis, Daniel Patrick Moynihan, Nancy Wilson, Pat Nixon

FAMOUS EVENTS: Federal Trade Commission established (1915); first National Book Awards (1950); *Gemini* becomes first spacecraft to dock in space (1968)

LUCKY NUMBER: 1

BIRTHSTONE: Aquamarine

POSITIVE TRAITS: Active, effective, poetic

NEGATIVE TRAITS: Dreamy, inconsistent, guilty

You are a take-charge type who specializes in turning honorable intentions into good deeds. At work, you're a paragon of efficiency, but at home you relax into your naturally reflective, poetic state. You are a romantic partner who enjoys cozy candlelit dinners and reading by the fire. Yet even though you're a dreamer, you are not impractical: Your ample common sense ensures that your family's every need will be met. You're a whiz with finances: Even when money is scarce, no one feels the pinch. You have a well-developed domestic streak and your home is probably shabby chic—more comfortable than elegant but not without a certain style. Friends and family tend to drop by frequently—and they are welcome.

ASTROLOGICAL SIGN: Pisces

PEOPLE BORN TODAY: Patrick Duffy, Lesley-Anne Down, Rob Lowe, Rudolf Nureyev, Nat "King" Cole, Kurt Russell

FAMOUS EVENTS: Feast of St. Patrick, who introduced Christianity to Ireland, established (432); submarine invented (1889); Golda Meir becomes prime minister of Israel (1969)

LUCKY NUMBER: 2

BIRTHSTONE: Aquamarine

POSITIVE TRAITS: Ethereal, transcendent, inspired

NEGATIVE TRAITS: Flighty, irresponsible, shortsighted

You seem touched by fairy dust, able to transcend the ordinary and endow all your actions with magical lightness and grace. Coworkers and friends find you creatively inspired, though difficult to pin down. You enchant romantic partners with your otherworldly sparkle, but may resist having your wings clipped by long-term commitment. Though the mundane but important responsibilities of marriage and parenthood may unnerve you, your affinity for children and your love of love will eventually win out. When they do, your fears will be dispelled when you discover that your playful and whimsical nature can thrive within a committed relationship. Even sprites like you get sick from time to time, so pay attention to minor symptoms before they mushroom into full-blown illness.

March 18

ASTROLOGICAL SIGN: Pisces

PEOPLE BORN TODAY: Vanessa Williams, George Plimpton, Wilson Pickett, Bonnie Blair, Charley Pride, Edgar Cayce

FAMOUS EVENTS: First recording made by Enrico Caruso (1902); electric razor invented (1931); first walk in space by cosmonaut Aleksei Leonov (1965)

LUCKY NUMBER: 3

BIRTHSTONE: Aquamarine

POSITIVE TRAITS: Resilient, hopeful, loyal

NEGATIVE TRAITS: Overly optimistic, clinging, reticent

You are the master of the comeback. No matter how many times adverse circumstances knock you out of the ring, you eventually return to fight another round, until you at last emerge the victor. You are blessed both with spiritual strength and with supportive family and friends; these sustain you between bouts and make your triumphs all the sweeter. You treasure your partner's loyalty and return it in full, and you teach your friends and family to hold on to their dreams and nurture hope in their hearts, no matter what the odds. Your recuperative powers are also remarkable, perhaps because of your unshakable belief that no matter how low you feel today, you'll be back on your feet tomorrow.

ASTROLOGICAL SIGN: Pisces

PEOPLE BORN TODAY: Glenn Close, Bruce Willis, Ornette Coleman, Irving Wallace, Ruth Pointer, Philip Roth

FAMOUS EVENTS: First U.S. bank robbery (1831); first televised Academy Awards (1953); Graceland purchased by Elvis Presley (1957)

LUCKY NUMBER: 4

BIRTHSTONE: Aquamarine

POSITIVE TRAITS: Hardworking, methodical, intense

NEGATIVE TRAITS: Unrealistic, oblivious, self-centered

You are both dreamy and dynamic, a fascinating combination of fantasy and fire. You cling to a personal image of how life should be, and you work tirelessly to realize it, which can cause you some difficulties with others, particularly if you act without taking their feelings and ideas into account. Your flights of fancy sometimes require grounding, which tends to leave you feeling thwarted and downcast. When this happens, share your feelings with your friends; you have plenty of them and they want to get to know you better. Many romantic partners will find your blend of vision and action seductive even if they don't take it seriously, but your ideal mate will believe in your dreams and your ability to make them come true.

March 20

ASTROLOGICAL SIGN: Pisces
PEOPLE BORN TODAY: Pat Riley, Spike Lee, William Hurt, Carl Reiner, Fred Rogers, Hal Linden
FAMOUS EVENTS: Failed attempt to kidnap President Lincoln by John Wilkes Booth (1865); John Lennon marries Yoko Ono (1969); Libby Riddles becomes first woman to win Iditarod Sled Dog Race (1985)
LUCKY NUMBER: 5
BIRTHSTONE: Aquamarine
POSITIVE TRAITS: Optimistic, perceptive, romantic
NEGATIVE TRAITS: Indecisive, cautious, insecure

Your positive outlook and sensitivity to others peg you as a gifted counselor, coach, diplomat, or mediator. You believe in the basic goodness of people and have a knack for building morale and getting people to work together as a team. Your mate can always rely on you for an emotional boost, but may have to prop you up when your optimism causes you to overshoot the mark. You are a practical and insightful adviser, helping those in your circle to face challenges head-on and to rebound quickly from setbacks. You love to cook or barbecue, especially for friends, who enjoy your high spirits and genius at the grill. Surrounded by friends, you know all is right with the world.

March 21

ASTROLOGICAL SIGN: Aries

PEOPLE BORN TODAY: Matthew Broderick, Timothy Dalton, Rosie O'Donnell, Gary Oldman, Al Freeman Jr., Johann Sebastian Bach

FAMOUS EVENTS: Thomas Jefferson appointed secretary of state (1790); first rock and roll concert held, in Cleveland (1952); civil rights march from Selma to Montgomery, Alabama, led by Dr. Martin Luther King Jr. (1965)

LUCKY NUMBER: 6

BIRTHSTONE: Diamond

POSITIVE TRAITS: Honest, direct, childlike

NEGATIVE TRAITS: Blunt, unbending, unsociable

You fire your thoughts and feelings at others with the force of a cannon, and are often so transparent that you needn't say anything at all to make your feelings known. You are eager to be liked, but unwilling to engage in pretense to win the good opinion of supervisors or social acquaintances. Partners privately appreciate your honesty, even though they may be publicly embarrassed by your bluntness. Though the right mate will understand that your tactlessness springs from your childlike nature rather than from any malicious intent, a thick skin is *de rigueur* for any partner of yours. You are also young at heart and a kindred spirit to children everywhere, but don't imitate their eating habits if you want to stay in shape.

March 22

ASTROLOGICAL SIGN: Aries
PEOPLE BORN TODAY: Stephen Sondheim, Marcel Marceau, Bob Costas, Matthew Modine, William Shatner, Andrew Lloyd Webber
FAMOUS EVENTS: First international airline service inaugurated (1919); first Beatles album released in Britain (1963); broccoli categorically rejected by President George Bush (1990)
LUCKY NUMBER: 7
BIRTHSTONE: Diamond
POSITIVE TRAITS: Straightforward, reliable, self-assured
NEGATIVE TRAITS: Literal, proud, autocratic

You are straightforward, dependable, and confident of reaching your goals, which you move toward with quiet and unwavering purpose. You steer clear of machinations and manipulation and of anyone you suspect of practicing them. Partners can count on you; if you say you'll call them, you will. Your mate may be frustrated by your refusal to talk out relationship issues, but you insist that your words and actions be taken at face value. Your impatience shows when others, less direct than you, beat around the bush instead of coming right out and saying what they have to say. Don't be offended if your mate asks you to get more in touch with your feelings; just do it and reap the rewards.

March 23

ASTROLOGICAL SIGN: Aries

PEOPLE BORN TODAY: Chaka Khan, Ric Ocasek, Akira Kurosawa, Moses Malone, Louie Anderson, Joan Crawford

FAMOUS EVENTS: "Give me liberty or give me death" speech delivered by Patrick Henry (1775); rivet patented (1794); Mexican presidential candidate Luis Donaldo Colosio assassinated (1994)

LUCKY NUMBER: 8

BIRTHSTONE: Diamond

POSITIVE TRAITS: Profound, inquisitive, progressive

NEGATIVE TRAITS: Stubborn, skeptical, unemotional

Your feet are firmly planted in the real world, but your mind is often engaged in exploring its fantastical fringes. New technology and scientific discoveries capture your imagination, and you are always the first to try out the latest gadget, program, or game. In love, you employ the scientific method, establishing a hypothesis about your partner and suspending judgment until all the facts are in. In the meantime, however, you don't hold back your affections. Though you tend to live mostly in your head, you're also tuned in to your body and have a highly developed appreciation for all things sensual. To relax, you get a charge out of socializing with like-minded friends, staying up late to discuss whatever is new under the sun.

March 24

ASTROLOGICAL SIGN: Aries

PEOPLE BORN TODAY: Steve McQueen, Bob Mackie, Donna Pescow, Roger Bannister, Kelly LeBrock, Denny McLain

FAMOUS EVENTS: Death of Queen Elizabeth I (1603); *Cat on a Hot Tin Roof* opens on Broadway (1955); Exxon *Valdez* oil spill disaster in Alaska (1989)

LUCKY NUMBER: 9

BIRTHSTONE: Diamond

POSITIVE TRAITS: Unassuming, affectionate, trusting

NEGATIVE TRAITS: Heedless, dreamer, thin-skinned

You enjoy ornament, decoration, and glittering façades, yet your nature is strictly no-frills. You are happiest when your achievements attract attention while your private life remains simple, steady, and filled with affection. You approach every new love relationship as if it were your first time out and your indefatigable optimism and enthusiasm make you a wonderful partner and sidekick. Because you are easily hurt, however, this same optimism can cause you some grief in matters of the heart. Nevertheless, because of your trusting, open nature, people of all types are drawn to you; among your wide circle of friends there is always someone eager to help you make the right connection or create an opportunity that makes your goals easier to attain.

March 25

ASTROLOGICAL SIGN: Aries

PEOPLE BORN TODAY: Aretha Franklin, Elton John, Sarah Jessica Parker, Nick Lowe, Gloria Steinem, Howard Cosell

FAMOUS EVENTS: Common Market established in Europe (1957); record fifth boxing championship won by Sugar Ray Robinson (1958); King Faisal of Saudi Arabia assassinated (1975)

LUCKY NUMBER: 1

BIRTHSTONE: Diamond

POSITIVE TRAITS: Active, audacious, individualistic

NEGATIVE TRAITS: Hypercritical, childish, touchy

You are a fully charged battery whose power supply never dips. Your electric energy and dynamic personality can help you surge to the top in your chosen field, as long as you keep a lid on your temper. You attract partners who, like you, want to be where the action is, but any lasting union will require a more conservative mate, who sees your volcanic outbursts as a reasonable price to pay for the excitement you bring to the relationship. Friends and family enjoy your spontaneity and applaud your enterprising nature, though your tendency to sulk when things don't go your way can put off those who know you less well. Don't confuse stamina with good health: eat well and exercise regularly.

March 26

ASTROLOGICAL SIGN: Aries

PEOPLE BORN TODAY: Diana Ross, Martin Short, Sandra Day O'Connor, Jennifer Grey, Joseph Campbell, Tennessee Williams

FAMOUS EVENTS: Death of Ludwig von Beethoven (1827); polio vaccine developed by Dr. Jonas Salk (1953); Camp David peace accords signed by Menachim Begin and Anwar Sadat (1979)

LUCKY NUMBER: 2

BIRTHSTONE: Diamond

POSITIVE TRAITS: Reliable, intuitive, mature

NEGATIVE TRAITS: Opinionated, overconfident, withdrawn

Like the postal service, you always deliver. You don't waste your breath making extravagant promises, you simply show up with the goods—on time. You cut straight to the heart of problems, using your intuition to sort out the real issues hovering beneath the surface of the superficial ones. Honesty, both emotional and intellectual, is your goal in any situation and though it can be painful, you insist on it. Because of your insights into human nature, and your ability to listen without passing judgment, friends and family seek you out in times of trouble. You are equally good at self-diagnosis, but where your health is concerned, seek outside opinions: If you suffer from anything more serious than a cold, call the doctor.

March 27

ASTROLOGICAL SIGN: Aries

PEOPLE BORN TODAY: Mariah Carey, Michael York, Arthur Mitchell, Cale Yarborough, Sarah Vaughan, Gloria Swanson, Quentin Tarantino

FAMOUS EVENTS: Ponce de Leon discovers Florida (1512); corkscrew patented (1860); first international radio transmission sent by Guglielmo Marconi (1899)

LUCKY NUMBER: 3

BIRTHSTONE: Diamond

POSITIVE TRAITS: Individualistic, stylish, exciting

NEGATIVE TRAITS: Melodramatic, attention-seeking, aloof

You have star quality, attracting attention wherever you go. Though you are aware of trends and experiment with innovations that intrigue you, you never cede your own singular style in matters of dress or behavior. Friends put up with your constant demand for attention because you are so entertaining and fun to be with. Your unique persona intrigues admirers, but you often find that you are more comfortable working a crowd than withstanding the intimate gaze of a lover. The right mate will share your sense of drama and know how to keep you interested and energized as you two fight for center stage. Sports bore you, whether you are a participant or a spectator. "Seeing and being seen," is your favorite pastime.

March 28

ASTROLOGICAL SIGN: Aries

PEOPLE BORN TODAY: Reba McEntire, Dianne Wiest, Ken Howard, Dirk Bogarde, Cheryl James (Salt of Salt-n-Pepa), Marlin Perkins

FAMOUS EVENTS: Crimean War started (1854); suicide by drowning of Virginia Woolf (1941); death of former president Dwight D. Eisenhower (1969)

LUCKY NUMBER: 4

BIRTHSTONE: Diamond

POSITIVE TRAITS: Focused, steady, family-oriented

NEGATIVE TRAITS: Narcissistic, oblivious, limited

Whatever chaos may be unfolding around you, you stick to your program and get the job done. Your ability to focus arises from the fact that your personal goals and your loved ones are your sole concerns; gossiping and meddling in the lives of others have no place on your agenda. You're the first one that friends and family think of when they need a confidant; a secret is safe with you and they know it. Because of your unsuspicious nature, you may not recognize manipulative behavior in others, which sometimes results in personal or professional setbacks. Your one vanity is your physique: You believe a strong body makes a strong mind (and a good impression) and you take pains to stay in shape.

March 29

ASTROLOGICAL SIGN: Aries

PEOPLE BORN TODAY: Elle MacPherson, Walt Frazier, Jennifer Capriati, Eric Idle, Pearl Bailey, Sam Walton

FAMOUS EVENTS: President James Madison's sister-in-law married in first White House wedding (1812); Coca-Cola invented (1886); presidential hopeful Bill Clinton admits to noninhaling marijuana use (1992)

LUCKY NUMBER: 5

BIRTHSTONE: Diamond

POSITIVE TRAITS: Deliberate, thorough, creative

NEGATIVE TRAITS: Wary, negative, reclusive

Slow and steady, that's your method of operation. No one can pull the wool over your eyes; you're cautious—too cautious some would say—and yet you have a knack for turning up good opportunities. You're the one who gets the best deal at the flea market, or secures the highest salary with the most perks. Your slowness to trust is a by-product of your astute skills at character analysis: You can detect a scam a mile away and know immediately when you are being manipulated. On the flip side, your wariness can tend to darken your outlook and make you unduly pessimistic. A lover you have utter faith in (and you wouldn't choose any other kind) can help to keep your suspicious tendencies in check.

March 30

ASTROLOGICAL SIGN: Aries

PEOPLE BORN TODAY: Paul Reiser, Celine Dion, Eric Clapton, Warren Beatty, Ian Ziering, Vincent van Gogh

FAMOUS EVENTS: First use of anesthesia for surgery (1842); Alaska purchased from Russia (1867); President Ronald Reagan and press secretary James Brady shot and wounded by John Hinckley Jr. (1981)

LUCKY NUMBER: 6

BIRTHSTONE: Diamond

POSITIVE TRAITS: Innovative, uncompromising, intense

NEGATIVE TRAITS: Uncooperative, antisocial, selfish

The freedom to chart your own course is essential to you. Around the house or around the workplace, you set your own agenda and create a personal environment that nurtures your own creative needs. Friends and romantic partners may think you selfish, but you're not: You are simply immersed in the pursuit of your personal goals, which you fear may never be attained if the needs of others take precedence over your own. When you do take the time to look outward, you are a warm and hospitable friend, eager to get up a party or simply spend time with your friends at home. Your ideal mate will have an independent streak as strong as your own, which should make for an interesting, if volatile, relationship.

March 31

ASTROLOGICAL SIGN: Aries
PEOPLE BORN TODAY: Albert Gore Jr., Leo Buscaglia, Liz Claiborne, Rene Descartes, Shirley Jones, Rhea Perlman, Franz Joseph Haydn, Octavio Paz
FAMOUS EVENTS: Jack Johnson becomes first African-American to win heavyweight boxing title (1878); U.S. inaugurates daylight saving time (1918)
LUCKY NUMBER: 7
BIRTHSTONE: Diamond
POSITIVE TRAITS: Energetic, loyal, stable
NEGATIVE TRAITS: Unambitious, self-effacing, cynical

A bird in the hand is worth two in the bush and then some, as far as you are concerned. In your estimation, a more promising job or a more appealing mate can never hold a candle to the one you already possess. Bosses and partners laud you for your loyalty, but in fact your stability springs from a profound sense of who you are. In love, your eye and your heart never wander because you find what is right for you the first time; trial and error are not your style. Though you may lack ambition, you do not lack vitality: You're frequently on the go and encouraging others to come along with you, which, because of your contagious enthusiasm, they readily do.

April 1

ASTROLOGICAL SIGN: Aries
PEOPLE BORN TODAY: Ali MacGraw, Debbie Reynolds, Jane Powell, Phil Niekro, David Eisenhower, Lon Chaney, Gil Scott-Heron, Toshiro Mifune
FAMOUS EVENTS: First woman signed by minor league baseball team (1931); Spanish Civil War ends (1939); Marvin Gaye fatally shot by his father (1984)
LUCKY NUMBER: 5
BIRTHSTONE: Diamond
POSITIVE TRAITS: Mature, responsible, conscientious
NEGATIVE TRAITS: Shy, self-doubting, workaholic

You do not seem to know your chronological age. As a child you demonstrated a mature sense of responsibility that told teachers and parents they could count on you; as an adult you are still very much the dependable one, doing your best to meet the expectations of others at work and at home. Your youthful demeanor gives you a wholesome appeal that attracts others, although your genuine shyness may prevent you from responding freely to their attentions. Any long-term mate will have to share you with your work, since it is impossible for you to leave any task undone. You will work harder at a shape-up routine if you enlist a personal trainer—and aim to please.

April 2

ASTROLOGICAL SIGN: Aries

PEOPLE BORN TODAY: Emmylou Harris, Marvin Gaye, Alec Guinness, Linda Hunt, Buddy Ebsen, Don Sutton

FAMOUS EVENTS: Radar patented by Watson Watt (1935); streaker steals the spotlight from Elizabeth Taylor at the Academy Awards (1974); Falkland Islands invaded by Argentina, starting conflict with Great Britain (1982)

LUCKY NUMBER: 6

BIRTHSTONE: Diamond

POSITIVE TRAITS: Utopian, noble, courageous

NEGATIVE TRAITS: Unrealistic, blinkered, naive

You are moved by the suffering of others, and whether you are fighting the demotion of a coworker, protesting political corruption, or standing up for a slighted child, you refuse to acknowledge the possibility of insurmountable obstacles. Your utopian worldview excites admiration in your friends and associates, who know that your intentions are pure even when they consider your efforts futile. You will inspire your more earthbound mate to new heights by pointing out undreamed-of possibilities. Those you hold dear are likely to share your idealism to some degree; your sunny optimism will help to discourage them from growing cynical as they mature. You can rally others to the cause even when your spirits are low—which is rare.

April 3

ASTROLOGICAL SIGN: Aries

PEOPLE BORN TODAY: Eddie Murphy, Melissa Etheridge, Marlon Brando, Marsha Mason, Alec Baldwin, Doris Day, Jane Goodall, Wayne Newton

FAMOUS EVENTS: Pony Express mail service initiated (1860); Jesse James shot by gang member Robert Ford (1882); F. Scott Fitzgerald and Zelda Sayre married (1920)

LUCKY NUMBER: 7

BIRTHSTONE: Diamond

POSITIVE TRAITS: Outgoing, tender, warm

NEGATIVE TRAITS: Exhibitionistic, spoiled, moody

As long as you are in the loop, you are content. You can't stand to be left out of things, and tend to sulk if you are. This rarely happens, however, since people respect your views and enjoy your company. You are an openhearted and giving mate, so long as your partner's gaze doesn't drift around the restaurant during a romantic dinner. Though you are exceedingly gregarious, affectionate, and tender-hearted, you sporadically need time off just to be by yourself—for no other reason than you want to be alone. Friends and lovers may feel shunned by this behavior if you surprise them with it. Let your natural kindness be your guide when your moods take over and all will be well.

April 4

ASTROLOGICAL SIGN: Aries
PEOPLE BORN TODAY: Maya Angelou, Robert Downey Jr., Nancy McKeon, Craig T. Nelson, A. Bartlett Giamatti, Muddy Waters, Anthony Perkins
FAMOUS EVENTS: North Atlantic Treaty Organization (NATO) founded (1949); Dr. Martin Luther King Jr. assassinated (1968); Pakistani president Zulfikar Ali Bhutto executed (1979)
LUCKY NUMBER: 8
BIRTHSTONE: Diamond
POSITIVE TRAITS: Clear-sighted, wise, influential
NEGATIVE TRAITS: Self-effacing, nomadic, changeable

At home, at work, and in your community, you have little trouble conceiving bold new ventures and recruiting others to your cause. Too often, however, you move on to the next crusade before the results are in, leaving others to garner most of the credit for your ideas. You will find greater satisfaction and financial rewards if you settle on a single goal and see it through. Your mate may be confused by your constant shifts in direction, but the energy you bring to the relationship—and the commitment—do a lot to compensate for any lack on your part. Your dedication and enthusiasm are sure to have a positive influence on everyone with whom you come in contact.

April 5

ASTROLOGICAL SIGN: Aries

PEOPLE BORN TODAY: Colin Powell, Bette Davis, Spencer Tracy, Gregory Peck, Melvyn Douglas, Booker T. Washington

FAMOUS EVENTS: Pocahontas and John Rolfe wed (1614); French Revolution leader Georges Danton guillotined (1794); Fran Phipps becomes first woman to reach the North Pole (1971)

LUCKY NUMBER: 9

BIRTHSTONE: Diamond

POSITIVE TRAITS: Forceful, charming, principled

NEGATIVE TRAITS: Overwhelming, unyielding, tempestuous

Your innate charisma wins you fans on the job and in society, but fame and fortune are not your top priorities: You value hard work and solid achievement more than money or popularity. Although you do not go out of your way to woo romantic partners, your principles only add to your appeal. You require a patient mate who accepts you as you are and soothes your ruffled feathers on the rare occasions when your wishes are thwarted. Those close to you may be taken aback at times by your forceful manner, but they know that you will keep every promise you make. You're in touch with your feelings and frequently rely on your inner voices to guide you through difficult situations.

April 6

ASTROLOGICAL SIGN: Aries

PEOPLE BORN TODAY: Billy Dee Williams, Barry Levinson, Merle Haggard, John Ratzenberger, Butch Cassidy, Marilu Henner

FAMOUS EVENTS: First modern Olympic Games opened (1896); U.S. declares war on Germany (1917); first Tony Awards presented (1947)

LUCKY NUMBER: 1

BIRTHSTONE: Diamond

POSITIVE TRAITS: Broad-minded, curious, creative

NEGATIVE TRAITS: Eccentric, unrealistic, out of touch

You carry the wide-eyed excitement and curiosity of childhood with you throughout your life. Whether you become a corporate chief or a corporate chef, your mind will remain open to new and better ways of performing your duties. Romantic partners see you as a bit flaky, but fun, and count on your imaginative skills to keep relationships from becoming stodgy and stale. You are everyone's favorite sidekick, and your knack for finding innovative ways of doing things extends to every facet of your life. This makes you a genie in the kitchen, a thrill in the bedroom, and a success in the workplace. Your energy isn't limitless, however, and you need more sleep than most to avoid burnout. Be sure you get it.

April 7

ASTROLOGICAL SIGN: Aries

PEOPLE BORN TODAY: Jerry Brown, James Garner, Francis Ford Coppola, Billie Holiday, Ravi Shankar, Percy Faith

FAMOUS EVENTS: First meeting of Edward, Prince of Wales and Wallis Simpson (1920); first long-distance television transmission (1927); first postage stamp featuring an African-American issued, in honor of Booker T. Washington (1940)

LUCKY NUMBER: 2

BIRTHSTONE: Diamond

POSITIVE TRAITS: Committed, enthusiastic, vibrant

NEGATIVE TRAITS: Subjective, demanding, rebellious

When an idea catches fire, you burn with an intensity that can drive you to extremes. You may run into trouble when you assume that friends or coworkers are as enthusiastically committed to your projects as you are. Romantic partners are attracted to your energy and passion, but may be scared off by your hotheaded displays; it takes a special mate to temper your wild-eyed fervor and bring your expectations down to earth. Unless parenthood becomes your obsession, your children may take a backseat to whatever cause holds you in its grip. Resist the pull of extremes in eating, drinking, and other diversions, to minimize the risk of addiction—and to keep your body as sharp as your mind.

April 8

ASTROLOGICAL SIGN: Aries

PEOPLE BORN TODAY: Julian Lennon, Betty Ford, Jim "Catfish" Hunter, Michael Bennett, Sonja Henie, Mary Pickford

FAMOUS EVENTS: Regular transatlantic steamship service begins (1838); Babe Ruth's home-run record broken by Hank Aaron (1974); Kurt Cobain commits suicide (1994)

LUCKY NUMBER: 3

BIRTHSTONE: Diamond

POSITIVE TRAITS: Caring, humanitarian, outspoken

NEGATIVE TRAITS: Private, shy, undemonstrative

You are more committed to the world at large than to any one individual. Family members, romantic partners, and the people you call friends may be frustrated in their attempts to achieve any real depth of understanding with you. You are easily moved and do not lack feelings, but you are seldom comfortable sharing them; you would rather express your kindness through humanitarian deeds that benefit as many people as possible. When you find a mate, it will probably be someone equally altruistic, and the two of you will direct a good deal of emotion outward rather than at each other. This isn't necessarily a bad thing: When you do finally connect with your partner, it will be exciting, and, in spite of your inhibitions, rewarding.

ASTROLOGICAL SIGN: Aries

PEOPLE BORN TODAY: Dennis Quaid, Keshia Knight Pulliam, Carl Perkins, Paulina Porizkova, Hugh Hefner, W. C. Fields

FAMOUS EVENTS: Civil War ended with Lee's official surrender to Grant (1865); first issue of *TV Guide* published (1953); Houston Astrodome opens (1965)

LUCKY NUMBER: 4

BIRTHSTONE: Diamond

POSITIVE TRAITS: Expansive, entertaining, sensual

NEGATIVE TRAITS: Excessive, unreliable, wild

Too much is not enough" is likely to be your motto. You drink deeply of all the pleasures life has to offer, then go looking for more. In business, your understanding of basic human nature can make you an accurate predictor of social trends and provide opportunities for profit. Romantic partners are seduced by your lavish lifestyle, but some may find your excesses too much of a good thing. Though you can be a lot of fun as a parent and friend, you're not always reliable; however you are generous, open, and affectionate, and, in most cases, these qualities more than offset your lack of dependability. You might attempt moderation: one glass of wine with dinner, one cream puff for dessert, and so on.

April 10

ASTROLOGICAL SIGN: Aries

PEOPLE BORN TODAY: Steven Seagal, John Madden, Brian Setzer, Omar Sharif, Don Meredith, Clare Boothe Luce

FAMOUS EVENTS: ASPCA incorporated (1866); first 3-D feature film premieres (1953); breakup of Beatles announced by Paul McCartney (1970)

LUCKY NUMBER: 5

BIRTHSTONE: Diamond

POSITIVE TRAITS: Courageous, dedicated, masterful

NEGATIVE TRAITS: Secretive, workaholic, phobic

You are an action hero or heroine, brave and daring but seldom reckless or foolish. Although you take considerable risks in business and finance, your private life may be punctuated by attacks of one phobia or another. (It is likely to be the little things—heights, airplanes, the dark—that push your panic button.) Your passion for work is equaled by your dedication to family and friends, who seek you out whenever they need a different, daring perspective. Your mate will applaud your boldness but may be less than enthralled with your unwillingness to share your thoughts and emotions. Your ideal mate will tolerate your reticence while coaxing you to come out of your shell and experience the joys of sharing and intimacy.

April 11

ASTROLOGICAL SIGN: Aries

PEOPLE BORN TODAY: Joel Grey, Louise Lasser, Bill Irwin, Hugh Carey, Oleg Cassini

FAMOUS EVENTS: French throne abdicated by Napoléon Bonaparte (1814); Buchenwald concentration camp liberated by Allied forces (1945); Jackie Robinson signed by Brooklyn Dodgers (1947)

LUCKY NUMBER: 6

BIRTHSTONE: Diamond

POSITIVE TRAITS: Wise, fair, diplomatic

NEGATIVE TRAITS: Impersonal, awkward, touchy

You possess the skills of an old-fashioned politician with more concern for ideas than for image, and in every facet of life you work to create a nurturing and peaceful environment. You're a great mediator, capable of bringing the most divergent viewpoints into harmony, and your poise and tact serve you well in any situation. In love, you tend to be cool—at first. You will never give your heart without first being absolutely certain that your affections are returned; when they are, you're as loyal—and romantic—as a mate could hope for. Your favorite diversion is planning get-togethers for several hundred of your closest friends, where your solid social graces keep everybody happily mingling for hours.

April 12

ASTROLOGICAL SIGN: Aries

PEOPLE BORN TODAY: David Letterman, Herbie Hancock, Shannen Doherty, Andy Garcia, David Cassidy, Vince Gill

FAMOUS EVENTS: Civil War begun by Confederate attack on Fort Sumter (1861); death of President Franklin D. Roosevelt (1945); Yuri Gagarin first man in space (1961)

LUCKY NUMBER: 7

BIRTHSTONE: Diamond

POSITIVE TRAITS: Well-informed, interested, communicative

NEGATIVE TRAITS: Opinionated, hectoring, distant

You are a human teletype machine, steadily cranking out the latest news to entertain and enlighten everyone around you. You seek an audience, not a confidant, and are often surrounded by a fascinated group of listeners. Romantic partners find you stimulating and fun, but any problems you have with your mate are likely to go unaddressed unless you occasionally share your own feelings as avidly as you do the morning news. Your elusiveness can cause friction; don't let it become a habit if you want your love to last. Because you spend a lot of time with your gaze glued to the news channel, position an exercise machine in front of the tube; you won't miss a thing and your body will thank you.

April 13

ASTROLOGICAL SIGN: Aries

PEOPLE BORN TODAY: Al Green, Seamus Heaney, Max Weinberg, Lanford Wilson, Eudora Welty, Cate Newell Stark, Thomas Jefferson

FAMOUS EVENTS: Jefferson Memorial dedicated (1943); Harold Washington elected Chicago's first black mayor (1983); underground flood in Chicago causes two hundred million dollars in damages (1992)

LUCKY NUMBER: 8

BIRTHSTONE: Diamond

POSITIVE TRAITS: Bold, powerful, reforming

NEGATIVE TRAITS: Reclusive, sensitive, odd

You are a reformer, willing to toil long and hard without recognition to effect the changes you consider vital. Your novel ideas may cause coworkers and acquaintances to regard you as an oddball at first, but later they will recognize the wisdom of your reforms and may even come to appreciate your slightly harebrained approach to problem solving. A like-minded mate will validate your vision and provide moral support when few others offer it. Because a stable relationship is the kind in which you are most comfortable, you give yourself over easily to love. Though you value solitude, you are really happiest "alone together" with your chosen mate, cooking, watching TV, or making love. Life is good to you.

April 14

ASTROLOGICAL SIGN: Aries

PEOPLE BORN TODAY: Emma Thompson, Julie Christie, Sir John Gielgud, Loretta Lynn, Anthony Perkins

FAMOUS EVENTS: President Abraham Lincoln assassinated (1865); *Titanic* sunk after colliding with iceberg, killing 1,517 (1912); Academy Award won by Hattie McDaniel, first African-American to receive Oscar (1940)

LUCKY NUMBER: 9

BIRTHSTONE: Diamond

POSITIVE TRAITS: Productive, respectful, conventional

NEGATIVE TRAITS: Fussy, careless, insecure

You follow in the footsteps of the greats, and often achieve such eminence that you find others following you. Devising radical new methods doesn't interest you; you aim only to reach heights already scaled by others. A stable home life and work situation and a steady, supportive mate will give you the security you need to soar in whatever professional or artistic endeavors you attempt. In return, you are a devoted partner, willing to give equal time to your mate's needs and desires. A partner who can appreciate your meticulous attention to detail and your intolerance for a mess of any kind will please you the most; and, if your union is to last, will be as emotionally receptive and responsive as you are.

April 15

ASTROLOGICAL SIGN: Aries

PEOPLE BORN TODAY: Dave Edmunds, Evelyn Ashford, Sir Neville Marriner, Roy Clark, Elizabeth Montgomery, Leonardo da Vinci

FAMOUS EVENTS: Ivory soap created by Harley Procter (1878); first handprints in Grauman's Theatre sidewalk made by Douglas Fairbanks, Mary Pickford, and Norma Talmadge (1927); first McDonald's restaurant opens (1955)

LUCKY NUMBER: 1

BIRTHSTONE: Diamond

POSITIVE TRAITS: Realistic, observant, clever

NEGATIVE TRAITS: Exacting, excitable, intense

You want to make your mark on the world—or at least your little part of it. When things fall short of your standards, you have a hard time keeping your hands off and resisting the urge to set things right. Your acute powers of observation make it possible for you to detect the missing link or vital piece of information needed to remedy any situation. Sometimes you take your talents to extremes, which can become a sore point with romantic partners, who want to be loved for who they are, not for their potential to become your fantasy mate. Nevertheless, you are well liked for your generosity, your high spirits, your loyalty, and your innate sense of fair play.

April 16

ASTROLOGICAL SIGN: Aries

PEOPLE BORN TODAY: Martin Lawrence, Ellen Barkin, Jon Cryer, Merce Cunningham, Kareem Abdul-Jabbar, Charlie Chaplin

FAMOUS EVENTS: Zoom lens patented (1947); Walter Cronkite debuts as *CBS Evening News* anchor (1962); *Apollo XVI* launched to the Moon (1972)

LUCKY NUMBER: 2

BIRTHSTONE: Diamond

POSITIVE TRAITS: Humorous, kind, charitable

NEGATIVE TRAITS: Unworldly, spacey, emotionally repressed

Friends and coworkers seem to regard you as a benign visitor from another planet. You are humorous, kindhearted, and high-minded—literally, since your head is often in the clouds. Strong emotions, whether positive or negative, make you uncomfortable, and you usually attempt to lighten intense moments with a joke. Your mate should be someone who shares your high ideals and dedication, so your preoccupation with social causes or community affairs won't cause him or her to feel neglected. You may be a somewhat lackadaisical parent when your children are young, but grow interested in their schoolwork and social activities as they mature. Your own physical pursuits should lean toward team sports rather than solitary fitness, since you need company to keep your attention from wandering.

ASTROLOGICAL SIGN: Aries

PEOPLE BORN TODAY: Boomer Esiason, Jan Hammer, Harry Reasoner, Olivia Hussey, William Holden, Isak Dinesen, J. P. Morgan

FAMOUS EVENTS: Martin Luther excommunicated (1521); Bay of Pigs invasion (1961); Jerrie Mock becomes first woman pilot to fly solo around the world (1964)

LUCKY NUMBER: 3

BIRTHSTONE: Diamond

POSITIVE TRAITS: Weighty, purposeful, affectionate

NEGATIVE TRAITS: Secretive, materialistic, moody

You are a quietly influential person who can reap great rewards in life. Though the security of a loving relationship with a mate is important to you, you are neither possessive nor dominating, preferring instead to let your mate enjoy a certain degree of independence. Though you tend to be moody, you most often look at the bright side of things—and prefer the company of those who do the same. You are wise enough not to subject others to your moods; instead you seek out a solitary refuge when your darker moments are upon you. You can take this too far, however, by refusing to share your ups and downs with your mate, thereby limiting the depth of your bonding.

April 18

ASTROLOGICAL SIGN: Aries

PEOPLE BORN TODAY: Conan O'Brien, James Woods, Rick Moranis, Eric Roberts, Hayley Mills, Clarence Darrow

FAMOUS EVENTS: Midnight ride taken by Paul Revere and compatriots (1775); San Francisco earthquake (1906); Grace Kelly and Prince Rainier wed (1956)

LUCKY NUMBER: 4

BIRTHSTONE: Diamond

POSITIVE TRAITS: Dignified, protective, loyal

NEGATIVE TRAITS: Proud, starchy, oversensitive

You're solid and dependable, proud and dignified. Though you are particularly vulnerable to assaults on your dignity or performance, they rarely occur. You are a true-blue friend to those who treat you with respect and understanding, and a loyal and protective partner in love. You are likely to choose a mate whose virtues include prudence and tact and who has a public persona that will harmonize with your sense of propriety. Your dignity doesn't preclude your having a good time; it's just that you won't ever have to spend the next day regretting embarrassing behavior. Because your horror of ungainliness may keep you from getting enough exercise, try "sweatin' to the oldies" with a videotape in the privacy of your living room, preferably with the curtains drawn.

April 19

ASTROLOGICAL SIGN: Aries
PEOPLE BORN TODAY: Dudley Moore, Paloma Picasso, Don Adams, Tim Curry, Elinor Donahue, Dick Sargent
FAMOUS EVENTS: First battle of the Revolutionary War begins at Lexington, Massachusetts (1775); first Boston Marathon (1897); longest recorded Major League home run hit by Mickey Mantle (1953)
LUCKY NUMBER: 5
BIRTHSTONE: Diamond
POSITIVE TRAITS: Committed, enduring, productive
NEGATIVE TRAITS: Forgetful, preachy, greedy

You possess enough physical stamina to be a long-distance runner and enough mental acuity to succeed in virtually anything. You are slow to commit to a career, a mate, a hobby—everything, in fact—but once you do, you stick to your choices like gum to a shoe. Most likely, your chosen mate and you will have identical goals, which you will enjoy moving toward together. Big on romance, you won't fall victim to dull routine just because you're part of a twosome; in fact, you will probably hone your seductive charms by finding creative ways to keep the fire going in your relationship. Probably your biggest asset is your natural good cheer: You always wake up on the right side of the bed.

April 20

ASTROLOGICAL SIGN: Aries

PEOPLE BORN TODAY: Daniel Day-Lewis, Jessica Lange, Don Mattingly, Luther Vandross, Ryan O'Neal, Tito Puente

FAMOUS EVENTS: New South Wales discovered by Captain James Cook (1770); radium discovered by Marie and Pierre Curie (1902); Pierre Trudeau sworn in as Canada's prime minister (1968)

LUCKY NUMBER: 6

BIRTHSTONE: Diamond

POSITIVE TRAITS: Charismatic, sensual, galvanizing

NEGATIVE TRAITS: Egotistical, stubborn, nutty

Charisma—you have it in spades. Because others follow your lead willingly, and even blindly on occasion, you have a well-developed ethical sense and only rarely do you succumb to the temptation to use your hypnotic personality *strictly* for personal gain. At home you are an exciting, passionate partner who can bring the romance of grand opera to a simple picnic lunch in the backyard. You're in tune to all your senses and glory in all the tastes, smells, sounds, and sights of your environment. Hugs and kisses are your basic sustenance, without which you would wither away; if you are not holding hands with your mate at the movies, something is dreadfully wrong. Perhaps you stubbornly insisted on sitting so far back in the theater?

April 21

ASTROLOGICAL SIGN: Taurus

PEOPLE BORN TODAY: Tony Danza, Andie McDowell, Charles Grodin, Patti LuPone, Queen Elizabeth II, Charlotte Brontë

FAMOUS EVENTS: Henry VIII ascends British throne (1509); German flying ace the Red Baron shot down (1918); first *successful* artificial heart implant (1982)

LUCKY NUMBER: 7

BIRTHSTONE: Emerald

POSITIVE TRAITS: Concerned, dynamic, intense

NEGATIVE TRAITS: Vulnerable, depressive, obsessive

Because you are willing to go that extra mile, you often end up in places few others ever get to. Though financial rewards are likely to come your way, they are not what motivates you; you want to push your personal envelope and discover what your true capabilities are. Intensely driven, you are not without a lighter side, which is what keeps you from succumbing to stresses inherent in your search for self-discovery. You know how to laugh, and how to make others laugh—frequently at your own expense. No matter how chaotic life gets in the outside world, your home will be a welcoming, relaxing refuge where you—and your partner, you *must* have a partner—can snuggle up and enjoy the fruits of your labor.

April 22

ASTROLOGICAL SIGN: Taurus

PEOPLE BORN TODAY: Jack Nicholson, Peter Frampton, Glen Campbell, Aaron Spelling, Charles Mingus, Yehudi Menuhin

FAMOUS EVENTS: First U.S. circus performance (1793); first pro basketball championship, won by Philadelphia Warriors (1947); New York World's Fair opens (1964)

LUCKY NUMBER: 8

BIRTHSTONE: Emerald

POSITIVE TRAITS: Clever, powerful, assertive

NEGATIVE TRAITS: Thoughtless, critical, controlling

Power and everything that bespeaks it are your goals. You devote your calculating wits and managerial skills to the pursuit of the best: best job, best car, best house. Friends and family find your ambitions laudable, and because you are lavish with praise and recognition of others, no one resents your successes. You tend to be suspicious where love is concerned and will only open up to a partner after a long, and sometimes frustrating, getting-to-know-you period. Your leisure activities also reflect your pursuit of the best; you undertake and enjoy searching out the best restaurant, the best coffee bar, or the best ski slope. Your health will improve if you ease up in your relentless drive for control.

April 23

ASTROLOGICAL SIGN: Taurus

PEOPLE BORN TODAY: Valerie Bertinelli, Jan Hooks, Roy Orbison, Shirley Temple Black, William Shakespeare, Lee Majors, Vladimir Nabokov

FAMOUS EVENTS: Deaths of Cervantes and Shakespeare (1616); first presidential mansion occupied by George and Martha Washington (1789); first Las Vegas performance of Elvis Presley (1956)

LUCKY NUMBER: 9

BIRTHSTONE: Emerald

POSITIVE TRAITS: Plucky, popular, accommodating

NEGATIVE TRAITS: Private, enigmatic, misleading

You are an enigma known only to your most intimate friends; others have either a false image of you, or little image at all. Their misreading doesn't bother you, however, as you are confident enough to let others paint the picture of you that pleases them most. You welcome the chance to open up to a partner, but be sure that your long-term mate is someone willing to sacrifice an infatuation with your surface charm for a deeper relationship with your more complicated true self. Though you tend to be restless, often finding it difficult to commit to a career, a plan of action, or a point of view, you are not flighty, and people can count on you to finish what you started.

April 24

ASTROLOGICAL SIGN: Taurus

PEOPLE BORN TODAY: Barbra Streisand, Shirley MacLaine, Jill Ireland, Robert Penn Warren, Michael O'Keefe, Eric Bogosian

FAMOUS EVENTS: First sighting of Halley's comet (1061); *La Marseillaise* composed (1792); Easter Rebellion begins in Ireland (1916)

LUCKY NUMBER: 1

BIRTHSTONE: Emerald

POSITIVE TRAITS: Nurturing, tender, emotional

NEGATIVE TRAITS: Fussy, brash, secretive

A devoted friend, coworker, and companion, you see it as your duty to make sure that others aren't too hot or too cold, too hungry or too full, too tired or too tense. Your solicitous behavior is alternately endearing and exasperating: Your mate will be grateful for your attentions, but don't risk draining the romance out of your relationship by assuming a parental role. You tend to cling to things, not out of neediness but out of nostalgia. It actually *pains* you to give up any part of your past, and your home is likely to be filled to the rafters with memorabilia, old clothes, trophies, and the like. Woe be to the person who suggests, or heaven forbid undertakes, to lighten you of these sentimental burdens.

April 25

ASTROLOGICAL SIGN: Taurus

PEOPLE BORN TODAY: Ella Fitzgerald, Al Pacino, Paul Mazursky, Talia Shire, Meadowlark Lemon, Edward R. Murrow

FAMOUS EVENTS: O. Henry imprisoned for embezzlement (1898); Allied landing at Gallipoli (1915); first guide dog for the blind employed (1928)

LUCKY NUMBER: 2

BIRTHSTONE: Emerald

POSITIVE TRAITS: Imposing, sensual, provocative

NEGATIVE TRAITS: Overpowering, earthbound, mundane

Regardless of your size, you make a big impression. Your physical and vocal presence turns heads when you enter a room, and friends and associates find your opinions hard to ignore. The more ethereal or spiritual aspects of life may be lost on you, since you tend to count as real only that which you can see and feel. Partners are attracted by your earthy sensuality and physical grace; few people are more at ease in their bodies than you are, and even fewer make the effort to physically satisfy their partners in the way that you do. Emotionally, you are very even—too even, some might argue—and rarely do you take the time, or feel the need, to get in touch with your feelings.

April 26

ASTROLOGICAL SIGN: Taurus
PEOPLE BORN TODAY: Carol Burnett, Michael Damian, Duane Eddy, Anita Loos, Bernard Malamud, John James Audubon
FAMOUS EVENTS: John Wilkes Booth (Lincoln's assassin) captured and shot (1865); Largest U.S. bank robbery, $3.3 million (1981); nuclear-reactor explosion at Chernobyl in Ukraine (1986)
LUCKY NUMBER: 3
BIRTHSTONE: Emerald
POSITIVE TRAITS: Dependable, pragmatic, imaginative
NEGATIVE TRAITS: Pessimistic, overly cautious, lazy

You are a pillar of common sense. You stand your ground when coworkers or friends try to sell you on half-baked schemes, gently but patiently pointing out the flaws in their logic. If you can take leave of logic long enough to listen to your heart, you are well on your way to a more balanced and healthy approach to life and love. Learn to give in to your whimsical side—you do have one!—and you may astonish yourself and others with your capacity for outlandishness. Your sense of humor is highly developed, almost never mean-spirited, and frequently directed at yourself—whom you often characterize publicly as a plodding dullard but secretly believe to be a curious, lovable dynamo.

ASTROLOGICAL SIGN: Taurus

PEOPLE BORN TODAY: Kate Pierson, Jack Klugman, Sheena Easton, Casey Kasem, Coretta Scott King, Ulysses S. Grant, Chuck Knox, Sandy Dennis

FAMOUS EVENTS: Magellan killed on final voyage (1521); Expo '67 opened in Montreal (1967); resignation of FBI director L. Patrick Gray (1973)

LUCKY NUMBER: 4

BIRTHSTONE: Emerald

POSITIVE TRAITS: Supportive, cooperative, charming

NEGATIVE TRAITS: Shy, serious, aloof

You are in your element as part of a crowd. When friends and coworkers relate to you one on one, they find you reserved and serious; it takes a project, party, or other group setting to set your dynamic energies in motion. When you do get revved up, however, all your social graces come into play. You're gregarious, funny, inventive, and willing to give almost anything a go—as long as it is legal. Friends consider you a "good catch" and probably play matchmaker for you, whether you like it or not. Though you are happier in a relationship than you are playing the field, you find creating intimacy to be hard work—or at least work that you are not well suited for.

April 28

ASTROLOGICAL SIGN: Taurus
PEOPLE BORN TODAY: Jay Leno, Ann-Margret, John Daly, Lionel Barrymore, James Monroe, Jack Nicholson, Blossom Dearie
FAMOUS EVENTS: Mutiny on the *Bounty* led by Fletcher Christian (1789); Mussolini executed (1945); *Kon-Tiki* expedition initiated by Thor Heyerdahl (1947)
LUCKY NUMBER: 5
BIRTHSTONE: Emerald
POSITIVE TRAITS: Honest, loyal, compassionate
NEGATIVE TRAITS: Stubborn, pushy, blunt

You're the first one friends, family, and colleagues call in a crisis, never doubting that you'll be there for them with a strong shoulder and a good solution. You're a tenacious worker, never giving up until you see light at the end of the tunnel. You appreciate honesty, even when it can be painful, and you try to be as forthcoming as possible with everyone you meet. Some may think you *too* forthcoming, but you would rather take the chance of offending someone than participating in deception of any kind. You are a generous and compassionate lover—and a passionate one too—and, as long as your partner is faithful, you will stick to your relationship with the same tenacity you stick to your principles.

April 29

ASTROLOGICAL SIGN: Taurus

PEOPLE BORN TODAY: Jerry Seinfeld, Michelle Pfeiffer, Andre Agassi, Carnie Wilson, Nora Dunn, Duke Ellington

FAMOUS EVENTS: Rubber patented (1813); Lou Gehrig set record for consecutive games played (1939); unconditional surrender of German army in Italy (1945); rioting in Los Angeles after acquittals in Rodney King beating trial (1992)

LUCKY NUMBER: 6

BIRTHSTONE: Emerald

POSITIVE TRAITS: Collected, poised, dignified

NEGATIVE TRAITS: Proud, pretentious, stiff

You have your act together and devote considerable energy to keeping it that way. Coworkers and love partners are unlikely to catch you with your pants down, or even your shoelaces untied. Keeping up a perfectly pressed front can be tiring, though, and your ideal mate will be one with whom you can let down your hair, have a good laugh at yourself, and share your hopes and dreams. Your manners are impeccable and you prefer the company of equally refined companions who know how to perform and appreciate life's little niceties. You are fortunate to have a sturdy constitution and a shapely physique in spite of the fact that you thumb your nose at all types of diets and fitness regimes.

April 30

ASTROLOGICAL SIGN: Taurus

PEOPLE BORN TODAY: Willie Nelson, Jill Clayburgh, Isiah Thomas, Cloris Leachman, Johnny Galecki, Gary Collins

FAMOUS EVENTS: George Washington becomes first president of U.S. (1789); Louisiana becomes the 18th state (1812); suicide of Adolf Hitler and Eva Braun (1945)

LUCKY NUMBER: 7

BIRTHSTONE: Emerald

POSITIVE TRAITS: Hardworking, committed, cheerful

NEGATIVE TRAITS: Blindly loyal, unyielding, rank-conscious

You don't know how to say no; you're the first person people think of when they need help and, whether you have the know-how or not, you gladly volunteer. Because you are a quick study, capable with your hands and equally capable with your mind, you come away from every task with more skills to your credit. Your natural good cheer makes you a joy to be around and your highly developed sense of humor ensures that you will be the center of attention. In romance, if you find yourself with a mate who requires your full attention and constant assistance, keep looking. You'll be happiest with a truly equal partner, someone emotionally secure and willing to give you personal space and affection with no strings attached.

May 1

ASTROLOGICAL SIGN: Taurus
PEOPLE BORN TODAY: Judy Collins, Rita Coolidge, Ray Parker Jr., Glenn Ford, Steve Cauthen, Jack Paar, Billie Owens
FAMOUS EVENTS: Premiere of *Citizen Kane* (1941); suicide of Nazi propaganda minister Joseph Goebbels (1945); Elvis Presley and Priscilla Beaulieu wed in Las Vegas (1967)
LUCKY NUMBER: 6
BIRTHSTONE: Emerald
POSITIVE TRAITS: Affectionate, calm, casual
NEGATIVE TRAITS: Clumsy, passive, tactless

You are a calm voice of reason, wondering what all the fuss is about as you mediate squabbles and head off hysterics. This can be a godsend, helping you and others maintain the proper perspective, but it can also be a handicap if it keeps you from pushing yourself forward at work or expressing your affection to loved ones. Use your emotional awareness to your advantage: Offer your mate regular reassurance that his or her love ranks first among the things you value. Your fondness for comedy and love of a good joke, even on yourself, makes you fun to be around. You are in no danger of becoming a physical fitness nut, but a brisk walk now and again won't do you any harm. Get out there and do it!

May 2

ASTROLOGICAL SIGN: Taurus

PEOPLE BORN TODAY: Larry Gatlin, Jenna Von Oy, Bianca Jagger, Benjamin Spock, Lesley Gore, Bing Crosby

FAMOUS EVENTS: Queen Anne Boleyn imprisoned in the Tower of London (1536); Stonewall Jackson fatally wounded by his own soldiers (1863); first science fiction film released (1902)

LUCKY NUMBER: 7

BIRTHSTONE: Emerald

POSITIVE TRAITS: Driving, cautious, generous

NEGATIVE TRAITS: Demanding, critical, harsh

Simply put, you shine. Whether you are whipping up an omelet or writing up a brief, your performance is of stellar quality. Friends and family recognize your talents and often emulate you. Though you appreciate the admiration, your natural modesty keeps it from going to your head. Instead, you seek the input and advice of others and enjoy probing into their opinions, which you then take into account when formulating your own ideas. Your private life is exactly that: private. Though you are relatively forthcoming with your partner, you are extremely reticent to expose yourself to others. You are, however, socially outgoing and your home is probably a welcoming home-away-from-home to your friends and your children's friends.

May 3

ASTROLOGICAL SIGN: Taurus

PEOPLE BORN TODAY: Greg Gumbel, Doug Henning, Engelbert Humperdinck, Golda Meir, Pete Seeger, Walter Slezak, May Sarton

FAMOUS EVENTS: First comic book published (1934); Margaret Mitchell wins Pulitzer Prize for *Gone with the Wind* (1937); Billy Jean King founds the Women's Sports Foundation (1984)

LUCKY NUMBER: 8

BIRTHSTONE: Emerald

POSITIVE TRAITS: Perspicacious, analytical, charming

NEGATIVE TRAITS: Negative, glib, self-deceiving

You are a born manager: You are the one who keeps everything running smoothly. Your office is well-organized, your house tidy, and your appointments kept on time. But you are not simply efficient; you have an eye for detail and create a pleasing environment wherever you go. Stubborn and strong-willed, you often find yourself at loggerheads with less systematic types, but your ability to look at yourself honestly keeps you from becoming rigid. You're wary in love, but once you trust someone, you are a generous, affectionate, and loyal partner. You have a tendency to work too hard and worry too much. A physical routine that soothes your mind as well as your body is just right for you. Tae kwon do, anyone?

May 4

ASTROLOGICAL SIGN: Taurus
PEOPLE BORN TODAY: Audrey Hepburn, Randy Travis, Nickolas Ashford, Pia Zadora, Maynard Ferguson, Roberta Peters, George Will
FAMOUS EVENTS: Al Capone convicted of tax evasion (1932); first Grammy Awards ceremony (1959); Margaret Thatcher becomes first woman prime minister of Great Britain (1979)
LUCKY NUMBER: 9
BIRTHSTONE: Emerald
POSITIVE TRAITS: Giving, caring, altruistic
NEGATIVE TRAITS: Self-sacrificing, stubborn, naive

You are as quick to perceive the goodness in others as you are slow to acknowledge your own. Though you are adept at summing people up, you are not judgmental; you simply see people as they are and let it go at that. Love partners are captivated by your easy charms and entertained by your acute perceptions, but they may start to squirm if you put them under the microscope too often. Though you are affectionate, you don't open up easily, and a bad romance can really knock you for a loop. You are much more comfortable with matters of the mind than matters of the heart, but once you find your soul mate, you will enjoy the pleasures of a deep and lasting union.

May 5

ASTROLOGICAL SIGN: Taurus
PEOPLE BORN TODAY: Michael Palin, James Beard, Tyrone Power, Karl Marx, Søren Kierkegaard, Tammy Wynette, Sigmund Freud, Arthur Hailey
FAMOUS EVENTS: Carnegie Hall opens (1891); introduction of Coco Chanel's perfume, Chanel No. 5 (1921); John Scopes arrested for teaching Darwin's theory of evolution (1925)
LUCKY NUMBER: 1
BIRTHSTONE: Emerald
POSITIVE TRAITS: Knowledgeable, skillful, generous
NEGATIVE TRAITS: Needy, didactic, hovering

Innovative ideas and how to implement them are your stock in trade. Friends and family know you are the one to call when they are stumped on a project or just need an infusion of energy to keep things going. You have energy enough for three and never seem to tire. Love means almost everything to you; you are most content being part of a couple and will do whatever is necessary to keep your relationship lively and on course. Your ideal partner will be as emotionally forthcoming as you are and share your sense of commitment. If you are lucky, your partner will also be as romantic and sentimental as you are, guaranteeing a life full of little celebrations and love fests.

May 6

ASTROLOGICAL SIGN: Taurus
PEOPLE BORN TODAY: Bob Seger, Willie Mays, Theodore H. White, Orson Welles, Rudolph Valentino
FAMOUS EVENTS: First Major League home run hit by Babe Ruth (1915); Hindenberg disaster (1937); four-minute-mile record broken by Roger Bannister (1954)
LUCKY NUMBER: 2
BIRTHSTONE: Emerald
POSITIVE TRAITS: Sensitive, artistic, empathetic
NEGATIVE TRAITS: Temperamental, excessive, overemotional

Your fine-tuned antenna is both a blessing and a curse. You are acutely sensitive to the feelings of your family, friends, and colleagues, but you can also be overly sensitive, which leads to misunderstandings and hurt feelings where none are necessary. You have a probing intelligence and particularly love a mystery, which gives you a chance to hone your analytical skills and draw on your considerable intuitive talents. You may not find the ideal mate for quite some time: You will not settle for anything less than the perfect union and you are willing to wait for happiness. In the meantime, your good nature and love of fun will ensure that time spent waiting for your soul mate to appear will not be dull.

May 7

ASTROLOGICAL SIGN: Taurus

PEOPLE BORN TODAY: Traci Lords, Robin Strasser, Johnny Unitas, Gary Cooper, Eva Peron, Robert Browning

FAMOUS EVENTS: First inaugural ball (1789); premiere of Beethoven's *Ninth Symphony* (1824); signing of German surrender at Rheims, ending World War II (1945)

LUCKY NUMBER: 3

BIRTHSTONE: Emerald

POSITIVE TRAITS: Elegant, aristocratic, discerning

NEGATIVE TRAITS: Perfectionistic, proud, superficial

Absolute perfection may not exist in this life, but that doesn't stop you from seeking it in your work and your surroundings. You set yourself the highest standards of speech, dress, and behavior and look for the same in friends and colleagues. Your elegant image attracts admirers, and the one who wins your heart will find you a loving, demonstrative, and sensual mate, willing and able to compromise when necessary to keep your relationship on track. Money can be a problem for you—not making it, keeping it. Your elegant style doesn't come cheap and you are an obsessive gift-giver, unable to resist that "little something" for friends and family. You work hard to stay in shape and work pays off—handsomely.

May 8

ASTROLOGICAL SIGN: Taurus

PEOPLE BORN TODAY: Harry S. Truman, Melissa Gilbert, Chris Frantz, Philip Bailey, Alex Van Halen, Thomas Pynchon, Beth Henley

FAMOUS EVENTS: Mississippi River discovered by de Soto (1541); Coca-Cola commercially introduced (1886); V-E Day celebration (1945)

LUCKY NUMBER: 4

BIRTHSTONE: Emerald

POSITIVE TRAITS: Logical, caring, ambitious

NEGATIVE TRAITS: Extravagant, judgmental, tough

Good luck follows you like a hungry dog, making it easier to realize your ambitions. However, no one should assume that it's just luck that makes you successful; you are a hard worker, painstaking in your methods and diligent in your follow-through. You tend to be liberal with your money, picking up the tab in restaurants, and buying extravagant gifts for friends and family, but your own material welfare always comes first. Basically kindhearted and caring, you also have a critical streak—and no compulsions about revealing it. Love is always on your agenda, and you know exactly what you want: a mate who will still be by your side in fifty years. With your luck, it just might happen.

May 9

ASTROLOGICAL SIGN: Taurus

PEOPLE BORN TODAY: Candice Bergen, Billy Joel, Glenda Jackson, Mike Wallace, Pancho Gonzalez, Albert Finney

FAMOUS EVENTS: Publication of first U.S. newspaper cartoon (1754); first airplane flight over North Pole (1926); birth control pill wins approval from FDA (1960); impeachment hearings on President Richard Nixon begin (1974)

LUCKY NUMBER: 5

BIRTHSTONE: Emerald

POSITIVE TRAITS: Honorable, ethical, fair

NEGATIVE TRAITS: Naive, judgmental, unrealistic

Your sense of honor almost seems a relic of more civilized times. A clear-cut code of personal behavior guides you through every challenge the modern world presents, from ethical dilemmas at work to matters of love and loyalty at home. You are not easily discouraged and rarely think about the time it will take you to achieve your goals; that you do eventually achieve them is all that matters. Romance is right up your alley; whether you are in a relationship or on the dating scene, few things please you more than setting in motion a romantic evening with all the trimmings. A partner who cannot appreciate your efforts will never win your heart, nor will anyone who trifles with it.

ASTROLOGICAL SIGN: Taurus

PEOPLE BORN TODAY: Bono, Fred Astaire, Barbara Woodhouse, Donovan, Phil and Steve Mahre, Judith Jamison

FAMOUS EVENTS: Explorer Amerigo Vespucci sets sail for the New World (1497); Victoria Woodhull becomes first woman nominated for U.S. presidency (1872); first observance of Mother's Day (1908)

LUCKY NUMBER: 6

BIRTHSTONE: Emerald

POSITIVE TRAITS: Original, inspired, independent

NEGATIVE TRAITS: Detached, eccentric, difficult

You seem to draw ideas and inspiration from a secret source that no one else can see. At work, your suggestions are often innovative and you are likely to adopt them even if others reject them. In your personal affairs, you also go your own way; even if you have a mate, you will not hesitate to pursue your own independent activities and interests. If you make the effort to include your loved ones in your own private world, they will regard you as a special, somewhat magical person. You strive to combine the purely physical with the highly imaginative, and in everything you do, you enjoy peering at the world through a kaleidoscope that provides a very different perspective from any other around.

May 11

ASTROLOGICAL SIGN: Taurus
PEOPLE BORN TODAY: Natasha Richardson, Martha Quinn, Eric Burdon, Salvador Dali, Martha Graham, Irving Berlin
FAMOUS EVENTS: Minnesota becomes the 32nd state (1858); combat troops ordered to Panama by President George Bush (1989); Nera White and Luisa Harris first women inducted into Basketball Hall of Fame (1992)
LUCKY NUMBER: 7
BIRTHSTONE: Emerald
POSITIVE TRAITS: Lighthearted, creative, distinctive
NEGATIVE TRAITS: Dreamy, distant, escapist

You dwell in a world of your own creation: You can turn job assignments into exciting contests and household chores into games. You also excel at adding flair to your physical environment through highly original decorating schemes and outrageous accessories. Unfortunately, you can so easily become immersed in your dream world that you lose touch with people on planet Earth. If you admit someone special into your enchanted realm, you will add youthfulness and sparkle to that person's existence. In addition, you are the perfect playmate for young people and will fully stimulate their imagination. Playing sports does not interest you half as much as dressing for them, and you are sure to be the funkiest fan in the stands.

May 12

ASTROLOGICAL SIGN: Taurus
PEOPLE BORN TODAY: Kim Fields, Emilio Estevez, Stephen Baldwin, Katharine Hepburn, George Carlin, Yogi Berra, Florence Nightingale
FAMOUS EVENTS: Coronation of King George VI broadcast on radio (1937); Sam Jones pitches first no-hitter at Wrigley Field in thirty-eight years (1955); first nonstop balloon flight across North America (1980)
LUCKY NUMBER: 8
BIRTHSTONE: Emerald
POSITIVE TRAITS: Observant, quick-witted, analytical
NEGATIVE TRAITS: Difficult, aloof, sarcastic

You have a sharp eye and a sharp tongue, but your well-honed, critical faculties can work to your advantage as long as you soften them with heart and humor. You have tremendous willpower; use it to curb your more biting observations and avoid making enemies and alienating friends. Show your generous side by giving others as much praise as criticism and learn to accept praise graciously yourself. Romantic partners do not escape your scrutiny, but once you are smitten, you will retract your claws and become your mate's greatest supporter. Though you are a passionate, playful lover, you can be emotionally aloof, regarding your feelings as merely fleeting and inconsequential—and not worth sharing. Give more to get more.

May 13

ASTROLOGICAL SIGN: Taurus

PEOPLE BORN TODAY: Stevie Wonder, Julianne Phillips, Harvey Keitel, Beatrice Arthur, Dennis Rodman, Daphne du Maurier

FAMOUS EVENTS: Sighting of the Virgin Mary reported at Fatima (1917); Pope John Paul II shot and wounded (1981); Guglielmo Marconi becomes first inductee into Radio Hall of Fame (1988)

LUCKY NUMBER: 9

BIRTHSTONE: Emerald

POSITIVE TRAITS: Impulsive, instinctive, electrifying

NEGATIVE TRAITS: Destructive, rebellious, wild

You are a wild child, following your instincts with behavior that can either electrify or shock people. You have difficulty abiding by social conventions and restrictions imposed by employers or other authority figures. At times you may wish you lived on a deserted island, but although you would love the freedom, you would miss having an audience—and someone to love. Your independence appeals to those who feel hemmed in, and your warmth and vitality can help a less impetuous partner get in touch with the emotional and impulsive side of life. Your health is likely to be excellent because you listen closely to your body's signals—eating when you are hungry, resting when you are tired, and seeking medical care whenever something feels amiss.

May 14

ASTROLOGICAL SIGN: Taurus

PEOPLE BORN TODAY: Kurt Browning, George Lucas, David Byrne, Shanice Wilson, Bobby Darin, Dante Aligheri

FAMOUS EVENTS: First vaccination against smallpox (1796); first Olympic games held in U.S. (1904); *Skylab*, first U.S. manned spacecraft launched (1973)

LUCKY NUMBER: 1

BIRTHSTONE: Emerald

POSITIVE TRAITS: Responsible, ambitious, expert

NEGATIVE TRAITS: Perfectionistic, unconfident, nervous

Whatever enterprise you undertake, you raise it to the next level. An indefatigable worker, you strive for excellence and usually achieve it. You bring the same perfectionism to relationships, knocking yourself out to win your partner's affection and admiration and often—too often—blaming yourself if a romance goes sour. Though your spunk, relaxed good looks, and generally cheerful manner draw people toward you, you can put them off by doubting your own likeability. Introspection is not your strong point. If you take the time to get to know yourself, if you truthfully assess your personal and professional achievements, your self-confidence will surge. Don't pooh-pooh your friends when they praise you; they are as sincere in their praise as you are deserving of it.

May 15

PEOPLE BORN TODAY: Pierce Brosnan, George Brett, Brian Eno, Richard Avedon, James Mason, Eddy Arnold

FAMOUS EVENTS: Cape Cod discovered (1602); two assassination attempts in one day survived by King George III (1800); first two female U.S. generals appointed by President Richard Nixon (1970)

LUCKY NUMBER: 2

BIRTHSTONE: Emerald

POSITIVE TRAITS: Clever, charming, imaginative

NEGATIVE TRAITS: Passive, shy, temperamental

You are most successful when you *act*. Too often your imaginative plans go to waste because you sit back waiting for others to solicit them. At work, you may have the brightest idea in the room, but no one will hear it unless the boss calls on you. Your charm and grace ensure you plenty of chances for romance, but you may also miss certain opportunities because you expect others to make the first move. Shake off this passivity and put yourself forward, and you can realize your greatest personal and professional dreams. Take the initiative in showing parental affection, too—don't let your children misinterpret your undemonstrativeness as indifference. Don't hang back when playing tennis, step right up to the baseline, and do the same in life.

May 16

ASTROLOGICAL SIGN: Taurus
PEOPLE BORN TODAY: Janet Jackson, Tori Spelling, Gabriela Sabatini, Lenny Kravitz, Liberace, Henry Fonda, Adrienne Rich
FAMOUS EVENTS: Marie Antoinette and Louis XVI wed (1770); first Academy Awards presented (1929); Junko Tabei becomes first woman to scale Mount Everest (1975)
LUCKY NUMBER: 3
BIRTHSTONE: Emerald
POSITIVE TRAITS: Spirited, sensual, expressive
NEGATIVE TRAITS: Moody, changeable, fickle

You are a classic free spirit, painting in the brightest colors on the largest canvases. You express your feelings without reservation both at work and at home, and you encourage coworkers and loved ones alike to open up to you. Your vitality and sensuality attract admirers in droves, but although you are a very sexy and stimulating mate, you are also far from the most stable one imaginable. You are warm and affectionate to all of your loved ones, but your rapidly changing moods can be distressing at times. Balance your volatility by making your home environment as secure and unchanging as possible. When flair, imagination, and a touch of the exotic are what is needed, you will be the first one called.

May 17

ASTROLOGICAL SIGN: Taurus

PEOPLE BORN TODAY: Enya, Sugar Ray Leonard, Kathleen Sullivan, Bob Saget, Dennis Hopper, Bill Paxton, Taj Mahal, Danny Manning

FAMOUS EVENTS: First Kentucky Derby (1875); first televised sports event (1939); school segregation banned by U.S. Supreme Court (1954)

LUCKY NUMBER: 4

BIRTHSTONE: Emerald

POSITIVE TRAITS: Dutiful, loving, reliable

NEGATIVE TRAITS: Sorrowful, critical, intolerant

You are a model of dedication and you know how to enjoy the rewards such a virtue brings to you. Though you encourage others to do their best and to reap their own rewards, you have little patience for those who slack off and shirk their obligations. You are not all work and no play, however, and friends can count you in whenever a good time is to be had. In love, you value commitment and loyalty much more than good looks, and you would rather be alone than settle for someone unworthy of your respect. You are likely, however, to spoil those you love and you go out of your way to let them know the depth of your feelings.

May 18

ASTROLOGICAL SIGN: Taurus

PEOPLE BORN TODAY: George Strait, Martika, Reggie Jackson, Pope John Paul II, Robert Morse, Perry Como

FAMOUS EVENTS: Montreal founded (1642); Abraham Lincoln nominated for presidency (1860); first baseball team walkout staged by Detroit Tigers (1912); Jacqueline Cochran becomes first woman pilot to break the sound barrier (1953)

LUCKY NUMBER: 5

BIRTHSTONE: Emerald

POSITIVE TRAITS: Compassionate, principled, upright

NEGATIVE TRAITS: Stern, vulnerable, melancholy

You see the world in black-and-white, and you commit yourself to an unwavering defense of what you believe to be right. You are as loyal to your principles as you are to people, and your incorruptibility makes you a sought-after business ally and treasured friend. Romantic partners who expect you to laugh off their misbehavior will be disappointed—and not just because of your principles: You love to be loved, but you also hate to be hurt and you recover slowly from emotional setbacks of any kind. Your long-term mate will likely be someone whose ethical standards are as exacting as your own and whose desire to love and commit is as high a priority as yours.

May 19

ASTROLOGICAL SIGN: Taurus

PEOPLE BORN TODAY: Pete Townshend, Grace Jones, Bill Laimbeer, Nora Ephron, Jim Lehrer, Malcolm X, Glenn Close, Lorraine Hansberry

FAMOUS EVENTS: Anne Boleyn beheaded (1536); first department store opens (1848); first conviction based on fingerprint evidence (1911); death of Jacqueline Kennedy Onassis (1994)

LUCKY NUMBER: 6

BIRTHSTONE: Emerald

POSITIVE TRAITS: Vital, fair-minded, decisive

NEGATIVE TRAITS: Opinionated, defensive, tardy

You are a force of nature, speaking out eloquently and acting decisively to right any injustices you observe. Though guardians of the status quo may resent your upsetting the applecart, they won't resent you; your zest for life and sense of fair play make sure of that. And the fact that your actions usually result in positive changes doesn't hurt your popularity either. You have the ability to shake others out of their complacency and into committed action. At home, you know how to relax. Being in love is your natural state of being, and you and your partner like nothing better than to have friends—and friends of friends—over for an evening of good food, good talk, and good fun.

May 20

ASTROLOGICAL SIGN: Taurus

PEOPLE BORN TODAY: Cher, Jimmy Stewart, Joe Cocker, Bobby Murcer, Dave Thomas, Mindy Cohn, Honoré de Balzac

FAMOUS EVENTS: Death of Christopher Columbus (1506); first railroad timetable published in a newspaper, the *Baltimore American* (1830); Amelia Earhart becomes first woman pilot to fly solo across the Atlantic (1932)

LUCKY NUMBER: 7

BIRTHSTONE: Emerald

POSITIVE TRAITS: Stylish, communicative, original

NEGATIVE TRAITS: Frustrated, excitable, verbose

When one of your highly original impulses strikes, you act on it—but not before you tell the entire world. Your fertile imagination and gift for communicating excitement make you a sparkplug on the job and a one-person party on the social scene. You stay up late and get up early; there is rarely enough time in a day for you to do everything on your agenda—but you try nonetheless. You are stylish and fashion-conscious and your ideal partner will be too. When you're feeling flush, shopping fits the bill perfectly, but you can be just as happy affirming your good looks and good taste in an afternoon spent window-shopping. You enjoy your life and feel connected to everyone in it.

May 21

ASTROLOGICAL SIGN: Taurus

PEOPLE BORN TODAY: Judge Reinhold, Mr. T, Leo Sayer, Ronnie Isley, Peggy Cass, Harold Robbins, Alexander Pope

FAMOUS EVENTS: First solo flight from New York to Paris completed by Charles Lindbergh (1927); Humphrey Bogart and Lauren Bacall wed (1945); Indian candidate for prime minister Rajiv Gandhi assassinated (1991)

LUCKY NUMBER: 8

BIRTHSTONE: Emerald

POSITIVE TRAITS: Bold, brave, achieving

NEGATIVE TRAITS: Conceited, defensive, caustic

You are fearless in the face of obstacles and single-minded in your pursuit of success. Your confidence may appear as conceit to jealous coworkers and romantic rivals, but it gives you an advantage in achieving your goals. No job seems too big for you, no challenge overwhelming. Your conviction that you are always right can spark arguments with love partners and put you on the defensive when they question your judgment. At home, you expect your word to be law for your mate and children. Your can-do attitude can lead you to accept too many responsibilities and impose unnecessary pressures on yourself. Avert the dangerous physical consequences of overstress by delegating some duties to trusted colleagues, friends, and family members.

May 22

ASTROLOGICAL SIGN: Gemini

PEOPLE BORN TODAY: Bernie Taupin, Susan Strasberg, Laurence Olivier, Paul Winfield, Arthur Conan Doyle, Richard Wagner

FAMOUS EVENTS: First public movie screening (1891); first visit to Russia by a U.S. president made by President Richard Nixon (1972); Janet Guthrie becomes first woman to qualify for the Indy 500 (1977)

LUCKY NUMBER: 9

BIRTHSTONE: Agate

POSITIVE TRAITS: Creative, commanding, inventive

NEGATIVE TRAITS: Hard-driving, obsessive, unreasonable

You have the vision to conceive ambitious projects and the drive to see them through. When you enlist coworkers or friends to assist you, you are a tough taskmaster and if your demands inspire mutiny in the ranks, you will plow onward alone if necessary. You can have trouble giving up on a dream even when your prospects of success seem dim. Your obsessiveness can be an impediment to romantic relationships, causing you to smother partners with too much affection or doggedly pursue them after they have lost interest. For long-term happiness with a mate, back off a bit to provide ample breathing room. If you make physical fitness a high priority, your willpower will enable you to whip yourself into shape in no time.

May 23

ASTROLOGICAL SIGN: Gemini

PEOPLE BORN TODAY: Joan Collins, Marvin Hagler, Alicia de Larrocha, John Newcombe, Rosemary Clooney, Robert Moog

FAMOUS EVENTS: Bifocals invented by Benjamin Franklin (1785); Rudyard Kipling becomes youngest winner of the Nobel Prize for Literature (1907); Bonnie and Clyde ambushed and killed (1934)

LUCKY NUMBER: 1

BIRTHSTONE: Agate

POSITIVE TRAITS: Clever, generous, innovative

NEGATIVE TRAITS: Unassertive, self-neglecting, wishful

You are a gifted problem solver, but you apply most of your ingenuity toward untying other people's knotty work challenges or personal woes. You are a generous friend who likes to help in practical ways. While you attack others' problems energetically, you tend to ignore or gloss over difficulties in your own life, and let needy coworkers and partners impose on you without complaining. Your loyalty to your mate is commendable, but it needn't preclude your speaking up for your own interests now and then. Allowing your own frustrations to fester can darken your outlook and ultimately damage the relationships you are trying to preserve with your silence. Letting your physical complaints go untreated can be even more risky—call the doctor promptly.

May 24

ASTROLOGICAL SIGN: Gemini
PEOPLE BORN TODAY: Priscilla Presley, Bob Dylan, Patti LaBelle, Roseanne Cash, Tommy Chong, Frank Oz
FAMOUS EVENTS: First telegraph message transmitted by Samuel F. B. Morse (1844); first night Major League baseball game played (1935); birth of twenty-two-pound newborn, heaviest baby ever (1982)
LUCKY NUMBER: 2
BIRTHSTONE: Agate
POSITIVE TRAITS: Concerned, observant, vocal
NEGATIVE TRAITS: Egotistical, biting, combative

You are a caring observer of society's failings and people's faults, and seldom hesitate to broadcast your views. Your biting criticisms get noticed by coworkers and friends, although your deafness to conflicting opinions can cost you their respect. Your gift for incisive observation attracts admiration from sharp-witted romantic partners, but beware of alienating them with one cutting remark too many. Your mate may have to play the role of diplomatic liaison between you and the world at large. Nevertheless, you are a staunch ally—in love in particular and in life in general. Fun is paramount to your well-being and you never lack partners to pursue it with. Your home is a haven, for friends, for family, and for you.

May 25

ASTROLOGICAL SIGN: Gemini

PEOPLE BORN TODAY: Dixie Carter, Ian McKellen, Beverly Sills, Miles Davis, Connie Sellecca, Robert Ludlum, Ralph Waldo Emerson

FAMOUS EVENTS: First insurance policy in U.S. advertised (1721); final career home run hit by Babe Ruth (1935); goal of putting man on the Moon set by President John F. Kennedy (1961)

LUCKY NUMBER: 3

BIRTHSTONE: Agate

POSITIVE TRAITS: Outspoken, independent, honorable

NEGATIVE TRAITS: Unforgiving, repressed, cool

You are tuned to your own inner voice. You conform to a strict personal code of behavior and stay true to your high ideals regardless of social shifts or pressure from less principled people. You expect friends and loved ones to meet your standards and can be slow to forgive them for their transgressions. You would rather claim a handful of worthy intimates and one unexceptionable mate than a roomful of casual acquaintances of unproved merit. Your children will have no doubt about your expectations of their behavior, and when they overstep your limits they will know it. Your firm principles don't mean you're buttoned up. On the contrary, you enjoy having fun with fashion, complementing your cool head with a cool look.

May 26

ASTROLOGICAL SIGN: Gemini
PEOPLE BORN TODAY: Sally Ride, John Wayne, Genie Francis, Stevie Nicks, Brent Musberger, Peggy Lee
FAMOUS EVENTS: Last battle of Civil War ends (1865); first appearance of Dow Jones Industrial Average (1896); percussionist Vicki Randle becomes first woman band member on the *Tonight* show (1992)
LUCKY NUMBER: 4
BIRTHSTONE: Agate
POSITIVE TRAITS: Upright, solicitous, warmhearted
NEGATIVE TRAITS: Hypocritical, rebellious, irresponsible

You uphold convention publicly, but tend to be a rebel privately, chafing against restrictions of all kinds. You preach to all who will listen the virtues of traditional arrangements like marriage and long-term employment, but are ambivalent about accepting such heavy responsibilities and may be more likely to opt for a single lifestyle or self-employment. Though you can be commitment-shy, you are a warmhearted and loving mate. If you become a parent, you can be relied on to shield your children from all real and perceived threats. You are happy in a structured environment as long as you don't feel tied down, and look forward to large family gatherings and visits to friends' homes, where you enjoy playing with their kids.

May 27

ASTROLOGICAL SIGN: Gemini

PEOPLE BORN TODAY: Dondre Whitfield, Pat Cash, Lisa Lopes, John Barth, Bruce Weitz, Ramsey Lewis, Vincent Price, Rachel Carson

FAMOUS EVENTS: Pop-up toaster patented (1919); Golden Gate Bridge opens (1937); the "unsinkable" German battleship *Bismarck* sinks (1941)

LUCKY NUMBER: 5

BIRTHSTONE: Agate

POSITIVE TRAITS: Elegant, witty, steady

NEGATIVE TRAITS: Outrageous, oblivious, self-indulgent

Because your elegance and sophistication brighten every affair, you are constantly sought after by acquaintances and colleagues who prize not only your loyal friendship but also your entertaining sparkle. *Bon mots* spring forth spontaneously and you can amuse and shock with little effort. You work tirelessly to attain career goals, but seldom step back to analyze your progress. Soliciting advice from a more observant mentor will set you back on the right track. In your personal life, you are exceedingly affectionate but you tend to tune out anything that sounds remotely like criticism, which can make you seem insensitive and arouse your mate's ire. To maintain harmony, try really listening to your partner instead of chanting "yes, dear" while staring at the TV.

ASTROLOGICAL SIGN: Gemini

PEOPLE BORN TODAY: Rudolph Giuliani, Gladys Knight, John Fogarty, Jerry West, Sondra Locke, Jim Thorpe

FAMOUS EVENTS: First full-color film, *On with the Show*, opens in New York City (1929); Amy Johnson makes first solo flight from England to Australia (1930); two monkeys sent into orbit by NASA (1959)

LUCKY NUMBER: 6

BIRTHSTONE: Agate

POSITIVE TRAITS: Initiating, dynamic, original

NEGATIVE TRAITS: Short-tempered, conceited, restless

Both at home and at work, you excel at concocting original schemes and are eager to see them bear fruit, then rush on to the next. Novelty and excitement are what you constantly crave, but although you readily share your ideas with others, you grow testy when they seem slow to catch on. Professionally, your impatience to assume a position of influence can draw resentment from colleagues who have paid their dues and feel that you should do the same. As a friend and adviser, you enjoy watching others learn new skills but may try too hard to rush their progress. Rushing is your problem in general; slowing down and trying to savor your accomplishments might be the most novel change of all.

ASTROLOGICAL SIGN: Gemini

PEOPLE BORN TODAY: Anthony Geary, Latoya Jackson, Eric Davis, Danny Elfman, Bob Hope, John F. Kennedy, Annette Bening

FAMOUS EVENTS: Constantinople captured by Turks (1453); summit of Mt. Everest reached by Edmund Hillary and Tenzing Norkay (1953); Tom Bradley elected first black mayor of Los Angeles (1973)

LUCKY NUMBER: 7

BIRTHSTONE: Agate

POSITIVE TRAITS: Mediating, affectionate, verbally adept

NEGATIVE TRAITS: Aggressive, procrastinating, mercurial

You have a way with people and a way with words. At work and among friends, you employ your diplomatic skills to resolve conflicts. Your wit and charm help you advance on the job and endow you with great romantic appeal. You are always "on," and entertain your mate with stimulating conversation and amusing observations even when the two of you are alone. Your desire to maintain your pleasant demeanor can lead you to repress anger, making the inevitable explosion all the more violent when it finally erupts. Try to deal with distressing issues as they come up instead of letting them build steam. You will be more likely to stay in good health if you turn eating and exercising into social occasions.

May 30

ASTROLOGICAL SIGN: Gemini

PEOPLE BORN TODAY: Wynonna Judd, Gale Sayers, Paola Fendi, Me' Blanc, Christine Jorgensen, Benny Goodman

FAMOUS EVENTS: Joan of Arc burned at the stake (1431); Decoration Day instituted to honor war dead (1868); first Indy 500 held (1911)

LUCKY NUMBER: 8

BIRTHSTONE: Agate

POSITIVE TRAITS: Prodigious, gifted, outstanding

NEGATIVE TRAITS: Mercurial, irresponsible, flighty

You have the talent to shine in a variety of fields; your challenge is to pick one only and commit yourself to it for the long haul. You master skills rapidly and then go in search of new challenges, but your insatiable hunger for change can lead you to ignore your obligations and let people down if you get bored and move on without seeing things through. Your enthusiasm and impulsiveness will charm romantic partners, but they may become a bit unnerved by your instability and doubt your ability to commit, which works against you as you are happiest in a close relationship. Thanks to your mercurial moods, though you are sometimes difficult and sometimes delightful, no partner will ever find you dull.

May 31

ASTROLOGICAL SIGN: Gemini

PEOPLE BORN TODAY: Brooke Shields, Clint Eastwood, Walt Whitman, Tom Berenger, Joe Namath, Prince Rainier of Monaco

FAMOUS EVENTS: Johnstown flood, worst in U.S. history, kills more than 2,200 people (1889); Adolf Eichmann hanged for Nazi war crimes (1962); resignation of House Speaker Jim Wright (1989)

LUCKY NUMBER: 9

BIRTHSTONE: Agate

POSITIVE TRAITS: Populist, down-to-earth, energetic

NEGATIVE TRAITS: Insecure, compulsive, proud

Down-to-earth in both your demeanor and your actions, you carry out your work and domestic responsibilities with a minimum of fuss and bother, and adjust easily to changing situations. You are happiest in an organized, aesthetically pleasing environment, and take pride in the fact that your home and workplace are often the envy of your friends and colleagues. Because you want to be understood clearly by everyone, you speak in terms that leave no room for misinterpretation. In relationships, you abhor game-playing and express your warm feelings with plenty of hugs and kisses and affectionate small talk. Your high energy, sunny disposition, and passion for communication can be contagious, and you have a knack for drawing people out.

June 1

ASTROLOGICAL SIGN: Gemini
PEOPLE BORN TODAY: Lisa Hartman, Jonathan Pryce, Frederica von Stade, Andy Griffith, Nelson Riddle, Marilyn Monroe
FAMOUS EVENTS: Kentucky becomes the 15th state (1792) and Tennessee becomes the 16th state (1796); North Pole located by Scottish explorer James Clark Ross (1831); *Sergeant Pepper's Lonely Hearts Club Band* released by the Beatles (1967)
LUCKY NUMBER: 7
BIRTHSTONE: Agate
POSITIVE TRAITS: Sharp, entertaining, discerning
NEGATIVE TRAITS: Scattered, impatient, uncentered

Chatty and entertaining, you are the perfect dinner party guest: conversing readily about the latest social trends, regaling your listeners with the opinions of experts, but rarely revealing your own. At work and in social settings, you tend to keep the focus on other people, and will often study and closely imitate the styles of those at the top in hopes of imitating their success. Only over the course of a long acquaintance will you gradually open up to friends and colleagues, but in a secure relationship with an accepting mate, you will gain self-confidence and settle into your own unique personality. Taking solo vacations will free you to be yourself among people who have no pre-conceptions about you.

ASTROLOGICAL SIGN: Gemini

PEOPLE BORN TODAY: Dana Carvey, Diana Canova, Barry Levinson, Sally Kellerman, Marvin Hamlisch, Charlie Watts, Thomas Hardy

FAMOUS EVENTS: Grover Cleveland, first president to marry in office, weds Frances Folsom (1886); Guglielmo Marconi patents his radio in U.S. (1896); Chinese student revolt in Tienanmen Square (1989)

LUCKY NUMBER: 8

BIRTHSTONE: Agate

POSITIVE TRAITS: Committed, ingenious, undaunted

NEGATIVE TRAITS: Complicating, trouble-seeking, self-defeating

Oh, what tangled webs you weave, just to test your ingenuity at unraveling them! You love to seek out challenges, and then overcome them with Houdini-like skill. Coworkers may balk, however, at your habit of injecting difficulties into simple procedures; and when life is running with bland smoothness, you may develop bad habits, like lateness and disorganization, that stack the odds against you. Yet when a real crisis arises, you will be the lifesaver who restores normalcy and order. Your enthusiasm for complications may attract you to troubled partners, so remember that you cannot change people: they can only change themselves. And if you choose a mate without serious problems, resist the temptation to cultivate excitement by planting the seeds of discord.

June 3

ASTROLOGICAL SIGN: Gemini

PEOPLE BORN TODAY: Larry McMurtry, Curtis Mayfield, Colleen Dewhurst, Allen Ginsberg, Tony Curtis, Josephine Baker

FAMOUS EVENTS: First baseball uniforms worn, by New York Knickerbockers (1852); Duke of Windsor, formerly King Edward VIII, wed to Wallis Warfield Simpson (1937); astronaut Edward White becomes first American to walk in space (1965)

LUCKY NUMBER: 9

BIRTHSTONE: Agate

POSITIVE TRAITS: Articulate, witty, persuasive

NEGATIVE TRAITS: Loquacious, argumentative, stubborn

Your magical way with words is a passport to personal happiness and worldly success: You use your impressive verbal skills to win business negotiations and woo romantic prospects. Friends are amused by your sharp wit, so long as you don't turn it against them. In love, your conversation goes beyond idle chatter; your feelings run deep, and you share them very freely. However, in lovers' quarrels and work disputes alike, you cling to your views and defend them fiercely, and you think nothing of filibustering until the other side folds and concedes your point. And although the gift of gab is your greatest weapon, it can also become your downfall, because others who possess it can effectively use words to influence or seduce *you*.

June 4

ASTROLOGICAL SIGN: Gemini
PEOPLE BORN TODAY: Andrea Jaeger, Parker Stevenson, Michelle Phillips, Robert Fulghum, "Dr. Ruth" Westheimer, Bruce Dern
FAMOUS EVENTS: First balloon flight by a woman, Marie Thible (1784); construction of White House completed (1800); first Pulitzer Prizes awarded (1917)
LUCKY NUMBER: 1
BIRTHSTONE: Agate
POSITIVE TRAITS: Intelligent, expressive, empathetic
NEGATIVE TRAITS: Critical, overintellectual, frustrated

You possess awesome intellectual abilities that can help you skyrocket in your career, along with the verbal skills that allow you to put your views front and center. These strengths can become weaknesses, however, if you lean on them so heavily that you neglect your emotional side. Try to accentuate the perceptive, feeling part of your nature buried deep within, especially in matters of the heart. Lovers need regular doses of warmth and even sentiment as well as the intellectual stimulation you so easily provide. Friends and family will also benefit from contact with your sensitive and nurturing side. You possess creative potential that may be lying dormant. Cultivate it, and develop fully all that is most human within you.

June 5

ASTROLOGICAL SIGN: Gemini

PEOPLE BORN TODAY: Kenny G, Marky Mark, Bill Moyers, Spalding Grey, Laurie Anderson, Richard Scarry, Federico García Lorca

FAMOUS EVENTS: George Harbo and Frank Samuelson become first to cross the Atlantic in a rowboat (1896); Senator Robert Kennedy assassinated (1968); first documented case of AIDS reported (1981)

LUCKY NUMBER: 2

BIRTHSTONE: Agate

POSITIVE TRAITS: Versatile, clever, curious

NEGATIVE TRAITS: High-strung, scattered, confused

You are an intellectual juggler, testing how many ideas and projects you can keep in the air simultaneously. Though you inevitably drop a few, your ability to get things done is phenomenal—and always in demand. You are a diverting conversationalist, able to enthrall others with your observations on a wide range of subjects. Your broad field of vision lets you keep track of social activities and work agendas with the reliability of a human daily planner. You cultivate many friendships and romantic interests and show genuine interest in each, but only after you have found the perfect partner will your passionate nature be revealed. Learn to trust your instincts as well as your intellect; you can't go wrong either way.

June 6

ASTROLOGICAL SIGN: Gemini

PEOPLE BORN TODAY: Bjorn Borg, Roy Innis, Amanda Pays, Harvey Fierstein, the Dalai Lama, Sandra Bernhard, Marian Wright Edelman

FAMOUS EVENTS: First helicopter tested (1936); Allied invasion of Normandy (1944); *Ed Sullivan Show* canceled after twenty-three-year run (1971)

LUCKY NUMBER: 3

BIRTHSTONE: Agate

POSITIVE TRAITS: Sincere, idealistic, caring

NEGATIVE TRAITS: Naive, opinionated, far-out

You know how to make things happen. Because of your commitment to progressive ideas, you strive to improve everyone's lot—at work, at home, and in society—and you have no trouble communicating your ideals forcefully to others. You are often accused of being impatient, but you're not; you just prefer to cut to the chase whenever possible. Though friends sometimes find you frustratingly inflexible, your compassion and good humor make up for any excessive stubbornness. Your chosen partner won't be disappointed, either—once you are secure in a relationship your madcap ways are a delight. Find a worthy outlet for your caring nature, but don't limit yourself to stuffing envelopes. Step up front and center—that's where you rightfully belong.

June 7

ASTROLOGICAL SIGN: Gemini
PEOPLE BORN TODAY: Prince, Tom Jones, Liam Neeson, Jessica Tandy, Nikki Giovanni, Paul Gauguin, Gwendolyn Brooks
FAMOUS EVENTS: Abraham Lincoln renominated for president (1864); Italy recognizes Vatican City in Rome as independent country (1929); first presidential address on color television given by President Dwight Eisenhower (1955)
LUCKY NUMBER: 4
BIRTHSTONE: Agate
POSITIVE TRAITS: Visionary, trendsetting, colorful
NEGATIVE TRAITS: Self-absorbed, careless, indulgent

You make a splash when you go out, even though you would rather stay home and plumb your own considerable depths. Somewhat shy in public, you save your real observations for your closest confidants. You take pains with your appearance and like to let your clothes do most of the talking in social situations. Your verve and style are a magnet for romantic partners, and those who can handle your fragile sensibility will reap the rewards of your unfeigned affections. Though introspective by nature, try not to shut others out, especially if you are to get all the attention you crave. Get more involved with the concerns of others; it will provide welcome distraction from whatever it is that haunts your tortured soul.

June 8

ASTROLOGICAL SIGN: Gemini

PEOPLE BORN TODAY: Joan Rivers, Keenen Ivory Wayans, Barbara Bush, Jerry Stiller, Sara Paretsky, Frank Lloyd Wright, Boz Scaggs, Leroy Neimant

FAMOUS EVENTS: Vacuum cleaner patented (1869); first U.S.–Australia airplane flight made (1928); Mickey Mantle's number retired by New York Yankees (1969)

LUCKY NUMBER: 5

BIRTHSTONE: Agate

POSITIVE TRAITS: Dedicated, skillful, independent

NEGATIVE TRAITS: Workaholic, intense, extreme

You dedicate yourself wholeheartedly to your life's work, whether running a company or raising a family, and no one can ever say you don't try hard enough. Because you are as conscientious about your responsibilities to family and friends as you are about your professional obligations, romantic partners are pleased by your integrity, industriousness, and complete devotion. The only complaint your loved ones are likely to make is that they don't see you enough. This is no idle complaint, as you are personable and fun to be around and your presence is sorely missed when you let work take over for too long a stretch. Keep your loved ones happy: Cultivate a sense of play. With your imagination, this should be a snap.

June 9

ASTROLOGICAL SIGN: Gemini
PEOPLE BORN TODAY: Michael J. Fox, Johnny Depp, Robert S. McNamara, Jackie Mason, Les Paul, Cole Porter, Jackie Wilson
FAMOUS EVENTS: St. Lawrence River discovered by Jacques Cartier (1534); first American book copyrighted (1790); death of Charles Dickens (1870)
LUCKY NUMBER: 6
BIRTHSTONE: Agate
POSITIVE TRAITS: Youthful, candid, forthright
NEGATIVE TRAITS: Childish, changeable, tactless

You are as definite in your views and as plain in your expressions as any first-grader. This forcefulness delights your friends and coworkers when you are pleased and dismays them when you are in a snit. When dining out with a romantic partner, you are unlikely to reserve your judgment of the food and service until you get home. Even when you are undeniably correct in your assessments, your lovers and friends may wish you would keep them to yourself, or at least moderate them with others' feelings in mind. Developing your "inner adult" will prevent you from hurting people you care about and release your mate from the obligation to play a parental role in your life.

June 10

ASTROLOGICAL SIGN: Gemini

PEOPLE BORN TODAY: Grace Mirabella, Maurice Sendak, F. Lee Bailey, Judy Garland, Robert Maxwell, Frederick Loewe, Saul Bellow, Howlin' Wolf, Prince Philip

FAMOUS EVENTS: First hanging of alleged witch in Salem, Massachusetts (1692); first emergency SOS signal transmitted (1909); Alcoholics Anonymous founded (1935)

LUCKY NUMBER: 7

BIRTHSTONE: Agate

POSITIVE TRAITS: Empathetic, humorous, bold

NEGATIVE TRAITS: Confused, nervous, self-destructive

Friends and coworkers are likely to think you haven't a care, because you keep up a happy and successful front. It is not that you are too proud to share your troubles, but that admitting them to others would mean admitting them to yourself, a frightening prospect for you. You underestimate your ability to cope, and you are capable of bold and daring action once you confront obstacles directly. Putting a good face on a bad situation can be especially dangerous where relationships are concerned. Don't ignore problems or let partners ride roughshod over you while pretending everything is fine. Your health is another area where warning signals must be heeded: Early diagnosis and prompt treatment are the best response to whatever ails you.

June 11

ASTROLOGICAL SIGN: Gemini

PEOPLE BORN TODAY: Joe Montana, Gene Wilder, Jacques Cousteau, Jackie Stewart, Adrienne Barbeau, William Styron, Vince Lombardi, Ben Johnson

FAMOUS EVENTS: Stove invented by Benjamin Franklin (1742); Sir Barton becomes first racehorse to win the Triple Crown (1919); first Alfred Hitchcock film released (1928)

LUCKY NUMBER: 8

BIRTHSTONE: Agate

POSITIVE TRAITS: Forceful, disciplined, optimistic

NEGATIVE TRAITS: Stubborn, relentless, tiring

You rush toward your goals with the force of a mighty river, wearing down any obstacles in your path and occasionally the patience of coworkers and friends. You're a hard worker—particularly when you can see the results of your labors—and it pays off. Your sense of fair play and willingness to pitch in make you a sought-after team player and you frequently find yourself among people who want to help you reach your goals. Romantic partners who don't believe in you 100 percent won't be in your life for long, nor will anyone who lacks your zest for living; you cannot abide being around morose or depressed types. When your soul mate arrives, the positive energy you radiate will light up both of your lives.

June 12

ASTROLOGICAL SIGN: Gemini

PEOPLE BORN TODAY: George Bush, Chick Corea, Timothy Busfield, Uta Hagen, Jim Nabors, Anne Frank, Djuna Barnes

FAMOUS EVENTS: First blood transfusion administered (1767); Baseball Hall of Fame opens in Cooperstown, New York (1939); MBE medals given to Beatles by Queen Elizabeth II (1965)

LUCKY NUMBER: 9

BIRTHSTONE: Agate

POSITIVE TRAITS: Positive, striving, decisive

NEGATIVE TRAITS: Shallow, judgmental, hasty

You make far-reaching plans for improving conditions, then marshal people effectively to carry them out. You like to be in charge, and because of your generous nature, you mistakenly assume that others are your equal in ability and commitment. Though you are more comfortable confronting external difficulties, you inspire love partners with your positive attitude, and tackle any relationship problems that arise with complete assurance. At the same time, you can be harshly judgmental when coworkers or loved ones don't measure up to the high standards you set. Pursuing self-knowledge and deepening your emotional awareness will keep all your relationships running smoothly. Others may think your goals and dreams are unrealistic, but don't worry: Your optimism is validated by your remarkable results.

June 13

ASTROLOGICAL SIGN: Gemini
PEOPLE BORN TODAY: Tim Allen, Ally Sheedy, Richard Thomas, W. B. Yeats, Malcolm McDowell, Basil Rathbone
FAMOUS EVENTS: Safety pin patented (1825); first ticker tape parade held, to honor Charles Lindbergh (1927); *Miranda* ruling passed by U.S. Supreme Court (1966)
LUCKY NUMBER: 1
BIRTHSTONE: Agate
POSITIVE TRAITS: Audacious, clever, imaginative
NEGATIVE TRAITS: Rash, deluded, extreme

You can often be found far out on a limb, taking a chance where no one else would dare. Though following your vivid imagination can lead you into dangerous straits, it often makes you an innovator and a pioneer. Heed your intuition: It may tell you which risks will pay off and which are likely to end in ruin. Your inner circle should include both those who fuel your wild dreams and those who can douse them with cold water when necessary. Your mate, if smart, will give you enough leeway to keep you happy but not get roped into your crazier schemes. Your appetite for adventure may drive you to perilous activities; think long and hard about the price to be paid for fleeting thrills.

June 14

ASTROLOGICAL SIGN: Gemini

PEOPLE BORN TODAY: Steffi Graf, Eric Heiden, Boy George, Donald Trump, Marla Gibbs, Harriet Beecher Stowe, Woody Guthrie, Jerry Rubin, Irving Stone

FAMOUS EVENTS: U.S. Army established by Congress (1775); Stars and Stripes voted first U.S. flag (1777); first presidential radio speech made by President Warren G. Harding (1922)

LUCKY NUMBER: 2

BIRTHSTONE: Agate

POSITIVE TRAITS: Bold, powerful, persistent

NEGATIVE TRAITS: Bossy, power-hungry, tense

You establish ambitious goals for yourself and plug away until you reach them; and although success will not be easy, it will eventually come. You may make a few enemies and a lot of rivals along the way, but your talents will be recognized for what they are: great. Relaxation is difficult for you, not to mention pointless, since nothing makes you happier than working hard and moving closer to your goals. Your friends tend to be those who can advance your aims or add glamour to your image, and you are happiest when you can return their favors. You share your feelings openly with your mate and expect the same in return; love is the one arena where you don't need to compete—you're a born winner.

June 15

ASTROLOGICAL SIGN: Gemini

PEOPLE BORN TODAY: Courtney Cox, Neil Patrick Harris, Mario Cuomo, Helen Hunt, Waylon Jennings, Jim Belushi, Billy Williams

FAMOUS EVENTS: Arkansas becomes 25th state (1836); first plastic (celluloid) patented (1869); Henry Flipper becomes first African-American to graduate from West Point (1877)

LUCKY NUMBER: 3

BIRTHSTONE: Agate

POSITIVE TRAITS: Appealing, attractive, quick-witted

NEGATIVE TRAITS: Calculating, misleading, unforgiving

With your personal magnetism and communicative gifts, you can easily bring others around to your point of view. Your quick mind arrives at conclusions rapidly, and you then devote your energies to winning the support of coworkers, friends, or family members who may turn resentful if they feel you've bamboozled them into accepting a questionable course of action. You are powerfully attractive to romantic partners, and enjoy wooing them with clever words as well as charming them with your irresistible smile. Your people skills may vault you to a position of influence; if you find yourself in power, it will be in your own best interest to observe a strict code of ethics and use your persuasive powers only to achieve the most high-minded ends.

June 16

ASTROLOGICAL SIGN: Gemini

PEOPLE BORN TODAY: Laurie Metcalf, Lamont Dozier, Joyce Carol Oates, Billy "Crash" Craddock, Erich Segal, Stan Laurel

FAMOUS EVENTS: "Bloomsday"—the day all the events occur in James Joyce's masterpiece *Ulysses* (1904); Alfred Hitchcock's film *Psycho* premieres in New York City (1960); first female cosmonaut launched into space (1963)

LUCKY NUMBER: 4

BIRTHSTONE: Agate

POSITIVE TRAITS: Prudent, methodical, earnest

NEGATIVE TRAITS: Choosy, parsimonious, inflexible

You are a methodical craftsperson who would rather have hard-earned respect than overnight acclaim. You plot your course carefully in your career and your personal life, laying firm foundations one brick at a time. You are most comfortable working in a structured environment where your goals are clear and you receive frequent feedback on your progress. You seldom rush into relationships, and are likely to audition scores of romantic partners before casting one in the all-important role of your mate. Financial security is of utmost importance to you; most likely, you have been building a nest egg since your first paper route or baby-sitting job. Leave a little room in your super-structured life for serendipitous joy to sneak in.

June 17

ASTROLOGICAL SIGN: Gemini

PEOPLE BORN TODAY: James Brown, Dan Jansen, Barry Manilow, Jason Patric, Dean Martin, Igor Stravinsky, Gwendolyn Brooks, Newt Gingrich

FAMOUS EVENTS: Watergate burglars arrested (1972); remains of President Zachary Taylor exhumed to test for signs of poisoning (1991); O. J. Simpson, in white Bronco, leads police on a low-speed, televised chase down Los Angeles freeways (1994)

LUCKY NUMBER: 5

BIRTHSTONE: Agate

POSITIVE TRAITS: Forceful, influential, demanding

NEGATIVE TRAITS: Deceptive, cool, hard to trust

You ask at least as much of yourself as you ask of others, and that's saying a lot. In any situation, you are likely to be a star performer and a forceful presence. You are happy to set an example, but too wrapped up in the pursuit of your own goals to serve as a mentor. Your vitality and masterful demeanor draws people toward you, but because you are emotionally aloof and physically undemonstrative, a successful relationship may prove difficult. Use your ability to concentrate to your advantage: Focus on your feelings and learn how to express them. You may find that you're not such a cool customer after all, and this could make all the difference in your future happiness.

June 18

ASTROLOGICAL SIGN: Gemini

PEOPLE BORN TODAY: Paul McCartney, Isabella Rossellini, Roger Ebert, Alison Moyet, Sammy Cahn, Carol Kane

FAMOUS EVENTS: Philadelphia founded by William Penn (1682); Napoleon defeated at Waterloo (1815); Dr. Sally Ride becomes first American woman launched into space, aboard *Challenger* (1983)

LUCKY NUMBER: 6

BIRTHSTONE: Agate

POSITIVE TRAITS: Shrewd, loyal, playful

NEGATIVE TRAITS: Egotistical, mercurial, bored

Your fun-loving personality and gentle charm conceal a hard head for business. Colleagues and higher-ups alike are likely to vote you Most Congenial, but you place as high a priority on meeting personal and professional goals as you do on being popular. Your lively social life lets you put material concerns aside and bask in your friends' affection. Though you thrive on attention, you're also good at reciprocating it, especially when it comes to offering practical advice or giving financial assistance. As sensible as you are, you need to be entertained. Your mate must be someone whose interests are as far-ranging as your own and who can amuse you with witty observations about your shared adventures.

June 19

ASTROLOGICAL SIGN: Gemini

PEOPLE BORN TODAY: Paula Abdul, Salman Rushdie, Kathleen Turner, Phylicia Rashad, Louis Jourdan, Lou Gehrig

FAMOUS EVENTS: First U.S. women's rights convention held (1848); first televised heavyweight boxing match (1946); Julius and Ethel Rosenberg executed for espionage (1953)

LUCKY NUMBER: 7

BIRTHSTONE: Agate

POSITIVE TRAITS: Courageous, committed, indefatigable

NEGATIVE TRAITS: Overambitious, stressed, antagonistic

You are at your best when rising to a challenge. Opposition to your plans or ideas, whether in your professional or personal life, brings out hidden reserves of resolve and courage. Whether you fight vociferously or quietly stand your ground, you are never cowed. Among friends, you enjoy engaging in debates about political or social issues. In love, you are passionate and committed, though your mate may find you stubborn and argumentative at times. Should your partner face difficulties, there is no one more loyal than you, and your own stamina and bravery are often what sees you through. Don't let your combative nature blind you; learn to put down your dukes and accept good fortune when it graces your life.

June 20

ASTROLOGICAL SIGN: Gemini
PEOPLE BORN TODAY: Nicole Kidman, John Goodman, Brian Wilson, Chet Atkins, Lillian Hellman, Errol Flynn, Danny Aiello, Lionel Richie, Cyndi Lauper
FAMOUS EVENTS: Queen Victoria ascends the British throne (1837); *Ed Sullivan Show* premieres (1948); third consecutive NBA championship won by Chicago Bulls (1993)
LUCKY NUMBER: 8
BIRTHSTONE: Agate
POSITIVE TRAITS: Exciting, dynamic, passionate
NEGATIVE TRAITS: Illogical, hypersensitive, uncontrolled

You are the straw that stirs the drink. Expressing your passionate feelings tends to churn up strong emotions in those around you. Indifference is anathema to you, and your easygoing companions a puzzle. Every event at work and on the home front elicits a Richter-scale reaction from you. You press friends and partners for reinforcement of your feelings, and because you love excitement, you sometimes provoke them into arguments just to enjoy the fireworks. You can also be a positive force by bringing loved ones' repressed emotions to the surface. Just as often, however, they must urge you to get a grip. A warmhearted but cool-headed mate can provide the balance you need to stay on an even keel.

June 21

ASTROLOGICAL SIGN: Gemini
PEOPLE BORN TODAY: Ray Davies, Juliette Lewis, Robert Pastorelli, Benazir Bhutto, Jean-Paul Sartre, Jane Russell, Mary McCarthy
FAMOUS EVENTS: First five-and-ten opened by F. W. Woolworth (1879); first long-playing record demonstrated (1948); last television appearance made by Elvis Presley (1977)
LUCKY NUMBER: 9
BIRTHSTONE: Agate
POSITIVE TRAITS: Intense, intellectual, sensual
NEGATIVE TRAITS: Excessive, controlling, materialistic

Though you were born on the longest day of the year, you rarely have enough time to meet your goals. You resist being pigeon-holed, and seek to distinguish yourself as a scholar, sportsperson, and sex symbol—all at the same time. Since this goal is nearly impossible, you risk driving yourself to exhaustion and despair in pursuit of it. If you set the bar equally high for your friends and romantic partners, you can become a controlling taskmaster. Try to appreciate the qualities that make others special and don't expect the perfection you seek for yourself. To avoid burnout, focus your physical and mental energies, which you have in abundance. Remember, you *can* have it all—but not all at once.

ASTROLOGICAL SIGN: Cancer

PEOPLE BORN TODAY: Meryl Streep, Kris Kristofferson, Todd Rundgren, Clyde Drexler, Tracy Pollan, Bill Blass, Anne Morrow Lindbergh

FAMOUS EVENTS: Congress creates the Department of Justice (1870); death of Judy Garland (1969); voting age lowered to 18 (1970)

LUCKY NUMBER: 1

BIRTHSTONE: Pearl

POSITIVE TRAITS: Imaginative, dramatic, sensitive

NEGATIVE TRAITS: Dreamy, delusional, detached

You have an imagination that lets you infuse everyday events with the excitement of grand opera. You see colleagues, friends, and lovers as costars in the ongoing saga of your life. This Walter Mittyesque approach lets you greet each ordinary day at work or evening at home with breathless anticipation. It may cause trouble, though, if you heighten the drama by spreading gossip or indulging in false speculation. You endear yourself to your mate by sincerely viewing him or her as a romantic figure long after the routine of daily life will have stripped away any illusions of glamour. Keep your feet on the ground by paying attention to other people's perceptions and perhaps occasionally subjecting yourself to the daily newspapers.

June 23

ASTROLOGICAL SIGN: Cancer

PEOPLE BORN TODAY: James Levine, June Carter Cash, Bob Fosse, Dr. Alfred Kinsey, Duke of Windsor (King Edward VIII), Empress Josephine of France, Anna Akhmatova

FAMOUS EVENTS: Friendship treaty signed by William Penn and Lenni Lenape Indians (1683); saxophone patented by Antoine Sax (1846); Taft-Hartley Act passed (1947)

LUCKY NUMBER: 2

BIRTHSTONE: Pearl

POSITIVE TRAITS: Romantic, devoted, thoughtful

NEGATIVE TRAITS: Gossipy, trivial, unrealistic

Love makes your world go 'round. You delight in discussing your own emotional attachments and are eager to hear friends' confidences, though your tendency to repeat them can be costly in human terms and make you appear untrustworthy—which you are not. You are prone to fall in love at first sight and mythologize your beloved to such a point that his or her real qualities, good and bad, may become unrecognizable. Your need for absolute devotion from a partner can scare away some potential mates, but your own ability to make a partner feel secure, loved, and pampered is downright remarkable. Don't underestimate the power of your fine sense of humor; it may be the one thing that can keep you from going over the top.

June 24

ASTROLOGICAL SIGN: Cancer

PEOPLE BORN TODAY: Mick Fleetwood, Nancy Allen, Norman Cousins, Jeff Beck, Michele Lee, Jack Dempsey, Ambrose Bierce, Josephine Bonaparte

FAMOUS EVENTS: North America sighted by explorer John Cabot (1497); coronation of King Henry VIII (1509); sighting of nine UFOs reported by Idaho pilot (1947)

LUCKY NUMBER: 3

BIRTHSTONE: Pearl

POSITIVE TRAITS: Spiritual, inspired, gifted

NEGATIVE TRAITS: Dominating, unethical, insensitive

You choose your own path, often attaining such success that others are moved to follow in your footsteps. Whatever you focus your energies on, whether it's your career, an avocation, or family life, you bring to it an almost supernatural level of proficiency. At work or at home, you can be counted on to solve stubborn problems with lightning flashes of inspiration. Regular doses of solitude help you to think creatively and formulate your plans. You are a caring friend and family member who keeps loved ones in your thoughts even though you may go for long periods without seeing them. Your talent and charm are potent lures to romantic partners, but they must learn to respect your priorities, which may not always put them first.

June 25

ASTROLOGICAL SIGN: Cancer

PEOPLE BORN TODAY: Carly Simon, George Michael, Sidney Lumet, Willis Reed, Phyllis George, George Orwell

FAMOUS EVENTS: General Custer and troops defeated at Battle of Little Big Horn (1876); Madame Marie Curie announces discovery of radium (1903); architect Stanford White shot by Harry Thaw (1906)

LUCKY NUMBER: 4

BIRTHSTONE: Pearl

POSITIVE TRAITS: Sensitive, creative, sympathetic

NEGATIVE TRAITS: Touchy, susceptible, insecure

You vibrate like a tuning fork to the slightest outside influence. Your sensitivity makes you a valuable team player, but you may be overly reliant on the approval of others, letting yourself be swept along by their wishes rather than risking their displeasure. In love you allow your partner to set the agenda, making choices about what the two of you will do and with whom you'll do it. In all your relationships your tendency to please others at the expense of your own desires may ultimately lead to a blowup when you can no longer suppress your needs. Avert disaster by aiming for equality with others on a day-to-day basis. Remember that it is possible to follow your own inner voice and still be loved.

June 26

ASTROLOGICAL SIGN: Cancer

PEOPLE BORN TODAY: Peter Lorre, Greg LeMond, Mick Jones, Dave Grusin, Billy Davis Jr., Babe Didrickson Zaharias, Pearl Buck

FAMOUS EVENTS: First movie theater opens in America (1896); bicycle patented (1918); *New York Daily News* begins publication (1919)

LUCKY NUMBER: 5

BIRTHSTONE: Pearl

POSITIVE TRAITS: Athletic, energetic, sensual

NEGATIVE TRAITS: Overprotective, overaggressive, vain

You love life's comforts and pleasures and are willing to work hard to provide them for your loved ones as well as yourself. Like the crab that symbolizes your astrological sign, you have a sturdy outer shell that lets you stand up to attack. You extend this protective ability to your colleagues, friends, and especially children, sometimes fighting their battles for them even if they would rather fend for themselves. You are a warm, loving, and sensual romantic partner with a flair for making a home environment that is at once secure and exciting. You enjoy sports of all kinds, and not just because you look good in tight-fitting sportswear; you enjoy testing your physical stamina and matching yourself against the competition.

June 27

ASTROLOGICAL SIGN: Cancer
PEOPLE BORN TODAY: Isabelle Adjani, Ross Perot, Bob Keeshan, Julia Duffy, Willie Mosconi, Helen Keller
FAMOUS EVENTS: Mormon leader Joseph Smith killed by antipolygamy mob (1844); "Happy Birthday" composed by Mildred J. Hill (1859); Korean conflict entered into by U.S. (1950)
LUCKY NUMBER: 6
BIRTHSTONE: Pearl
POSITIVE TRAITS: Competitive, driven, persuasive
NEGATIVE TRAITS: Guarded, defensive, inflexible

You are a watchdog, devoted to defending yourself and your interests against attack. Those who criticize or argue with you may often find themselves involved in a fierce fight, though close companions know that your bark is worse than your bite. You sometimes alienate coworkers and acquaintances by being needlessly aggressive, reacting to threats that exist only in your imagination. Though you are a loyal mate, you can be quick to take offense at criticism—even the constructive kind—and your defensiveness may cause unnecessary rifts in your relationship. You sometimes put so much of your energy into protecting your current assets or relationships that you miss out on opportunities to develop new ones. Relax and let the world pet you occasionally.

June 28

ASTROLOGICAL SIGN: Cancer
PEOPLE BORN TODAY: Mary Stuart Masterson, John Cusack, Mel Brooks, Luigi Pirandello, Gilda Radner, Richard Rodgers
FAMOUS EVENTS: Coronation of Queen Victoria (1838); first dog show, in Newcastle, England (1859); Archduke Franz Ferdinand assassinated, beginning World War I (1914)
LUCKY NUMBER: 7
BIRTHSTONE: Pearl
POSITIVE TRAITS: Funny, warm, appealing
NEGATIVE TRAITS: Irrational, disorganized, outspoken

People count on you to break the tension at a business meeting or crack the ice at a stiff social gathering, and your keen eye and sharp wit win widespread admiration. You often interject "zingers" into conversations, though not from any lack of tact or insight: Your eyebrow-raisers are precisely calculated to achieve their desired effect, which is to put you in the spotlight. Occasionally, however, you put your foot in your mouth by taking easy shots that offend their targets. You are as at ease in romantic situations as you are in social ones. Partners are impressed by your cleverness and your emotional accessibility. For love to last, though, any potential mate will have to be content with a supporting role—at least in public.

June 29

ASTROLOGICAL SIGN: Cancer
PEOPLE BORN TODAY: Richard Lewis, Stokely Carmichael, Gary Busey, Slim Pickens, Robert Evans, Antoine de Saint-Exupéry
FAMOUS EVENTS: Shakespeare's Globe Theater destroyed by fire (1613); Charlie Dumas becomes first high jumper to break seven feet (1956); Marilyn Monroe and Arthur Miller wed (1956)
LUCKY NUMBER: 8
BIRTHSTONE: Pearl
POSITIVE TRAITS: Imaginative, giving, empathetic
NEGATIVE TRAITS: Self-sacrificing, inconsistent, frustrated

Helping others is of paramount importance to you. Although you are ambitious, your career and personal goals are driven by your desire to make a difference in the lives of others. You work hard to fulfill the expectations of a respected parent, teacher, or spouse, and to provide a comfortable life for your loved ones, but you are not afraid to take the time you need to recharge your batteries—even if these bouts of inertia look like laziness. You have so many solid accomplishments that you don't have to worry about appearances. Because you are an exceedingly generous mate, you frequently have to temper your giving impulses in order to allow your partner and/or children to stand on their own.

June 30

ASTROLOGICAL SIGN: Cancer

PEOPLE BORN TODAY: Mike Tyson, Czeslaw Milosz, Lena Horne, Buddy Rich, David Allan Grier, Susan Hayward

FAMOUS EVENTS: Tightrope walk across Niagara Falls by Charles Blondin (1859); first woman graduates from a U.S. law school (1870); *Gone with the Wind* published (1936)

LUCKY NUMBER: 9

BIRTHSTONE: Pearl

POSITIVE TRAITS: Tough, savvy, driven

NEGATIVE TRAITS: Suspicious, angry, reclusive

You are slow to trust and even slower to reveal yourself, not because you are emotionally repressed but because your savvy, intellectual approach to situations has brought you so much success. You learn the ropes quickly on the job and in social situations; colleagues and acquaintances consider you a cool customer who can show flashes of fire when crossed. Your inner circle, however, is privy to glimpses of your true and tender self, and values your loyalty as a friend. Partners know you as a closet romantic allergic to public displays of affection, but as demonstrative as a puppy in private. Surrounding yourself with people you can count on will keep you from becoming too aloof and disconnected—and help to temper your rages.

July 1

ASTROLOGICAL SIGN: Cancer

PEOPLE BORN TODAY: Princess Diana, George Sand, Deborah Harry, Dan Aykroyd, Twyla Tharp, Carl Lewis

FAMOUS EVENTS: First adhesive postage stamps issued (1847); Battle of Gettysburg begins (1863); first U.S. zoo opens, in Philadelphia (1874)

LUCKY NUMBER: 8

BIRTHSTONE: Pearl

POSITIVE TRAITS: Generous, altruistic, ambitious

NEGATIVE TRAITS: Insecure, self-doubting, withdrawn

You give so much to others—constantly putting yourself in their shoes and helping to shoulder their burdens—that you occasionally need a boost yourself. After building morale at work and bolstering the self-esteem of friends with encouragement and praise, you then throw yourself into social causes that let you iron out inequalities and try to provide a fair deal for everyone. You may be drawn to romantic partners who doubt their desirability, in the hope that your affections will reinforce their fragile egos, but since you, too, are prone to periods of insecurity and depression, it would be unwise to pair yourself with a chronically needy mate. Be sure your partner is capable of giving as well as taking emotional support.

July 2

ASTROLOGICAL SIGN: Cancer

PEOPLE BORN TODAY: Cheryl Ladd, Jose Canseco, Herman Hesse, Richard Petty, Imelda Marcos, Thurgood Marshall

FAMOUS EVENTS: President James Garfield assassinated (1881); Amelia Earhart vanishes over Pacific Ocean (1937); Civil Rights Act signed by President Lyndon B. Johnson, banning racial discrimination (1964)

LUCKY NUMBER: 9

BIRTHSTONE: Pearl

POSITIVE TRAITS: Capable, bright, responsible

NEGATIVE TRAITS: Touchy, oversensitive, insecure

Although your public persona is colorful and capable, you are plagued by private doubts. You second-guess your decisions and question your choices even when they succeed, which they almost always do. You constantly come through for friends and coworkers, but your natural modesty makes it difficult for you to accept the praise you so richly deserve. Though you attract lovers effortlessly, you are never sure whether your sweetheart loves you for yourself or for an image far removed from the real you. Whoever succeeds in getting close to you must handle your fragile feelings with kid gloves, but those efforts will be rewarded by your deep devotion and imaginative approach to romance. Reach out: You don't have to suffer your insecurities in silence.

July 3

ASTROLOGICAL SIGN: Cancer

PEOPLE BORN TODAY: Tom Cruise, Franz Kafka, Tom Stoppard, Betty Buckley, Ken Russell, George M. Cohan, M. F. K. Fisher

FAMOUS EVENTS: First automobile test-driven by Karl Benz (1886); radio debut of Abbott and Costello (1940); Richard Branson and Per Lindstrand cross the Atlantic in hot-air balloon (1987)

LUCKY NUMBER: 1

BIRTHSTONE: Pearl

POSITIVE TRAITS: Penetrating, insightful, revealing

NEGATIVE TRAITS: Detached, snobbish, superior

You are a keen observer of human nature, and the foibles and follies of your fellows seldom go unremarked when you are around. Your knack for seeing through people's behavior to their underlying motivations makes you both more cynical and more forgiving than others; you hold new acquaintances at arm's length until you determine what they want. Romantic partners who try to sweet-talk you or arouse your jealousy are more likely to make you laugh, but when you do find lasting love, you accept your mate's flaws and share your own failings openly. You will engage yourself more fully in life if you remember that you belong to the same species as the creatures whose actions you find so absurd.

July 4

ASTROLOGICAL SIGN: Cancer

PEOPLE BORN TODAY: Geraldo Rivera, Leona Helmsley, George Steinbrenner, Pam Shriver, twins Esther and Pauline Friedman (Ann Landers and Abigail Van Buren), Neil Simon

FAMOUS EVENTS: Declaration of Independence adopted (1776); deaths of John Adams and Thomas Jefferson (1826); Yankee Stadium farewell speech made by Lou Gehrig (1939)

LUCKY NUMBER: 2

BIRTHSTONE: Pearl

POSITIVE TRAITS: Industrious, principled, generous

NEGATIVE TRAITS: Demanding, autocratic, egotistical

Without apology or shame, you think you know what's best for everyone. Both at work and at home, you set strict ground rules meant to be followed to the letter; and because you are utterly loyal to your extended family of relatives, friends, and associates, you expect the same dedication in return. When they chafe under your restrictions, therefore, you are genuinely hurt and puzzled: Don't they realize you have their best interests at heart? The mild-mannered and compliant façade you adopt for romantic partners cannot last, because your long-term mate must be completely devoted and willing to let you arrange every detail of your life together. In return, however, you will supply unstinting generosity and abundant displays of affection.

July 5

ASTROLOGICAL SIGN: Cancer
PEOPLE BORN TODAY: Huey Lewis, Robbie Robertson, Katherine Helmond, Rich Gossage, Shirley Knight, P. T. Barnum
FAMOUS EVENTS: First travel agency started by Thomas Cook (1841); bikini swimsuit debuts (1946); first Wimbledon singles victory by an African-American, Arthur Ashe (1975)
LUCKY NUMBER: 3
BIRTHSTONE: Pearl
POSITIVE TRAITS: Entertaining, fun, sociable
NEGATIVE TRAITS: Wild, excessive, mercurial

Born in the wake of Independence Day, you are a real firecracker. With your flair for fun, your imaginative ideas, and your restless enthusiasm for new acquaintances and activities, you light up both the workplace and any social gatherings you may attend. Your circle of friends is wide, but pals may have trouble keeping up with your explosive pace; you are highly attractive to romantic partners, but your mercurial mood swings can test your mate's patience. It will take someone special to hold your attention for long, and you will resist any attempts to settle down and add stability to your life. Don't: In the long run you will find a more centered existence far more fulfilling. You may even like it.

July 6

ASTROLOGICAL SIGN: Cancer

PEOPLE BORN TODAY: Sylvester Stallone, Nancy Reagan, Merv Griffin, Beatrix Potter, Janet Leigh, Frida Kahlo

FAMOUS EVENTS: Sir Thomas More beheaded for treason by King Henry VIII (1535); rabies treatment successfully tested by Dr. Louis Pasteur (1885); first Wimbledon singles victory by an African-American woman, Althea Gibson (1957)

LUCKY NUMBER: 4

BIRTHSTONE: Pearl

POSITIVE TRAITS: Charismatic, passionate, intense

NEGATIVE TRAITS: Needy, obsessive, one-track

You burn with intensity about every aspect of life, and find it impossible to be casual about responsibilities or personal commitments. Compromise is also not easy for you, so although you are highly reliable, your passionate attachment to your own ideas and plans can lead to clashes with others. You are a devoted friend, attached to your kindergarten buddies for life; and although you are equally dedicated to romantic partners, and pledge allegiance with impressive sincerity, you fall in love too easily. Beware of scaring off prospects by seeming too needy and learn to let go of unpromising relationships. Your strong instincts are a good guide, but try to remember that every situation presents a variety of workable options, and not just one.

July 7

ASTROLOGICAL SIGN: Cancer

PEOPLE BORN TODAY: Ringo Starr, Michelle Kwan, Satchel Paige, Shelley Duvall, Marc Chagall, Gian Carlo Menotti

FAMOUS EVENTS: Traveler's checks patented (1891); Mother Cabrini, first American saint, canonized (1946); Sandra Day O'Connor becomes first woman appointed to the U.S. Supreme Court (1981)

LUCKY NUMBER: 5

BIRTHSTONE: Pearl

POSITIVE TRAITS: Fanciful, childlike, romantic

NEGATIVE TRAITS: Quixotic, naive, delusional

You're a beautiful dreamer—tilting at windmills, dwelling in a lovely realm of imagination, still in touch with the idealism that many people abandon with the onset of adult responsibilities. Deception and scheming are foreign to you; yet you are the one who typically points out the emperor's lack of clothing. Your innate honesty and political ineptness may limit your rise up the social or professional ladder, but romantic partners are touched by your ingenuousness and lifted out of their mundane lives by your creative approach to life. Nevertheless, for your own peace of mind, you must step out from behind your veil of dreams and attempt to see the world as it really is—then make the best of it.

July 8

ASTROLOGICAL SIGN: Cancer
PEOPLE BORN TODAY: Anjelica Huston, Kevin Bacon, Cynthia Gregory, Phil Gramm, Marty Feldman, Nelson Rockefeller
FAMOUS EVENTS: Percy Bysshe Shelley drowned in sailing accident (1822); ice-cream sundae invented (1881); first issue of *Wall Street Journal* (1889)
LUCKY NUMBER: 6
BIRTHSTONE: Pearl
POSITIVE TRAITS: Understanding, sensible, well-prepared
NEGATIVE TRAITS: Sober, defensive, too accepting

You clearly see the challenges lying before you and do your best to meet, forestall, or overcome them. Painfully aware of life's trials and tribulations, you want to shield the people you care about from these same blows. Your practical brand of caring makes you quick to intercede with help and advice in an effort to spare others needless heartache (or headaches). Though they may appreciate your sincere concern, they also at times may resent your interference or feel you underestimate their abilities. Romantic partners can rely on you for emotional support, but there, too, you must refrain from making their problems your own and treating them like children. With children themselves, you are a natural nurturer, if a tad overprotective.

ASTROLOGICAL SIGN: Cancer

PEOPLE BORN TODAY: Jimmy Smits, Tom Hanks, O. J. Simpson, Kelly McGillis, John Tesh, Brian Dennehy, Dame Barbara Cartland

FAMOUS EVENTS: Two trains collide in worst U.S. train disaster (1918); comic strips read over radio by New York's mayor Fiorello LaGuardia during newspaper strike (1945); *American Bandstand*, with Dick Clark, premieres on television (1956)

LUCKY NUMBER: 7

BIRTHSTONE: Pearl

POSITIVE TRAITS: Involved, seeking, persistent

NEGATIVE TRAITS: Discouraged, eccentric, unrealistic

You long to taste everything that life has to offer. You are always seeking out novel ideas on the job and in your personal pursuits, and your sociability and openness to different points of view make you very popular: Friends know they can confide their craziest-sounding plans to you without fear of ridicule. Your choice of romantic partners runs to those who share your curiosity or who come from backgrounds that differ drastically from your own. Because you believe that anything is possible, you have a tendency to become downhearted when your efforts fail, although you almost never concede defeat. You keep coming back: "If at first you don't succeed, try something else" is a philosophy that serves you well.

July 10

ASTROLOGICAL SIGN: Cancer

PEOPLE BORN TODAY: Arthur Ashe, Virginia Wade, Arlo Guthrie, Roger Craig, Jean Kerr, Jake LaMotta

FAMOUS EVENTS: John Scopes defended by Clarence Darrow in the "monkey" trial about evolution (1925); color motion pictures demonstrated by George Eastman (1928); first Beatles film, *A Hard Day's Night*, premieres (1964)

LUCKY NUMBER: 8

BIRTHSTONE: Pearl

POSITIVE TRAITS: Studious, sensitive, purposeful

NEGATIVE TRAITS: Self-sacrificing, passive, reclusive

You learn your lessons well from the victories and missteps of others, and plot your actions accordingly. More dynamic coworkers and friends may regard you as passive but you're not: you're steady and purposeful. When others' impetuous actions land them in hot water, you readily help them out while vowing silently not to imitate their mistakes. Equally, you size up romantic partners from a distance before making any moves, and indeed may wait until you are sure of their intentions before declaring your own. Even your long-term mate may find you something of a mystery, and struggle to draw out your feelings and opinions. By all means look before you leap—but not so long that you spend your life on the sidelines.

July 11

ASTROLOGICAL SIGN: Cancer

PEOPLE BORN TODAY: Sela Ward, Richie Sambora, Debbie Dunning, Leon Spinks, Suzanne Vega, Yul Brynner, E. B. White

FAMOUS EVENTS: Alexander Hamilton fatally shot in duel with Vice President Aaron Burr (1804); Major League debut of Babe Ruth (1914); first woman ordered to pay alimony (1981)

LUCKY NUMBER: 9

BIRTHSTONE: Pearl

POSITIVE TRAITS: Sociable, communicative, team player

NEGATIVE TRAITS: Superficial, gossipy, image-conscious

You are in the swim at work and on the social scene. Because you are often the first to recognize new trends and fashions, people come to you for ideas—and you have plenty to give them. You are happiest and most productive in a group environment where your dynamic relationships with coworkers keep you excited and energized; and in private life you incessantly join organizations that let you socialize with like-minded people. Your large pool of acquaintances provides plenty of opportunities for romance and your ability to put others at their ease guarantees your popularity. Being part of a couple is a key personal goal for you, and you prefer to plan joint activities with your mate rather than pursue individual interests.

July 12

ASTROLOGICAL SIGN: Cancer
PEOPLE BORN TODAY: Kristi Yamaguchi, Bill Cosby, Mel Harris, Richard Simmons, Milton Berle, Andrew Wyeth
FAMOUS EVENTS: Niagara Falls crossed on tightrope by Maria Spelterina (1876); Charles Stewart Rolls, aviator and cofounder of Rolls-Royce, killed in Britain's first plane crash (1910); first integrated baseball All-Star game played (1949)
LUCKY NUMBER: 1
BIRTHSTONE: Pearl
POSITIVE TRAITS: Humorous, caring, strong-minded
NEGATIVE TRAITS: Overpowering, stubborn, uncooperative

Your gentle, humorous manner may lead people to think that you're a pushover, but nothing could be further from the truth. You hold profound convictions from which you refuse to be dissuaded; many have tried, all have failed. Your loyalty isn't limited to your convictions, either; you are a steadfast and reliable friend as well, even though your tendency to orchestrate their lives may not always win you high marks. Ally yourself with those who share your principles and devote your time and unfailing energy to doing things rather than talking about them. Romantic partners who let you take the lead may appeal to you in the beginning, but for a successful long-term relationship, find your match—and let the fireworks begin.

July 13

ASTROLOGICAL SIGN: Cancer

PEOPLE BORN TODAY: Harrison Ford, Patrick Stewart, Jack Kemp, Spud Webb, Louise Mandrell, Cheech Marin

FAMOUS EVENTS: Newly completed Buckingham Palace occupied by Queen Victoria (1837); *Women's Wear Daily* debuts (1910); first record made by Frank Sinatra (1939)

LUCKY NUMBER: 2

BIRTHSTONE: Pearl

POSITIVE TRAITS: Strong, gutsy, direct

NEGATIVE TRAITS: Inflexible, discouraged, doubting

It ain't over till it's over": Failure, to you, is just a phase you pass through on your way to ultimate success. Whenever you suffer professional or personal setbacks, you chalk them up to experience and waste no time starting over. You're no blind optimist; rather you're indefatigable because your imagination never fails you; you never lack for a different idea, a new approach, or a better way. Little intimidates you, but you can be awkward in romantic situations, which require you to lay aside your action-oriented approach for a more subtle style of relating. Because you do not suffer fools gladly—if at all—you should surround yourself with people, and most of all with a mate, who are straightforward, principled, and reliable.

July 14

You cast a spell over others with your dramatic presence and your wizardry with words and images. Whether communicating with a crowd or a small circle of friends, you know how to package your ideas for maximum impact and influence; and regardless of what career or cause you embrace, you bring to it the abilities of an advertising pro. You win the hearts of romantic partners by divining their hidden desires and promising to fulfill them, but if you expect to hold their lasting affections, you must balance this seductive gift with solid results. Don't cheat yourself out of meaningful relationships by trying too hard to please; let others get to know the real you and your relationships will be rooted in fact, not fantasy.

July 15

ASTROLOGICAL SIGN: Cancer
PEOPLE BORN TODAY: Kim Alexis, Linda Ronstadt, Forest Whitaker, Brigitte Nielsen, Alex Karras, Iris Murdoch, Jean-Bertrand Aristide
FAMOUS EVENTS: Washington Bradley pitches the first no-hitter (1876); first around-the-world solo flight completed (1933); record for continuous flight set, 111 hours (1986)
LUCKY NUMBER: 4
BIRTHSTONE: Pearl
POSITIVE TRAITS: Catalyzing, exciting, stimulating
NEGATIVE TRAITS: Disruptive, negative, manipulative

You are equal parts performer and muse whose charismatic presence and imaginative ideas have a profound effect on others. It may simply be desire to please you that drives coworkers and friends to achieve impressive deeds, or it could be that they want to test themselves against your formidable accomplishments. When others do well, you're usually the first to pop the champagne and lavish the praise, which makes you even more popular. Romance can cause you some trouble; potential partners are particularly susceptible to your magnetic charms, and you have a tendency to take advantage of your power and their vulnerability. Ask yourself each morning not only what you want to accomplish, but what effect it will have on those you care about.

July 16

ASTROLOGICAL SIGN: Cancer

PEOPLE BORN TODAY: Rubén Blades, Margaret Court, Pinchas Zuckerman, Ginger Rogers, Barbara Stanwyck, "Shoeless" Joe Jackson

FAMOUS EVENTS: Russian czar Nicholas II and family murdered by Bolsheviks (1918); first use of parking meters, in Oklahoma City (1935); first atomic bomb tested in New Mexico (1945)

LUCKY NUMBER: 5

BIRTHSTONE: Pearl

POSITIVE TRAITS: Intense, encouraging, loyal

NEGATIVE TRAITS: Restless, obsessive, preachy

You dream big dreams—and they come true. Though you exhibit an unpretentious and down-to-earth demeanor and rarely draw attention to yourself, you never lose sight of your grandiose ambitions. A supportive friend, you encourage others to follow their wildest fantasies just as you chase your own. In fact, you pursue, and sometimes succeed in capturing, romantic partners whom others might consider out of your league in terms of stature, education, wealth, or even physical appearance. Whether or not you succeed romantically, you remain loyal and friendly to all the people you admire and develop many lasting connections. You aim high, setting goals for yourself that continually force you to test your mettle, and more often than not, you succeed.

July 17

ASTROLOGICAL SIGN: Cancer

PEOPLE BORN TODAY: Donald Sutherland, Phoebe Snow, Diahann Carroll, Phyllis Diller, Dawn Upshaw, James Cagney, Camilla Parker-Bowles

FAMOUS EVENTS: Hundred Years' War between Britain and France begins (1453); final Allied summit of World War II at Potsdam (1945); first stealth bomber test flight (1989)

LUCKY NUMBER: 6

BIRTHSTONE: Pearl

POSITIVE TRAITS: Capable, directed, self-sufficient

NEGATIVE TRAITS: Isolated, egotistical, workaholic

You strive to be without peer in your chosen field—and to have others acknowledge your mastery. Your confidence makes you a disciplined self-starter in any task you undertake, and you impress others with your steady professionalism. Once you win the respect of associates and acquaintances for your cool efficiency, you can direct your efforts toward gaining recognition for your creativity as well. You resent friends typecasting you as the smart or reliable one, and spend too much time trying to acquaint them with the full spectrum of your good qualities. Your self-sufficiency can make you seem unapproachable to romantic partners, but you are capable of great devotion to a mate whose faith in you is equal to your own.

July 18

ASTROLOGICAL SIGN: Cancer

PEOPLE BORN TODAY: Nelson Mandela, Hunter S. Thompson, Dick Button, Clifford Odets, William Makepeace Thackeray, John Glenn, Richard Branson

FAMOUS EVENTS: Ty Cobb gets his 4,000th hit (1927); Spanish Civil War started (1936); arrival in Ireland of Los Angeles–bound pilot Douglas "Wrong Way" Corrigan (1938)

LUCKY NUMBER: 7

BIRTHSTONE: Pearl

POSITIVE TRAITS: Bold, fearless, adventurous

NEGATIVE TRAITS: Radical, childish, extreme

Determined to make your voice heard, you are unlikely to embrace conventional methods in your professional or personal life. When you find a better way, you boldly speak out to let others know about it. Higher-ups may dread your candid outbursts, but coworkers applaud your courage in pointing out the truth. Friends may regard you as eccentric, but because they like you so much, they are willing to assume that there is a method to your apparent madness. Your hunger for the spotlight can cause problems in romantic relationships unless you grant your partner equal time; and although your mate may back you to the hilt in your pursuit of truth and justice, there are moments when your significant other should be your only "cause."

ASTROLOGICAL SIGN: Cancer

PEOPLE BORN TODAY: Ilie Nastase, George McGovern, Vikki Carr, Richard Jordan, Edgar Degas

FAMOUS EVENTS: V-for-victory hand sign introduced by Winston Churchill (1940); Geraldine Ferraro becomes first woman nominated for vice president by major political party, the Democrats (1984); Caroline Kennedy and Edwin Schlossberg wed (1986)

LUCKY NUMBER: 8

BIRTHSTONE: Pearl

POSITIVE TRAITS: Modest, deliberate, thoughtful

NEGATIVE TRAITS: Cranky, insecure, excessive

Because you expect a great deal of yourself, you strive daily for self-improvement and are painfully aware of your inadequacies, even to the point of exaggerating them and imagining shortcomings where none exist. You sometimes fend off criticism by lashing out at others first, so your friends may feel that they are constantly on the defensive with you. Those who know you best, however, realize that your harshest judgments are reserved for yourself. Your seductive playfulness is a pleasant surprise to romantic partners, and more than compensates for the occasional tantrum they will have to tolerate. A mate who shores up your self-esteem can free you to be as kind and gracious as you were always meant to be.

July 20

ASTROLOGICAL SIGN: Cancer
PEOPLE BORN TODAY: Carlos Santana, Natalie Wood, Chuck Daly, Diana Rigg, Tony Oliva, Sir Edmund Hillary, Elizabeth Dole
FAMOUS EVENTS: Assassination attempt survived by Adolf Hitler (1944); first Moon walk, by *Apollo XI* astronauts Armstrong and Aldrin (1969); *Viking I* becomes first U.S. spacecraft to land on Mars (1976)
LUCKY NUMBER: 9
BIRTHSTONE: Pearl
POSITIVE TRAITS: Daring, adventurous, achieving
NEGATIVE TRAITS: Inattentive, unstable, struggling

Like a snake, you must periodically shed your old skin for a new one. You are exhilarated, rather than daunted, by fresh challenges and difficulties; keeping the same job, domestic situation, or daily routine for long periods of time can be stifling to your spirit. No matter how comfortable your position may seem to an outsider, you are inevitably overcome by restlessness and must move on. Friends provide an emotional anchor throughout your constantly changing personal and professional life, and even take vicarious pleasure in your adventures. Because nothing scares you more than boredom, your romantic alliances can be intense; your partner must be a chameleon and an adventurer to keep you interested—and a miracle worker to keep you at home.

July 21

ASTROLOGICAL SIGN: Cancer
PEOPLE BORN TODAY: Robin Williams, Cat Stevens, Janet Reno, Jon Lovitz, Isaac Stern, Ernest Hemingway
FAMOUS EVENTS: *The New Orleans Tribune* debuts, first daily African-American newspaper (1864); astronauts Armstrong and Aldrin return safely from first Moon walk (1969); Governor Michael Dukakis nominated for presidency (1988)
LUCKY NUMBER: 1
BIRTHSTONE: Pearl
POSITIVE TRAITS: Vital, sensual, thrilling
NEGATIVE TRAITS: Reckless, violent, disruptive

Others may be allergic to conflict, but you're an addict; when trouble begins to brew, you jump into the vat headfirst. This tendency to thrust yourself into battle, whether it concerns you or not, creates as many admirers as it does enemies. But even more than the thrill of battle, you love to win. And because you are a genuinely creative problem solver, you frequently do win, though you are often downcast if victory comes too easily. Romantic partners seeking constant harmony are not for you; you enjoy a relationship peppered with disagreements and spiced with reconciliations and you're not above creating a little trouble to keep the adrenaline flowing. A lasting union may prove elusive if your intended lacks the fighting spirit.

July 22

ASTROLOGICAL SIGN: Cancer

PEOPLE BORN TODAY: Danny Glover, Alex Trebek, Oscar de la Renta, Rose Fitzgerald Kennedy, Edward Hopper, Stephen Vincent Benét

FAMOUS EVENTS: "America the Beautiful" written as poem by Katharine Lee Bates (1893); John Dillinger shot by federal agents (1934); mass wedding of 2,200 couples performed by Rev. Sun Myung Moon at Madison Square Garden (1982)

LUCKY NUMBER: 2

BIRTHSTONE: Pearl

POSITIVE TRAITS: Brave, striving, dutiful

NEGATIVE TRAITS: Long-suffering, driven, repressed

You are a master at coping with whatever life dishes out; when a crisis arises, you come through with flying colors. Even in the most difficult times you keep up a brave front and provide sturdy support for your friends, family, and associates, but you also know how to get others to help themselves, and you do it. Though romantic partners, too, may lean heavily on you, you wear your responsibilities lightly, and your sunny nature and natural good cheer rarely flag. It's only when you wear yourself out that you tend to become downcast; your ideal partner will see the warning signs and take you away for a relaxing weekend, or lock the doors and be your loving slave until your energy and optimism return.

July 23

Astrological sign: Leo

People born today: Woody Harrelson, Belinda Montgomery, Calvert de Forrest (Larry "Bud" Melman), Coral Browne, Don Drysdale, Pee-wee Reese, Raymond Chandler

Famous events: Salvation Army founded by William Booth (1865); rock and roll banned from Iran by Ayatollah Khomeini (1979); Vanessa Williams gives up Miss America title after nude photos published in *Penthouse* (1984)

Lucky number: 3

Birthstone: Ruby

Positive traits: Emotional, sympathetic, warm

Negative traits: Fragile, stressed, oversensitive

You are a soft touch for anyone with a sob story, providing a shoulder to cry on and even material assistance, yet when your own spirits are low you are often too shy to seek the same comfort. You are known for your good taste and artistic talents; your home is your palette and your work draws rave reviews. Your house is always the one where people congregate, and your office always the one where people stop and shoot the breeze. Though partners gravitate readily to your warmth, and you know how to keep a lover satisfied, don't cheat yourself out of the same attentions you so generously provide: Hold out for the special someone who is willing and able to reciprocate.

July 24

ASTROLOGICAL SIGN: Leo

PEOPLE BORN TODAY: Michael Richards, Lynda Carter, Karl Malone, Bella Abzug, Amelia Earhart, Peter Yates, Simón Bolívar

FAMOUS EVENTS: Mormon followers led to Salt Lake City by Brigham Young (1847); U.S. conducts first underwater nuclear test, at Bikini Atoll (1946); Mount Fuji climbed by ninety-one-year-old Hulda Crooks (1987)

LUCKY NUMBER: 4

BIRTHSTONE: Ruby

POSITIVE TRAITS: Charismatic, inspiring, original

NEGATIVE TRAITS: Eccentric, fickle, irrational

You are a true original and an invigorating presence in the lives of all who know you. Though colleagues and acquaintances may secretly think you an oddball, they admire your daring ways and find themselves irresistibly drawn to you. And although few of your friends would choose to flout convention as wildly as you do, none of them would ever throw a bash without you: You are practically a party on your own. Romantic partners swarm to you; they want to get close in the hope of understanding what makes you tick and perhaps vicariously capturing some of your magic. It will be hard for you to find a mate as compelling as yourself, but once you do, you will begin a life of unrelenting passion and adventure.

July 25

ASTROLOGICAL SIGN: Leo
PEOPLE BORN TODAY: Iman, Roger Clinton, Barbara Harris, Walter Payton, Estelle Getty, Jerry Paris
FAMOUS EVENTS: Austrian chancellor Engelbert Dollfuss killed by Nazis (1934); first test-tube baby conceived, Louise Joy Brown, (1978); first space walk by a woman, cosmonaut Svetlana Savitskaya (1984)
LUCKY NUMBER: 5
BIRTHSTONE: Ruby
POSITIVE TRAITS: Creative, noble, fair
NEGATIVE TRAITS: Impractical, moody, self-critical

You often fall short of your goals, but only because you set them so high. You aspire to great feats at home and at work, and although you may accomplish 99 percent of what you set out to do, you consider your efforts a failure unless you achieve the remaining 1 percent. Others are not nearly so uncharitable; friends see you as a dynamo capable of things they can only imagine, and romantic partners prize you for the purity of your motives and your innate generosity, as well as your sturdiness and devotion. Your desire for perfection springs from the noblest of motives, but it can also be self-destructive. Pay more attention to others' opinions of yourself and less to your own: You'll live longer, and wear a bigger smile on your face.

July 26

ASTROLOGICAL SIGN: Leo

PEOPLE BORN TODAY: Sandra Bullock, Dorothy Hamill, Mick Jagger, Helen Mirren, Stanley Kubrick, Kevin Spacey, Carl Jung, Aldous Huxley

FAMOUS EVENTS: Benjamin Franklin becomes first postmaster general (1775); President Truman signs an order integrating the U.S. armed forces (1946); first solo sail by a woman across the Pacific completed by Sharon Adams (1969)

LUCKY NUMBER: 5

BIRTHSTONE: Ruby

POSITIVE TRAITS: Honest, confident, worldly

NEGATIVE TRAITS: Uncompromising, egocentric, outrageous

You have unshakable confidence in yourself and rarely betray a shred of self-doubt. A wise observer of human nature and social trends, you base your beliefs on observation rather than on any cherished illusions, but you also offer your opinions unhesitatingly as fact, expecting agreement and acknowledgment from associates and acquaintances. Those who populate your inner circle know that you are not omniscient, and they delight in pointing out your lapses. Romantic partners tend to be awed by your self-assurance, an effect you work hard to preserve as long as possible. Long-term happiness, however, will require a mate as strong and self-assured as you are, one who is unafraid to puncture your ego when it becomes overinflated.

July 27

ASTROLOGICAL SIGN: Leo

PEOPLE BORN TODAY: Peggy Fleming, Bugs Bunny, Maureen McGovern, Jerry Van Dyke, Bobbie Gentry, Norman Lear, Leo Durocher

FAMOUS EVENTS: Tobacco plant imported from England by Sir Walter Raleigh (1586); suicide of Vincent van Gogh (1890); insulin discovered by Dr. Frederick Banting (1921)

LUCKY NUMBER: 6

BIRTHSTONE: Ruby

POSITIVE TRAITS: Authoritative, generous, assured

NEGATIVE TRAITS: Tense, close, distant

You are a masterly director of others in your professional and personal realms, in command both of the encompassing vision needed for victory and of the tactics that will assure it. Your style can mislead friends and romantic partners into assuming that you are hard as steel when the truth is just the opposite. You have a heart of gold, but you refuse to wear it on your sleeve. You show your love by doing, not by emoting, and for those whom you love, this is more than enough. Though children may find your no-nonsense attitude a bit intimidating, they respond eagerly to your can-do attitude and you're the one they call first to play a new game or help put on a puppet show.

July 28

ASTROLOGICAL SIGN: Leo

PEOPLE BORN TODAY: Jacqueline Kennedy Onassis, Bill Bradley, Sally Struthers, Vida Blue, Marcel Duchamp, John Ashbery

FAMOUS EVENTS: King Henry VIII wed to fifth wife, Catherine Howard (1540); mail by rail begins in U.S. (1862); first transatlantic cable, sent by Queen Victoria to President Andrew Johnson (1866)

LUCKY NUMBER: 7

BIRTHSTONE: Ruby

POSITIVE TRAITS: Resolute, modest, thoughtful

NEGATIVE TRAITS: Underappreciated, misunderstood, lonely

You exemplify professional excellence and personal integrity. Because you believe in doing things the right way whether people are watching or not, you may prefer to work independently; and although you can express your beliefs articulately, you would rather lead by example than make hollow speeches. (Indeed you are too modest to trumpet your own attributes, so you often find them praised by your fan club of friends and associates.) The self-reliance on which you pride yourself, however, can lead to loneliness unless you forge lasting emotional connections. Romantic partners find you admirable, but your reluctance to appear needy can mask your loving nature. A long-term mate who shares life's daily joys and woes will recognize and return your true warmth.

July 29

ASTROLOGICAL SIGN: Leo

PEOPLE BORN TODAY: Peter Jennings, Patti Scialfa, Wil Wheaton, Ken Burns, Paul Taylor

FAMOUS EVENTS: NASA created (1958); Bob Dylan seriously injured in motorcycle accident (1966); Prince Charles wed to Lady Diana Spencer (1981)

LUCKY NUMBER: 8

BIRTHSTONE: Ruby

POSITIVE TRAITS: Group-oriented, cooperative, reliable

NEGATIVE TRAITS: Generalizing, shy, conformist

You do your best to be one of the gang, whether on the job or in a social setting. Though your contributions are usually of pivotal importance, you resist being singled out with attention or praise. You tend to undervalue yourself and overvalue others, which in the end can cloud your judgment. Learn to accept praise when it is due; the worst that can happen is that your self-esteem will rise to match your abilities. You are attracted to people who fit in seamlessly with your social crowd, which can cause you to overlook potential partners who are less conformist in their outlook but nonetheless appreciate your sunny disposition and innate modesty. Your skill with words is also enticing; you can't resist embellishing a good story.

July 30

ASTROLOGICAL SIGN: Leo

PEOPLE BORN TODAY: Laurence Fishburne, Emily Brontë, Arnold Schwarzenegger, Patricia Schroeder, David Sanborn

FAMOUS EVENTS: U.S. Navy women's auxiliary (WAVES) created (1942); Medicare bill signed by President Lyndon Johnson (1965); Jimmy Hoffa last seen before disappearance (1975)

LUCKY NUMBER: 9

BIRTHSTONE: Ruby

POSITIVE TRAITS: Imposing, forceful, sensual

NEGATIVE TRAITS: Mundane, materialistic, uninspired

Feet firmly planted in the vaunted "real" world, you set ambitious material goals for yourself: physical fitness, financial success, all the trappings of affluence. In your book, professional praise and romantic endearments come in a distant second to substantial gifts and cold hard cash. So do spiritual pursuits, although you are unfailingly fair and moral in your dealings with others, and indeed you are a rock that they can rely on. You are true to your word, dead-set against playing games, and make a strong impression on romantic partners, who are delighted with your solid dependability. Don't neglect your friends: You need their influence to help you appreciate the good things in life that do not show up on a balance sheet.

July 31

ASTROLOGICAL SIGN: Leo

PEOPLE BORN TODAY: Primo Levi, Wesley Snipes, Sherry Lansing, Stanley Jordan, Evonne Goolagong, William Bennett, Casey Stengel

FAMOUS EVENTS: U.S. patent office opens (1790); first roar of Leo, the lion, heard at opening of MGM's first talkie (1928); Idlewild Airport, later renamed John F. Kennedy International, dedicated (1948)

LUCKY NUMBER: 1

BIRTHSTONE: Ruby

POSITIVE TRAITS: Articulate, artistic, industrious

NEGATIVE TRAITS: Haughty, perfectionistic, overworked

You are an articulate observer who can sum up people with precise description or accurate mimicry. Little escapes your eagle eye, and you are quick to catch others' mistakes; but because you correct your own missteps before anyone notices them, you may give the impression of focusing only on others' faults. In fact your industriousness conceals a keen sense of humor and fun that emerge when you relax among friends. You have a well-developed aesthetic sense and enjoy being surrounded by attractive objects and people, and physical beauty is also a high priority in your choice of romantic partners. For a long-term mate, however, you should seek someone who shares both your strong work ethic and your artistic sensibilities.

August 1

ASTROLOGICAL SIGN: Leo

PEOPLE BORN TODAY: Jerry Garcia, Tempestt Bledsoe, Alfonse d'Amato, Robert Cray, Yves St. Laurent, Dom DeLuise, Herman Melville

FAMOUS EVENTS: Oxygen discovered (1774); first San Francisco cable car tested (1873); MTV channel debuts (1981)

LUCKY NUMBER: 9

BIRTHSTONE: Ruby

POSITIVE TRAITS: Impassioned, original, communicative

NEGATIVE TRAITS: Unbending, extremist, meddlesome

You speak out passionately whenever you are confronted with adverse or harmful conditions and when you see an opportunity for improvement, you take it. Though you hope others will accept the wisdom of your ideas, you're not a crusader. In fact, it is often your *joie de vivre* rather than your ideas that influences people; it certainly is your main attraction. You are likely to have friends in every field, and your social calendar is always filled in. Though you can be somewhat unbending, your good nature easily compensates for it. You're loving and fun to be around; the only problem is everyone wants to be around you. Finding time to single out a partner and shape a meaningful relationship will take dedication.

August 2

ASTROLOGICAL SIGN: Leo

PEOPLE BORN TODAY: Cynthia Stevenson, Carroll O'Connor, Linda Fratianne, Eddie Furlong, Peter O'Toole, James Baldwin

FAMOUS EVENTS: First escalator patented (1892); Navy Lt. John F. Kennedy rescues fellow *PT-109* crew members (1943); Dr. Martin Luther King Jr. honored by new federal holiday (1983)

LUCKY NUMBER: 1

BIRTHSTONE: Ruby

POSITIVE TRAITS: Confident, focused, persistent

NEGATIVE TRAITS: Tactless, uncompromising, aloof

Life is not a popularity contest for you; developing your talents and earning rewards for them are much more meaningful to you than being liked. An affable manner comes naturally to you, but it by no means bespeaks a need for approval. You are confident of your ability to reach your personal and professional goals and adamant in your refusal to be thrown off track. You're creative and flexible, capable of switching tactics when necessary but always keeping your eyes on the prize. Though your friendships center around shared ambitions rather than shared feelings, you're a loyal and reliable friend. Romance can be elusive but it doesn't have to be, particularly if you opt for love over admiration—at least some of the time.

August 3

ASTROLOGICAL SIGN: Leo

PEOPLE BORN TODAY: Martha Stewart, Tony Bennett, Jomarie Payton, Martin Sheen, Victoria Jackson, Maggie Kuhn

FAMOUS EVENTS: Christopher Columbus embarks on voyage to the New World (1492); Calvin Coolidge sworn in as thirtieth president, upon death of Warren G. Harding (1923); illegal strike declared by air traffic controllers (1981)

LUCKY NUMBER: 2

BIRTHSTONE: Ruby

POSITIVE TRAITS: High-minded, purposeful, inspiring

NEGATIVE TRAITS: Self-important, unrealistic, demanding

You have a hearty appetite for living and for leadership. You can't resist getting involved in other people's problems and take pleasure in pointing out solutions that might have escaped them. Pitching in on tough jobs and difficult chores makes you feel useful and virtuous. Friends know they can count on you for a helping hand, but may tire at times of your know-it-all attitude. Your pragmatism may befuddle romantic partners, particularly if you offer advice when they are simply looking for sympathy. If you choose a mate with the same roll-up-your-sleeves approach to life that you have, there will be little the two of you can't do—and do well—to make your life together a success.

August 4

ASTROLOGICAL SIGN: Leo

PEOPLE BORN TODAY: Mary Decker Slaney, Roger Clemens, Richard Belzer, Queen Mother Elizabeth, Helen Thomas, Louis Armstrong, Percy Bysshe Shelley

FAMOUS EVENTS: Freedom of the press established by acquittal of John Peter Zenger in libel trial (1735); all U.S. and Canadian telephone lines silenced for one minute to observe death of Alexander Graham Bell (1922); Anne Frank and family captured by gestapo (1944)

LUCKY NUMBER: 3

BIRTHSTONE: Ruby

POSITIVE TRAITS: Bold, unconventional, striking

NEGATIVE TRAITS: Thoughtless, sarcastic, heedless

You reserve the right to take the road less traveled, even if you find nothing wrong with the well-trodden path. You often espouse unconventional views, and take pleasure in the attention these views attract. You are an articulate critic, given to well-honed barbs, which can often be wounding to others. Neither diplomacy nor salesmanship come naturally to you, so life in the corporate world will not be easy. You're a rebel but not a loner, developing love-hate relationships with friends and romantic partners and resisting their influence even as you crave their attention. Learn to discern between singularity and self-sabotage.

August 5

ASTROLOGICAL SIGN: Leo
PEOPLE BORN TODAY: Patrick Ewing, Jonathan Silverman, Loni Anderson, Neil Armstrong, John Huston, Guy de Maupassant
FAMOUS EVENTS: First federal income tax established (1861); first radio broadcast of Major League baseball game (1921); Marilyn Monroe dies of barbiturate overdose (1962)
LUCKY NUMBER: 4
BIRTHSTONE: Ruby
POSITIVE TRAITS: Cool, controlled, determined
NEGATIVE TRAITS: Blunt, aggressive, provocative

You know how to keep a cool head; when people and events rattle your nerves, you don't let it show. Those in the know, however, understand that your unruffled exterior masks deep emotions and strong sensitivities. You can startle colleagues and acquaintances with your bluntly stated views, though your friends and family know enough to duck for cover when they ask your opinion. Few people are as effective as you can be in a crisis. However, when it comes to the day-to-day operations of your business or family life, you tend to let others take the helm. Though you risk alienating romantic partners if you don't consider their feelings before opening fire, your sensuous nature and emotional honesty save the day.

August 6

ASTROLOGICAL SIGN: Leo

PEOPLE BORN TODAY: David Robinson, Lucille Ball, Robert Mitchum, Kenneth D. Flappan, Andy Warhol, Louella Parsons, Alfred, Lord Tennyson

FAMOUS EVENTS: First execution by electric chair (1890); first swimming of English Channel by a woman, Gertrude Ederle (1926); death of Pope Paul VI (1978)

LUCKY NUMBER: 5

BIRTHSTONE: Ruby

POSITIVE TRAITS: Creative, ambitious, hopeful

NEGATIVE TRAITS: Obsessive, nosy, hardened

You work hard and play hard—big projects and even bigger parties are your stock in trade. You concoct grand schemes and go all out to make them happen, astounding others with your guts and your energy. Skeptics seldom deter you, though you can be temporarily derailed by genuine setbacks and disappointments. Optimistic, you bet against the odds repeatedly, even though your lack of caution gets you into a jam. Your unquenchable interest in others makes you a desirable friend and romantic partner; you listen as much as you talk and know how to create an environment in which others feel warm and secure. Accept that your partner's dreams are not always going to be your dreams—and your love boat won't sink.

August 7

ASTROLOGICAL SIGN: Leo

PEOPLE BORN TODAY: Garrison Keillor, Alberto Salazar, Rodney Crowell, Rahsaan Roland Kirk, Don Larsen, Ralph Bunche

FAMOUS EVENTS: Order of the Purple Heart established by General George Washington (1782); first mile run in under four minutes run by Roger Bannister (1954); tightrope walk between World Trade Center twin towers performed by Philippe Petit (1974)

LUCKY NUMBER: 6

BIRTHSTONE: Ruby

POSITIVE TRAITS: Talkative, charming, droll

NEGATIVE TRAITS: Shy, emotionally guarded, insecure

You can charm the birds out of the trees, but you wouldn't confide in them if you thought they might "sing." You regale coworkers and friends with colorful stories, occasionally stretching the truth for dramatic effect. Even your constant companions may feel they don't really know you, since you dwell in a realm of private feelings and fantasies, which you seldom or never share. Your lively wit readily captivates romantic partners, but once you start to feel serious about someone, it can take you forever to declare your feelings. You're a surprise package, revealing your many-faceted personality and hidden talents slowly over the years. Building a cheering section of trusted intimates will give you the confidence to open up sooner.

August 8

ASTROLOGICAL SIGN: Leo

PEOPLE BORN TODAY: David Evans ("The Edge"), Deborah Norville, Dustin Hoffman, Mel Tillis, Esther Williams, Connie Stevens

FAMOUS EVENTS: Mimeograph patented by Thomas Edison (1876); Great Train Robbery committed in England (1963); first border point between Israel and Jordan opened (1994)

LUCKY NUMBER: 7

BIRTHSTONE: Ruby

POSITIVE TRAITS: Talented, versatile, adaptable

NEGATIVE TRAITS: Self-demanding, perfectionistic, overconfident

You are a quick study and a hard worker. Because you appear to be a natural at whatever you do, people often think that success comes easily to you and don't give you enough credit for your diligence and perseverance—and your talent. You are liable to drive yourself too hard without realizing it, which can adversely affect your health. While you may demand the same bravura performance from yourself when tossing a salad as when completing an important project, even you need to let up and relax occasionally. Your all-around excellence can be intimidating to love partners and friends alike, so be sure to let them see your human qualities as well as your heroic ones as often as possible.

August 9

ASTROLOGICAL SIGN: Leo

PEOPLE BORN TODAY: Whitney Houston, Deion Sanders, Melanie Griffith, Sam Elliott, David Steinberg, Rod Laver, Hurricane Jackson, Ken Norton

FAMOUS EVENTS: King Edward VII crowned (1902); Jesse Owens wins four gold medals at Berlin Olympics (1936); Richard M. Nixon resigns (1974)

LUCKY NUMBER: 8

BIRTHSTONE: Ruby

POSITIVE TRAITS: Disciplined, dynamic, supportive

NEGATIVE TRAITS: Overbearing, difficult, moody

You are an ambitious achiever. People look to you naturally for leadership and guidance; you only have to let them follow. You are an inspiring mentor to those with less experience or know-how and you have limitless patience. Because you enjoy giving advice to others—and being looked up to—you may be miffed if they ignore you or assert their independence and follow their own advice. You come on strong with romantic partners, frequently telling them what course to follow in their personal and professional lives. Though your intentions are good, be careful not to let concern turn into control. Your love can feel like a straitjacket if you don't allow others the same freedom you claim as your inalienable right.

August 10

ASTROLOGICAL SIGN: Leo

PEOPLE BORN TODAY: Rosanna Arquette, Bobby Hatfield, Patti Austin, Ronnie Spector, Eddie Fisher, Jimmy Dean, Herbert Hoover

FAMOUS EVENTS: Smithsonian Institution chartered by Congress (1846); polio contracted by Franklin D. Roosevelt (1921); Michael Jackson purchases the rights to the Beatles' music for $47.5 million (1985)

LUCKY NUMBER: 9

BIRTHSTONE: Ruby

POSITIVE TRAITS: Giving, entertaining, sociable

NEGATIVE TRAITS: Vulnerable, insecure, overly eager

You are a people-pleaser—appreciated at work, popular among your friends, and admired by loved ones. You carefully cultivate your public persona, aiming to delight others with your energetic presence and charming manner. Because you place a high priority on others' approval, you put on a happy face regardless of your real feelings, which, in the end, cheats others out of getting to know the real you. Learn to accept that your friends will still care for you even when you're having a bad hair day or can't come up with a clever comeback. Catering to others' desires can make you lose touch with your own. Strike a balance and your natural good nature will lead to success in life and love.

ASTROLOGICAL SIGN: Leo

PEOPLE BORN TODAY: Alex Haley, Joe Jackson, Eric Carmen, Jerry Falwell, Claus von Bulow, Hulk Hogan, Louise Bogan

FAMOUS EVENTS: First Ascot races held (1711); death of steel scion and philanthropist Andrew Carnegie (1919); first color TV broadcast of a baseball game (1951)

LUCKY NUMBER: 1

BIRTHSTONE: Ruby

POSITIVE TRAITS: Observant, incisive, enlightening

NEGATIVE TRAITS: Egocentric, judgmental, scathing

You are a perceptive observer and commentator who requires an attentive audience to be happy. In work situations and personal relationships, you cut to the heart of any problem and eagerly share with others what you have uncovered. Even among those you consider your friends, you are quick to discern manipulative or unworthy behavior and never hesitate to confront them with your discoveries. Though you can be harshly judgmental and scathing in your criticism, you are quick to acknowledge the good in others and are as lavish with praise as you are with criticism. Your reluctance to accept others at face value can be a barrier to intimacy in love relationships. You might want to move out of that glass house before casting another stone.

August 12

ASTROLOGICAL SIGN: Leo

PEOPLE BORN TODAY: Pete Sampras, Mark Knopfler, Pat Metheny, Porter Wagoner, Jane Wyatt, Christy Mathewson

FAMOUS EVENTS: First use of disinfectant in surgery by Dr. Joseph Lister (1827); sewing machine patented by Isaac Singer (1891); gold-medal-winning record claimed by U.S. at close of Los Angeles Olympics (1984)

LUCKY NUMBER: 2

BIRTHSTONE: Ruby

POSITIVE TRAITS: Masterful, prodigious, energetic

NEGATIVE TRAITS: Unrelenting, strict, tiring

You are a virtuoso in your chosen field—whether it's raising children, raising crops, or raising buildings. You toil behind the scenes to stay on top of your game, reading up on the latest research and trading knowledge with others who have attained your same degree of success. Though you wish everyone could shine as brightly as you, you would miss being at the top of the heap if they did. You are a magnet for romantic attention, but an inflated ego and a tendency to put relationships on the back burner can curtail your ability to find happiness in love. You do best with a mate who appreciates your accomplishments, relates to you as an equal, and doesn't object when you steal the spotlight.

August 13

ASTROLOGICAL SIGN: Leo

PEOPLE BORN TODAY: Danny Bonaduce, Dan Fogelberg, Fidel Castro, Alfred Hitchcock, Bert Lahr, Annie Oakley, Kathleen Battle

FAMOUS EVENTS: Long-distance air speed record set (1930); Walt Disney's *Bambi* premieres at Radio City Music Hall (1934); first roller derby held (1935)

LUCKY NUMBER: 3

BIRTHSTONE: Ruby

POSITIVE TRAITS: Bold, daring, revolutionary

NEGATIVE TRAITS: Brash, upsetting, self-doubting

Controversy and conflict are your constant companions, and it can be hard to tell whether they come looking for you or you go searching for them. Your urge to break with convention pushes you to make waves at work and at home, but you refuse to be knocked down when the tide of opinion turns against you. Those who start out shaking their heads at your brashness often end up admiring your bravery, and your gutsy approach to life guarantees you a wide circle of friends. Your outgoing personality, deeply felt passions, and zest for life are enticing to romantic partners, but the essential insecurity they hide must be revealed if your dreams for intimacy and true love are to come true.

ASTROLOGICAL SIGN: Leo

PEOPLE BORN TODAY: Magic Johnson, Gary Larson, Susan St. James, Steve Martin, Danielle Steel, Russell Baker, David Crosby, Lina Wertmüller

FAMOUS EVENTS: Social Security established (1935); unconditional surrender of Japan to Allied forces (1945); English Channel crossed in bathtub by Bill Neal (1982)

LUCKY NUMBER: 4

BIRTHSTONE: Ruby

POSITIVE TRAITS: Amusing, appealing, revealing

NEGATIVE TRAITS: Eccentric, controversial, critical

Motivated by honesty, you state the obvious and never hesitate to say what others are reluctant to say. Though you have a somewhat skewed view of the universe, your perceptions often stimulate others to think more deeply about what they previously took for granted. You are inspired by a desire to strip away layers of folly and artifice to reveal the truth and this desire more often than not lands you in hot water with friends, family, lovers, and colleagues. Though romantic partners enjoy your emotional honesty and thoughtful approach to life, your zest for examining every aspect of their behavior and personality under a microscope might scare them off. Try not to turn your loved one into a lab specimen and all could go well.

August 15

ASTROLOGICAL SIGN: Leo

PEOPLE BORN TODAY: Julia Child, Linda Ellerbee, Rose Marie, Ethel Barrymore, T. E. Lawrence (Lawrence of Arabia), Napoleon Bonaparte, Vernon Jordan, Oscar Peterson

FAMOUS EVENTS: King Macbeth of Scotland murdered (1057); premiere of *The Wizard of Oz* (1939); opening of Woodstock Festival (1969)

LUCKY NUMBER: 5

BIRTHSTONE: Ruby

POSITIVE TRAITS: Imposing, powerful, magnanimous

NEGATIVE TRAITS: Dictatorial, imperious, immodest

You are a bold adventurer and leader, sallying forth without an ounce of self-doubt. Your courage and confidence conspire to make you a commanding, near-heroic figure to your coworkers and friends. If you are uncertain of the proper procedure in any situation, you wing it with élan. Your optimism and ambition are sweeping enough to include great plans for all your intimates and allies, and you generously share the fruits of your success. You are both friend and role model to many in your social circle. Romantic partners bask in your regal presence, but risk losing their identities in your shadow. Be magnanimous enough to grant your mate a say on all issues, even if it's usually your word that ends up becoming law.

August 16

ASTROLOGICAL SIGN: Leo

PEOPLE BORN TODAY: Madonna, Timothy Hutton, J. T. Taylor, Kathie Lee Gifford, Frank Gifford, Eydie Gorme

FAMOUS EVENTS: Death of Babe Ruth at age fifty-three (1948); death of Elvis Presley at age forty-two (1977); Madonna and Sean Penn wed (1985)

LUCKY NUMBER: 6

BIRTHSTONE: Ruby

POSITIVE TRAITS: Exciting, energetic, motivated

NEGATIVE TRAITS: Driven, foolhardy, exhibitionistic

You are a powerhouse of energy and enthusiasm. In any situation you aim for the top and usually get there. Innate confidence assists you in all that you do, but can sometimes cause you to ignore advice and resist direction. Your high energy is tempered by a strong sense of conscience, which keeps you from acting in a way hurtful to others. In love, you are the pursuer rather than the pursued, and the object of your affections is never in doubt as to your feelings. Because you insist on retaining your independence, setting mutual goals with your partner may be difficult. If your mate is strong-willed and energetic—in other words, a lot like you—things will probably turn out fine.

August 17

ASTROLOGICAL SIGN: Leo

PEOPLE BORN TODAY: Sean Penn, Belinda Carlisle, Robert DeNiro, Jim Courier, Christian Laettner, Mae West

FAMOUS EVENTS: First steamship crossing of Atlantic begins (1833); Pulitzer Prize established by Joseph Pulitzer (1903); first balloon crossing of Atlantic completed (1978)

LUCKY NUMBER: 7

BIRTHSTONE: Ruby

POSITIVE TRAITS: Deep, intense, assured

NEGATIVE TRAITS: Volcanic, superior, scornful

Your impassive exterior may not reveal the fiery emotions that churn inside you, but neither does it project false gaiety or an eagerness to please that you seldom feel. Because you are a deep thinker, pondering matters thoroughly before making a move, your contributions to any endeavor have great weight and impact. At home or at work, you work best in a bright, orderly, and clutter-free environment and you do whatever is necessary to create it. Though you rarely come up short in the humor department, you can easily be annoyed by the frivolous antics of friends and colleagues. A patient and persuasive partner, capable of drawing out your passions and quelling your occasional rages, will be amply rewarded by your love, trust, and unswerving loyalty.

August 18

ASTROLOGICAL SIGN: Leo

PEOPLE BORN TODAY: Christian Slater, Patrick Swayze, Madeleine Stowe, Malcolm-Jamal Warner, Robert Redford, Shelley Winters

FAMOUS EVENTS: Vladimir Nabokov's novel *Lolita* published (1958); Beatles drummer Pete Best replaced by Ringo Starr (1962); Larry Bird announces his retirement from basketball (1992)

LUCKY NUMBER: 8

BIRTHSTONE: Ruby

POSITIVE TRAITS: Big-hearted, tolerant, striving

NEGATIVE TRAITS: Contentious, oversensitive, overworking

You have courage and confidence enough to withstand any curves life throws your way. You know how to bounce back—and you do it quickly. Though you are not insensitive to the pain of professional or personal setbacks, you remain undaunted and eager to embrace any new situation. Your need to surmount all obstacles can cause you to overextend yourself; your odds for success will increase greatly if you take time off to recharge your batteries. Friends and family treasure your empathy—they know you think of their problems as your own. Romantic partners find in you the kind of generous and sensitive mate that they had only dreamed of before, and you are a natural for a nurturing long-term union.

August 19

ASTROLOGICAL SIGN: Leo
PEOPLE BORN TODAY: Bill Clinton, John Stamos, Peter Gallagher, Gene Roddenberry, Malcolm Forbes, Coco Chanel, Ogden Nash
FAMOUS EVENTS: Adolf Hitler elected president of Germany (1934); Spanish poet Federico García Lorca murdered by Franco sympathizers (1936); U-2 pilot Francis Gary Powers sentenced to Soviet prison term for spying (1960)
LUCKY NUMBER: 9
BIRTHSTONE: Ruby
POSITIVE TRAITS: Ebullient, accommodating, popular
NEGATIVE TRAITS: Guarded, unconfiding, manipulative

The thoughts and feelings you exhibit among friends and colleagues may be genuine, but they are hardly the whole story. You carefully edit your ideas before sharing them, revealing only those that will favorably impress your chosen audience. This skill helps you preserve your image regardless of the results—good or bad—that your performance yields. Only a handful of confidants are privy to the "unscripted" you, and they feel privileged to be accepted into your private world. Romantic partners may be drawn in quickly by your sunny ingenuous façade, but where lasting and real intimacy is the goal, things will develop much more slowly. Letting your guard down will become easier once you can accept that your loved ones love you too.

August 20

ASTROLOGICAL SIGN: Leo
PEOPLE BORN TODAY: Peter Horton, Connie Chung, Robert Plant, Isaac Hayes, Graig Nettles, Jacqueline Susann, Don King
FAMOUS EVENTS: Alaska discovered by Vitus Bering (1741); Tchaikovsky's *1812 Overture* premieres (1882); Russian revolutionary Leon Trotsky assassinated (1940)
LUCKY NUMBER: 1
BIRTHSTONE: Ruby
POSITIVE TRAITS: Creative, romantic, adventurous
NEGATIVE TRAITS: Unrealistic, deluded, addictive

Your intellect is your ticket to the realm of the imagination. Though you may secretly yearn for a luxurious "peel-me-a-grape" lifestyle, you toil dutifully at the tasks at hand, satisfying your yearning for the exotic by experimenting with foreign foods, fashions, and literature, and traveling to far-off lands as often as your schedule and budget allow. Friends may mock your fantasy life, but they probably envy your imagination, which enables you to infuse excitement into your day-to-day existence. In love you want the full-scale romantic treatment, but have a tendency to overestimate the ability of moonlight and roses to sustain a relationship. Keep your feet on the ground and it won't matter if your head is in the clouds.

August 21

ASTROLOGICAL SIGN: Leo

PEOPLE BORN TODAY: Wilt Chamberlain, Kenny Rogers, Princess Margaret, Jim McMahon, Harry Smith, William "Count" Basie

FAMOUS EVENTS: Rebellion against slavery started by Nat Turner (1831); Hawaii becomes 50th state (1959); political leader Benigno Aquino murdered in Philippines (1983)

LUCKY NUMBER: 2

BIRTHSTONE: Ruby

POSITIVE TRAITS: Attractive, purposeful, group-oriented

NEGATIVE TRAITS: Self-indulgent, egotistical, excessive

Everyone likes you, but not everyone takes you seriously. You long to be recognized for your intellectual contributions but are more likely to attract attention for your other attributes, such as your beauty, grace, or athletic ability. Put your innate appeal to work for you and use your captivating looks, voice, or manners to garner attention that you can redirect as you wish. You attract love partners so easily that you may be tempted to play the field longer than you should and let your perfect match slip away; this would be a disaster since you are a naturally giving partner who will thrive in a committed and caring relationship. Channel your creative energy into charitable or community-based activities that strengthen your spirit.

August 22

ASTROLOGICAL SIGN: Leo
PEOPLE BORN TODAY: Norman Schwarzkopf, Debbi Peterson, Bill Parcells, Valerie Harper, Ray Bradbury, Dorothy Parker, Carl Yastrzemski
FAMOUS EVENTS: Title of first female American newspaper editor assumed by Ann Franklin (1762); first America's Cup race (1851); strikeout record set by Nolan Ryan (1989)
LUCKY NUMBER: 3
BIRTHSTONE: Ruby
POSITIVE TRAITS: Bold, ingenious, pragmatic
NEGATIVE TRAITS: Controlling, proud, stubborn

You are that rare creature who is simultaneously creative and commanding. Your imagination is broad enough to embrace unthought-of possibilities in any endeavor that you undertake. You then effectively marshal other people and your own energies to execute your inspirations. You bring flair to the most mundane chores and can make work seem like fun for others. In personal as well as professional relationships, you give orders much more readily than you take them, and cooperate halfheartedly when someone else is in the driver's seat. Your warmth and sociability lend themselves well to romance, yet with even the most compatible mate you are not happy unless you are free to pursue your own interests and express your unique personality.

August 23

ASTROLOGICAL SIGN: Virgo

PEOPLE BORN TODAY: Gene Kelly, Shelley Long, River Phoenix, Antonia Novello, Keith Moon, Rick Springfield, Mark Russell

FAMOUS EVENTS: Sacco and Vanzetti executed (1927); John Lennon and Cynthia Powell wed (1962); defection of Bolshoi Ballet star Alexander Godunov (1979)

LUCKY NUMBER: 4

BIRTHSTONE: Sapphire

POSITIVE TRAITS: Precise, reliant, stylish

NEGATIVE TRAITS: Perfectionistic, restrained, timid

Dependable, that's what you are. You pay as much attention to the process as to the product, whether you are carrying out a work assignment, baking a cake, or combing the dog. Though your acute eye and fine touch are invaluable, they can sometimes cloud your view of the big picture; you can become so focused on the particulars that you lose your direction. Friends and colleagues count on you to keep them organized, and your mate counts on you for the smooth running of the household. You are happy to comply, as long as your efforts are rewarded with gratitude and, occasionally, with praise. Get out into the world more and let your sense of style and zest for life work for you.

August 24

ASTROLOGICAL SIGN: Virgo

PEOPLE BORN TODAY: Marlee Matlin, Cal Ripken Jr., A. S. Byatt, Joe Regalbuto, Steve Guttenberg, Claudia Schiffer, Jorge Luis Borges

FAMOUS EVENTS: Pompeii buried by lava from eruption of Mount Vesuvius (A.D. 79); first nonstop flight across the U.S. by a woman made by Amelia Earhart (1932); Miami devastated by Hurricane Andrew (1992)

LUCKY NUMBER: 5

BIRTHSTONE: Sapphire

POSITIVE TRAITS: Sharp-witted, wary, probing

NEGATIVE TRAITS: Suspicious, niggling, defensive

You take nothing at face value. Exhaustive reports and personal vouchers can't stop you from searching beneath the surface of people and events to uncover what might be hidden. Your questioning mind makes you hard to deceive in work and in relationships, and you can be a formidable adversary for those who try to manipulate you. Less perceptive friends may rely heavily on your opinions, presenting their potential partners in love or business to you for your inspection and approval. In your own love life, it can be hard for you to connect with others because you so rarely let down your guard. The right partner will know how to break down your defenses—and build up your trust—at least in them.

August 25

ASTROLOGICAL SIGN: Virgo

PEOPLE BORN TODAY: Elvis Costello, Ivan the Terrible, Sean Connery, Anne Archer, Tom Skerritt, Leonard Bernstein

FAMOUS EVENTS: English Channel first swum, by Matthew Webb (1875); Paris freed from Nazi occupation (1944); 100-meter-dash world record set by Carl Lewis (1991)

LUCKY NUMBER: 6

BIRTHSTONE: Sapphire

POSITIVE TRAITS: Outgoing, showy, vital

NEGATIVE TRAITS: Vain, unsure, praise-seeking

A polished image and savvy social skills are the capital you draw on to advance yourself in the world at large. Though seductive and self-assured on the outside, inside you worry that you are not as attractive, clever, or accomplished as others, and you knock yourself out trying to prove that you are. Casual acquaintances may denigrate you for your apparent conceit, but close friends, of which you have many, are aware of your insecurities and know how to smooth them over. Your reluctance to take emotional risks can cause you to relate to love partners on a superficial level, but the right mate will be tender with your fragile heart and lead you slowly down the road to intimacy.

ASTROLOGICAL SIGN: Virgo
PEOPLE BORN TODAY: Macaulay Culkin, Branford Marsalis, Geraldine Ferraro, Valerie Simpson, Ben Bradlee, Irving R. Levine
FAMOUS EVENTS: Artillery first used in battle (1346); first baseball game airs on television (1939); Marilyn Monroe signed to film contract (1946)
LUCKY NUMBER: 7
BIRTHSTONE: Sapphire
POSITIVE TRAITS: Inspired, resourceful, cheerful
NEGATIVE TRAITS: Self-effacing, foolish, clumsy

You have undeniable star potential, yet you are more comfortable playing a lesser role. You set high standards for yourself, hoping to master your specialty well enough to carry out your part of any task admirably and reliably. Being singled out for individual recognition at work or in personal endeavors makes you ill at ease, even when the attention is well deserved and hard earned. When engaging in sports or games with friends, you want your team to triumph so that everyone can be satisfied and happy. In love, you find it easy to connect and are seldom without a partner to encourage and adore. You were born to be happy, and most of the time you are—aren't you?

August 27

ASTROLOGICAL SIGN: Virgo

PEOPLE BORN TODAY: Pee-wee Herman, Barbara Bach, Daryl Dragon, Mother Teresa, Tuesday Weld, Lyndon Baines Johnson, Alice Coltrane, Confucius

FAMOUS EVENTS: First oil well in U.S. drilled (1859); only meeting of Elvis Presley and the Beatles (1965); first solo voyage around the world embarked on by Sir Francis Chichester (1966)

LUCKY NUMBER: 8

BIRTHSTONE: Sapphire

POSITIVE TRAITS: Altruistic, giving, generous

NEGATIVE TRAITS: Hardened, domineering, driven

You are happiest when you make others happy, whether improving their lot in life or just giving them a good laugh. You gravitate toward a career in which you can perform a valuable service, rather than merely work for your own ego gratification and financial gain. You can be a hard taskmaster, driving others to work hard for your ideals. If your job doesn't satisfy your generous urges, you may devote yourself to a charitable cause or just become an exceptionally giving friend, partner, and parent. If your kindness toward loved ones or strangers goes unappreciated, you may become cynical, though you are unlikely to stop caring altogether. A materially or emotionally needy mate may appeal to your caregiver inclinations, but beware of submerging your own needs for another's.

August 28

ASTROLOGICAL SIGN: Virgo
PEOPLE BORN TODAY: Scott Hamilton, Jason Priestley, Emma Samms, Roxie Roker, Lou Piniella, Charles Boyer, Johann Wolfgang von Goethe
FAMOUS EVENTS: United Parcel Service (UPS) founded (1907); march on Washington, biggest civil rights rally ever (1963); concert at Forest Hills Tennis Stadium given by Beatles (1964)
LUCKY NUMBER: 9
BIRTHSTONE: Sapphire
POSITIVE TRAITS: Knowledgeable, humorous, respected
NEGATIVE TRAITS: Strict, demanding, judgmental

With your mix of craftsmanlike skill and communicative ability, you can rack up a résumé of impressive achievements and become a respected spokesperson for your profession or interest group. Your informed comments on a wide range of subjects are likely to be grounded in your personal experience or extensive research; you wouldn't dream of talking off the top of your head or of winging your way through anything. Friends regard you with a mixture of affection and awe, though they may unrealistically expect you to have the answer to their every question. Love partners may at first find you intimidating with your air of unrelenting perfectionism, but they warm up to you as you reveal your lively sense of humor and love of all things sensuous.

ASTROLOGICAL SIGN: Virgo

PEOPLE BORN TODAY: Michael Jackson, Rebecca DeMornay, Richard Gere, Robin Leach, Ingrid Bergman, Charlie Parker

FAMOUS EVENTS: Senate record for filibustering set by Strom Thurmond, twenty-four hours (1957); National League RBI record set by Hank Aaron (1971); around-the-world sail completed by Charles Burton and Sir Randolph Fiennes (1982)

LUCKY NUMBER: 1

BIRTHSTONE: Sapphire

POSITIVE TRAITS: Innovative, disciplined, individualistic

NEGATIVE TRAITS: Unrealistic, withdrawn, self-critical

Your fantastic imagination can fire you toward the heights of achievement in your professional and personal life. You set ambitious goals for yourself and move toward them with a rigorous self-discipline that amazes your associates and acquaintances alike. Though you have wonderfully creative and artistic abilities, you thrive on routines and schedules and will impose structure whenever you find it lacking. Friends beg to be penciled into your agenda, since they delight in your company and enjoy your surprisingly wicked sense of humor. Partners have a tough time competing with your professional priorities, and may accuse you of using your work or other time-consuming interests as an excuse to avoid developing intimacy and facing your (ungrounded) fears of inadequacy as a mate.

August 30

ASTROLOGICAL SIGN: Virgo

PEOPLE BORN TODAY: Peggy Lipton, Michael Chiklis, Elizabeth Ashley, John Phillips, Jean-Claude Killy, Ted Williams, Robert Crumb

FAMOUS EVENTS: First White House baby, Ester Cleveland, born to Frances and President Grover Cleveland (1893); Lt. Col. Guion Bluford Jr. becomes first African-American astronaut launched into space (1983); Leona Helmsley convicted of tax evasion (1989)

LUCKY NUMBER: 2

BIRTHSTONE: Sapphire

POSITIVE TRAITS: Responsible, nurturing, protective

NEGATIVE TRAITS: Overburdened, dictatorial, frustrated

Your role as a parent figure extends far beyond any children you may have. Coworkers, friends, and siblings all look to you to keep them focused, solvent, and generally out of trouble's way. You assume responsibility with ease at work, and efficiently dispatch others to do your bidding. While you welcome professional obligations, you may occasionally resent carrying the same burdens home. You are a magnet for flighty friends who need you to make sure they show up for work, write to their mothers, and pay their taxes. You may attract romantic partners with a similar bent, though a mate who is nearly as serious and dutiful as you will help make your home a place of refuge from the heavy load you take on elsewhere.

August 31

ASTROLOGICAL SIGN: Virgo

PEOPLE BORN TODAY: Van Morrison, Itzhak Perlman, Paul Winter, Edwin Moses, Alan Jay Lerner, Maria Montessori, Daniel Schorr, Eldridge Cleaver

FAMOUS EVENTS: Laurence Olivier and Vivien Leigh wed (1940); first *CBS Evening News* broadcast anchored by Walter Cronkite (1963); first run across Canada by a woman completed by Carallyn Bowes (1976)

LUCKY NUMBER: 3

BIRTHSTONE: Sapphire

POSITIVE TRAITS: Energetic, exciting, alive

NEGATIVE TRAITS: Critical, cranky, stressed

While you don't exude Hollywood glamour, you radiate energy and excitement. You may attain leader status on the job and in society without even trying. Friends never make social plans without consulting you, and you expect them to solicit your opinions on every major decision. When attention turns toward someone else, you may become cranky—though you are not really mean-spirited. Love partners are turned on by your sense of humor and appetite for romance. Your long-term mate must be prepared to lavish attention and affection on you and generally make you feel like the most important person in the household, if not the world. Protecting yourself from the draining effects of emotional stress and overwork will let your light shine even brighter.

September 1

ASTROLOGICAL SIGN: Virgo

PEOPLE BORN TODAY: Gloria Estefan, Dee Dee Myers, Lily Tomlin, Leonard Slatkin, Ann Richards, Alan Dershowitz, Rocky Marciano

FAMOUS EVENTS: Germany invades Poland (1939); world chess championship won by Bobby Fischer (1972); Rock and Roll Hall of Fame opens (1995)

LUCKY NUMBER: 1

BIRTHSTONE: Sapphire

POSITIVE TRAITS: Industrious, courageous, dynamic

NEGATIVE TRAITS: Stern, perfectionistic, overworked

Though preoccupied with work, you are no dull grind: You simply find honest effort stimulating and carry out your duties with a contagious excitement. Because you take pleasure in having your mettle tested, challenges of any sort please you. No matter how unfamiliar you are with the territory, you never shrink from a task. More curious than a cat, you quiz everyone you meet, from chefs to cab drivers, as you go about your daily routine. Intimates value your industriousness—you're a dynamo around the house—and your willingness to listen. Your unflagging interest in people makes you a bit of a flirt; nevertheless, you are a straightforward and affectionate partner, expressing your needs and goals openly and expecting the same in return.

September 2

ASTROLOGICAL SIGN: Virgo

PEOPLE BORN TODAY: Jimmy Connors, Joan Kennedy, Christa McAuliffe, Mark Harmon, Terry Bradshaw, Peter Ueberroth, Keanu Reeves

FAMOUS EVENTS: Last day Julian calendar used in Britain and colonies (1752); World War II officially ends when Japan signs peace treaty (1945); two consecutive holes-in-one shot by Norman Manley (1964)

LUCKY NUMBER: 2

BIRTHSTONE: Sapphire

POSITIVE TRAITS: Idealistic, ambitious, lively

NEGATIVE TRAITS: Temperamental, unrealistic, stubborn

You remain true to your high ideals, and are willing to brave career setbacks and personal unpopularity if you must. On the rare occasions when you let yourself be talked into compromising your integrity, you ultimately rebel in a fiery display of independence. Although your friends can count on you for honest feedback on their ideas, they may be infuriated by your stubbornness in even the smallest matters. Your idealism and vitality make you an attractive romantic partner—especially your physical vitality—but your mate will need forbearance to put up with your exacting standards and mercurial moods. You should recognize that getting along with others, while not a high ideal in itself, can be indispensable to achieving your aims.

September 3

ASTROLOGICAL SIGN: Virgo

PEOPLE BORN TODAY: Charlie Sheen, Al Jardine, Pierre Troisgros, Kitty Carlisle, Dixie Lee Ray, Louis Sullivan, Sarah Orne Jewett, Alison Lurie

FAMOUS EVENTS: Penny newspaper, the *New York Sun*, launched (1833); first professional football game played (1895); England and France declare war on Germany (1939)

LUCKY NUMBER: 3

BIRTHSTONE: Sapphire

POSITIVE TRAITS: Eager, excelling, trailblazing

NEGATIVE TRAITS: Impatient, hasty, attention-hungry

Your desire for excellence and accolades drives you to distinguish yourself both on the job and on the social scene. An overachiever, you are often the first to meet a goal; but even when you aren't, your performance will frequently outshine all others. Everything about you reflects your strive for perfection, but your easygoing and unassuming personality makes it almost impossible for anyone to resent you—for long. In fact, you have numerous friends whom you delight in introducing to the hottest new restaurants and the trendiest activities. If you keep your more flamboyant tendencies in check and share the spotlight from time to time, the right partner will find you irresistible—and excellence in love will be yours as well.

September 4

ASTROLOGICAL SIGN: Virgo

PEOPLE BORN TODAY: Ione Skye, Martin Chambers, Judith Ivey, Tom Watson, Richard Wright, Mitzi Gaynor

FAMOUS EVENTS: City of Los Angeles founded (1781); first commercial electric lighting turned on in Grand Central Station by Thomas Edison (1882); record seventh gold medal won by swimmer Mark Spitz at Munich Olympics (1972)

LUCKY NUMBER: 4

BIRTHSTONE: Sapphire

POSITIVE TRAITS: Diligent, thoughtful, responsible

NEGATIVE TRAITS: Perfectionistic, pedestrian, fussy

You bring the exacting precision of a Swiss watchmaker to everything you do. Everyone looks to you for the last word on proper procedures, whether it's writing a report or trimming a sail. You tend to be a homebody, but even there you execute your tasks with professional skill, equipping yourself with the correct tools and masterfully imitating a chef in the kitchen or a plumber in the bathroom. Friends may become exasperated with your insistence on perfection, but that won't keep them from seeking you out time and again when something needs to be done—and done right. Romantic partners wish you would loosen up, but your ideal mate will recognize how truly creative you are and appreciate your willingness to commit.

September 5

ASTROLOGICAL SIGN: Virgo

PEOPLE BORN TODAY: Raquel Welch, Bob Newhart, John Cage, Darryl F. Zanuck, Louis XIV, Arthur Koestler, Jesse James, Werner Erhard

FAMOUS EVENTS: First Labor Day parade held (1882); Israeli athletes taken hostage by Arab terrorists at Munich Olympics (1972); first woman, Ann Meyers, signed to NBA contract (1979)

LUCKY NUMBER: 5

BIRTHSTONE: Sapphire

POSITIVE TRAITS: Flamboyant, exciting, visionary

NEGATIVE TRAITS: Unrealistic, self-indulgent, over-the-top

You are filled with ambitious dreams and fantastic schemes, and the drive and determination to make them come true. Friends, coworkers, and family members are fired by your creative approach to problem solving, your contagious sense of humor, and your lively enthusiasm. Your tendency to splurge may cause you some financial problems, but your basic common sense will keep you out of bankruptcy court. Life in the fast lane suits your temperament perfectly, but your body may need a slower pace from time to time. Your life-is-a-party attitude ensures plenty of romance in your life, but if you don't ease up on the accelerator now and then, you may blindly speed by your one true love. And that would be a disaster—for both of you.

September 6

ASTROLOGICAL SIGN: Virgo

PEOPLE BORN TODAY: Jane Curtin, Swoosie Kurtz, David Allen Coe, Joanne Worley, Joseph P. Kennedy, Jane Addams

FAMOUS EVENTS: Pilgrims set sail on the *Mayflower* (1620); President William McKinley assassinated (1901); defection of Czech tennis champion Martina Navratilova (1975)

LUCKY NUMBER: 6

BIRTHSTONE: Sapphire

POSITIVE TRAITS: Committed, caring, organized

NEGATIVE TRAITS: Self-sacrificing, alienated, autocratic

You're a born caregiver. At home or at work you take others under your wing, providing shelter and protection until they can learn to fly on their own. Your cheery, unpretentious manner allows people to accept your ministrations without feeling embarrassed or demeaned. People genuinely like you; you have the ability to make them feel good about themselves. Children especially find you appealing, and because you never talk down to them, they look up to you. Since you're a giver not a taker, you have difficulty asserting your needs. Your ideal mate will be one who can easily read your mind and intuit your feelings—and then follow through with whatever the situation calls for. Loving is easy for you; *being* loved may take some getting used to.

September 7

ASTROLOGICAL SIGN: Virgo

PEOPLE BORN TODAY: Chrissie Hynde, Julie Kavner, Corbin Bernsen, Sonny Rollins, Buddy Holly, Grandma Moses, Elia Kazan, Al Maguire

FAMOUS EVENTS: First submarine used in warfare (1776); first use of boxing gloves in a prizefight (1892); first Miss America crowned (1921)

LUCKY NUMBER: 7

BIRTHSTONE: Sapphire

POSITIVE TRAITS: Feisty, industrious, persistent

NEGATIVE TRAITS: Aggressive, ruthless, driven

You're a steamroller. When you make up your mind to do something, you let nothing stand in your way. You are fiercely loyal to friends and family and even relish a good skirmish on their behalf—particularly when you and your adversaries are evenly matched. Your friends respect the steely strength that lies behind your easygoing façade, and know better than to try to talk you out of any decisions you may make. In romantic situations, you are impetuous, bodacious, and plucky. Once you have set your cap for someone, you are almost impossible to resist. But why would anyone want to? Your powers of seduction are awesome and your combative tendencies easily held in check when love comes through the door.

ASTROLOGICAL SIGN: Virgo
PEOPLE BORN TODAY: Jonathan Taylor Thomas, Heather Thomas, Sid Caesar, Peter Sellers, Patsy Cline, Ann Beattie
FAMOUS EVENTS: First recorded birth of sextuplets (1866); *Star Trek* premieres (1966); Richard Nixon pardoned by President Gerald Ford (1974)
LUCKY NUMBER: 8
BIRTHSTONE: Sapphire
POSITIVE TRAITS: Inventive, original, commanding
NEGATIVE TRAITS: Difficult, temperamental, vain

You are a wellspring of creativity; your ideas and schemes are highly original and often completely unconventional. Friends have a hard time keeping up with you, but try nonetheless because they find your company so stimulating. Whether it is true or not, you come across as completely self-confident and self-reliant, which often hinders your ability to forge a long-term relationship since potential partners may find it difficult to imagine where they fit in your self-contained universe. In spite of this, your social life is a whirlwind; you are famous for your inability to resist an invitation. Late-to-bed and early-to-rise is your motto: You need all the hours you can get to satisfy your lust for life.

September 9

ASTROLOGICAL SIGN: Virgo

PEOPLE BORN TODAY: Hugh Grant, Kristy McNichol, Michael Keaton, Tom Wopat, Joe Theismann, Otis Redding, Leo Tolstoy

FAMOUS EVENTS: Hot dog invented (1884); perfect game pitched by Sandy Koufax (1965); Ellis Island Museum of Immigration opens (1990)

LUCKY NUMBER: 9

BIRTHSTONE: Sapphire

POSITIVE TRAITS: Exacting, striving, perceptive

NEGATIVE TRAITS: Unsure, impressionable, passive

When your stellar performance is rewarded with a leadership role, you find yourself set adrift; your innate modesty makes you much more comfortable as a team player or second-in-command. You are an intrepid companion, willing to take part in any adventures your numerous friends might cook up. And because you are extremely perceptive and deeply empathetic, friends and family often make you their confidant, though you wish they would not. You have a highly developed sense of privacy and are often amazed by the way in which others reveal their innermost thoughts. In a secure relationship, however, you are an open book—and your partner might as well be too, since you are adept at reading even the most subtly nuanced behavior.

September 10

ASTROLOGICAL SIGN: Virgo

PEOPLE BORN TODAY: Amy Irving, Joe Perry, Jose Feliciano, Charles Kuralt, Arnold Palmer, Roger Maris, Harry Connick Jr., Stephen Jay Gould

FAMOUS EVENTS: War of 1812 won by U.S. (1813); sewing machine patented by Elias Howe (1846); first coast-to-coast highway opens (1913)

LUCKY NUMBER: 1

BIRTHSTONE: Sapphire

POSITIVE TRAITS: Sensible, farsighted, artistic

NEGATIVE TRAITS: Predictable, edgy, isolated

Long-range planning, that's your specialty. Allowing for individual quirks and for every conceivable possibility, you are seldom caught by surprise. Indeed, you often come to the rescue of others, pointing out their pitfalls or snatching them back from the brink of disaster. You are patient, slow to criticize, and accepting of others' faults and foibles—up to a point. When that point is reached, you are not afraid to vent your feelings and let the world know that you resent being cast as the responsible one while those around you goof off at your expense. Romantic partners rely on you—perhaps more than they should—and often consider you their safety net. Don't let others have all the fun; go a little crazy.

September 11

ASTROLOGICAL SIGN: Virgo

PEOPLE BORN TODAY: Lola Falana, Brian DePalma, Tom Landry, Paul "Bear" Bryant, D. H. Lawrence, O. Henry, Mickey Hart

FAMOUS EVENTS: Hudson River discovered by Henry Hudson (1609); Alexander Hamilton named first U.S. secretary of the treasury (1789); Boulder Dam dedicated by President Franklin D. Roosevelt (1936)

LUCKY NUMBER: 2

BIRTHSTONE: Sapphire

POSITIVE TRAITS: Exciting, motivating, imaginative

NEGATIVE TRAITS: Insistent, dominating, fretful

You see the potential in others, even the kind of dramatic success they might not dare to imagine, and take pleasure in helping them realize it. Friends are grateful for the vision and push you provide, and reward you amply with loyalty and affection. Romantic partners likewise appreciate your belief in them, but they may feel like puppets on a string unless you grant them a measure of autonomy and show respect for their judgment, which you do more often than not. Your kind of active caring is all too rare, but it can tempt you to live vicariously, garnering more praise for coaching others to greatness than for your own substantial achievements. Don't let your own star qualities lie dormant.

September 12

ASTROLOGICAL SIGN: Virgo

PEOPLE BORN TODAY: Barry White, Peter Scolari, Maria Muldaur, Gerry Beckley, Jesse Owens, Maurice Chevalier, H. L. Mencken

FAMOUS EVENTS: "The Star-Spangled Banner" composed by Francis Scott Key (1814); Alice Stebbins Wells becomes first female police officer in U.S. (1910); Senator John F. Kennedy weds Jacqueline Bouvier (1953)

LUCKY NUMBER: 3

BIRTHSTONE: Sapphire

POSITIVE TRAITS: Pragmatic, charming, clever

NEGATIVE TRAITS: Mistrustful, skeptical, opportunistic

You pride yourself on your worldliness, navigating even the most treacherous social waters with skill and aplomb, and taking infinite delight in the machinations of your fellow human beings. Greed and malice hold no power to shock you, though unsolicited kindness and generosity move you deeply. You are unfailingly responsive to friends and family members and your quick wit and social graces keep you at the top of everyone's invitation list. You are a trustworthy mate who knows human failings well enough to sidestep most of them yourself, though you can be a bit too detached emotionally. Keep the rest of the world at a distance—if you must—but let your loved ones see that your inner graces are as developed as your outer ones.

September 13

ASTROLOGICAL SIGN: Virgo
PEOPLE BORN TODAY: Judith Martin ("Miss Manners"), Nell Carter, Jacqueline Bisset, Arnold Schönberg, Claudette Colbert, Sherwood Anderson, Roald Dahl
FAMOUS EVENTS: First helicopter flight (1939); Margaret Chase Smith elected to U.S. Senate, becoming first woman to serve in both houses of Congress (1948); eight winning horses ridden by jockey Pat Day (1989)
LUCKY NUMBER: 4
BIRTHSTONE: Sapphire
POSITIVE TRAITS: Self-assured, individualistic, innovative
NEGATIVE TRAITS: Anachronistic, superior, isolated

You care more about being true to yourself than about being in step with current trends, and your remarkable habits are either noticeably dated or distinctly ahead of their time. Exceedingly self-confident, you neither care for the opinions of others nor do you solicit them. Friends may gently mock you for your oddball methods, but more than likely they suspect you've got the right idea—and admire you for it. Depending on where you fall on the time continuum, you are likely to attract romantic partners whose manners are a genteel throwback to a previous era or whose lifestyle choices are frankly futuristic. Hold on to your principles, and eventually you will make mere followers of fashion think twice about their own choices.

ASTROLOGICAL SIGN: Virgo

PEOPLE BORN TODAY: Faith Ford, Jean Smart, Joe Penny, Zoe Caldwell, Kate Millett, Margaret Sanger

FAMOUS EVENTS: Isadora Duncan strangled by scarf caught in auto wheel (1927); Princess Grace of Monaco fatally injured in car accident (1982); first solo balloon crossing of the Atlantic, by Joe Kittinger (1984)

LUCKY NUMBER: 5

BIRTHSTONE: Sapphire

POSITIVE TRAITS: Constructive, optimistic, probing

NEGATIVE TRAITS: Critical, confrontational, carping

When a difficult situation needs to be turned around, you're the one to call. With your finely honed critical faculties, you probe until you reach the root of any trouble. When friends bring you their problems, which they often do, you seldom limit yourself to expressions of sympathy. Instead, you dissect their problems and prescribe a step-by-step solution—even if that solution requires them to turn their lives upside down. You take the same creative approach to your own problems and seldom settle for compromises or halfway solutions. You expect your romantic relationships to play a positive role in your life, and you won't be happy until you find a mate as willing as you are to shake things up if the situation calls for it.

September 15

ASTROLOGICAL SIGN: Virgo

PEOPLE BORN TODAY: Oliver Stone, Tommy Lee Jones, Prince Harry of Britain, Dan Marino, Bobby Short, Agatha Christie, Jean Renoir, Fay Wray

FAMOUS EVENTS: Greenpeace founded (1971); record fourth world heavyweight title won by Muhammad Ali (1978); first issue of *USA Today* published (1982)

LUCKY NUMBER: 6

BIRTHSTONE: Sapphire

POSITIVE TRAITS: Dynamic, creative, versatile

NEGATIVE TRAITS: Self-righteous, suspicious, aggressive

You are a bundle of contradictions for whom nothing is simple. High energy impels you to action, but your suspicious nature inclines you to hang back. The path you trace to your goals is likely to be an elaborate one filled with twists and turns as well as determination and hard work. You have a close-knit circle of friends whom you regard as allies in a treacherous world, but your tendency to mistrust and second-guess even them can be destructive. Romantic partners are entranced by your ambitious plans and creative spirit, but may grow disillusioned by your inevitable stalls and diversions. Your perfect mate will be easy-going and even-tempered, looking to you for excitement—but not stability.

September 16

ASTROLOGICAL SIGN: Virgo
PEOPLE BORN TODAY: Richard Marx, Orel Hershiser, David Copperfield, Lauren Bacall, B. B. King, Peter Falk, John Knowles
FAMOUS EVENTS: First use of Great Seal of the United States (1782); General Motors founded by William Durant (1908); first animal (baboon) heart transplanted into human (1984)
LUCKY NUMBER: 7
BIRTHSTONE: Sapphire
POSITIVE TRAITS: Stylish, confident, uncompromising
NEGATIVE TRAITS: Blunt, unsparing, attention-grabbing

You present yourself to the world just as you are, feeling no need to conform to the expectations of those around you. Supremely self-confident, you are convinced that whoever hooks up with you, in business or in love, is getting the deal of a lifetime. Though you do not insist on a leadership role yourself, you won't commit to a project unless you admire the people in charge. When friends ask your opinion you offer it readily—too readily sometimes—and with little concern for their feelings. Although this leads to frequent fence-mending, it has no effect on your impulsive candor. You are a generous and warm-hearted partner in love, so long as your mate makes no effort to muzzle you or change your ways.

September 17

ASTROLOGICAL SIGN: Virgo

PEOPLE BORN TODAY: Rita Rudner, Adam Weinstein, William Carlos Williams, John Ritter, Anne Bancroft, Hank Williams, Perry Weinstein, Orlando Cepeda, Ken Kesey

FAMOUS EVENTS: U.S. Constitution signed (1787); first transcontinental airplane flight made by C. P. Rogers (1911); *M★A★S★H* television series premieres (1972); Vanessa Williams crowned first African-American Miss America (1983)

LUCKY NUMBER: 8

BIRTHSTONE: Sapphire

POSITIVE TRAITS: Witty, sensitive, articulate

NEGATIVE TRAITS: Critical, fussy, superficial

You are a hard worker with a keen eye for detail. Your light touch and refined tastes are evident in any place you spend some time. Though you frequently surpass others' expectations, you just as often fall short of your own lofty standards. Fear of insolvency fuels your professional drive, yet your industrious habits and high-octane creativity make serious money worries unlikely. When you meet that special someone, you are quick to lower your defenses and raise your charms, both of which you have in abundance. Extend to yourself the same patience and understanding you show coworkers and loved ones, and realize that your best is more than good enough. Take the time to appreciate the beauty you have created around you.

September 18

ASTROLOGICAL SIGN: Virgo

PEOPLE BORN TODAY: Ryne Sandberg, Holly Robinson, Robert Blake, Agnes DeMille, Greta Garbo, Samuel Johnson

FAMOUS EVENTS: Cornerstone of capitol laid by George Washington (1793); first broadcast over CBS radio network (1927); Jimi Hendrix dies from drug overdose (1970)

LUCKY NUMBER: 9

BIRTHSTONE: Sapphire

POSITIVE TRAITS: Profound, productive, indomitable

NEGATIVE TRAITS: Cynical, argumentative, reclusive

Your ability to overcome any obstacle thrown in your path will bolster your self-confidence and result in an impressive list of accomplishments. Though you may find domestic happiness elusive and even publicly pronounce it overrated, you privately yearn for a committed and passionate relationship. When discouraged or hurt by people who are unwilling or unable to understand your emotional depths, you seek comfort in the world of books and ideas, and in the steady perfection of your chosen craft. This brings you intellectual and financial rewards but stymies your romantic life. Curb your cynicism and put some of your creative energy into your search for a mate, and your days of being lonely and misunderstood may come to an end.

September 19

ASTROLOGICAL SIGN: Virgo

PEOPLE BORN TODAY: Joan Lunden, Jeremy Irons, Twiggy, Adam West, Zandra Rhodes, Cass Elliot

FAMOUS EVENTS: Death of President James Garfield following assassination attempt two months earlier (1881); first underground nuclear test, in U.S. (1957); Simon and Garfunkel reunited for free Central Park concert (1981)

LUCKY NUMBER: 1

BIRTHSTONE: Sapphire

POSITIVE TRAITS: Refined, wise, resilient

NEGATIVE TRAITS: Mercurial, excessive, distant

Fifteen minutes of fame won't satisfy you. Your gaze and your goals are fixed on long-term prosperity and financial stability—and the creature comforts they can bring. You succeed by staying abreast of trends without becoming associated with any particular passing fad. Adaptability and common sense are your hallmarks and they serve you well. Friends consider you a sage and seek out your advice, which they are wise to follow. Your personal style is classically elegant and gets you a great deal of admiration, which you thrive on. Your long-term mate will have to be vigilant to keep up with your rapidly changing interests, but not to worry: Your loyalty to loved ones far exceeds your allegiance to ideas.

September 20

ASTROLOGICAL SIGN: Virgo

PEOPLE BORN TODAY: Sophia Loren, Anne Meara, Red Auerbach, Jelly Roll Morton, Alexander the Great, Upton Sinclair

FAMOUS EVENTS: First electric range patented (1859); flashbulb patented (1930); Bobby Riggs trounced by Billie Jean King in "Battle of the Sexes" tennis match (1973); Jim Croce killed in plane crash (1973)

LUCKY NUMBER: 2

BIRTHSTONE: Sapphire

POSITIVE TRAITS: Ambitious, practical, astute

NEGATIVE TRAITS: Self-centered, condescending, disdainful

You are a born leader. Though your exuberant and outgoing personality might lead outsiders to assume you are all emotion, those who know you well are impressed by your diplomatic, conceptual, and analytical abilities. Your skills are in great demand, and because you have difficulty saying no, you are often roped into more projects than you can possibly handle, which raises your stress factor considerably. You run domestic affairs with the same aplomb, combining your organizational skills with your keen sensitivity to human nature that makes you a natural both with children and adults. Friends recognize you as both a kindhearted supporter and a hardworking ally in any project. Your romantic and nurturing qualities keep love partners content and assured of their importance in your life.

September 21

ASTROLOGICAL SIGN: Virgo

PEOPLE BORN TODAY: Ricki Lake, Bill Murray, Cecil Fielder, Stephen King, Marsha Norman, Larry Hagman, H. G. Wells

FAMOUS EVENTS: Canada given to Sir Alexander Stirling by King James (1621); first gasoline-powered automobile driven (1893); longest punt in NFL history, ninety-eight yards, made by Steve O'Neal (1969)

LUCKY NUMBER: 3

BIRTHSTONE: Sapphire

POSITIVE TRAITS: Curious, seeking, accepting

NEGATIVE TRAITS: Vindictive, thrill-seeking, self-destructive

You savor all the shadings of life and rarely shy away from its underside. Indeed, you are fascinated by the darker side of coworkers, friends, and social acquaintances, and because you are curious but not judgmental, people often tell you things that might better be kept secret. You enjoy a cathartic cry as much as a belly laugh, and your circle of friends represents a wide spectrum of lifestyles and attitudes. Romantic partners will share your lust for life and, more likely than not, lead you willingly into unfamiliar waters. Once you decide to drop anchor and settle into a long-term relationship, you will probably opt for a partner whose mood swings and erratic behavior keep you slightly off balance—and completely enthralled.

September 22

ASTROLOGICAL SIGN: Virgo

PEOPLE BORN TODAY: Shari Belafonte, Bonnie Hunt, Scott Baio, Joan Jett, Lynn Herring, Tommy Lasorda, Catherine Oxenberg, Eric von Stroheim

FAMOUS EVENTS: U.S. spy Capt. Nathan Hale executed by British (1776); office of postmaster general created (1789); President Gerald Ford escapes assassination attempt by Sara Jane Moore (1975)

LUCKY NUMBER: 4

BIRTHSTONE: Sapphire

POSITIVE TRAITS: Purposeful, strong-willed, mature

NEGATIVE TRAITS: Wary, isolated, willful

Being one of the crowd holds little appeal for you. Resolutely indifferent to peer pressure, you focus single-mindedly on your particular goals, charting a clear course and devoting most of your energy to staying on it. Though this self-absorption can put people off, you are willing to interact with them—in your own time and on your own terms. If they are willing to wait—and they should be—they will benefit from that same single-minded attention focused on them. You don't make friends quickly or easily, but those you do cultivate will become friends for life. Because you avoid social situations and don't know how to flirt, let your friends play matchmaker; they, at least, can enumerate your (many) good points.

September 23

ASTROLOGICAL SIGN: Libra
PEOPLE BORN TODAY: Bruce Springsteen, Ray Charles, Mary Kay Place, Julio Iglesias, Mickey Rooney, Victoria Woodhull, John Coltrane
FAMOUS EVENTS: Neptune discovered by Johann Gottfried Galle (1846); first airmail flight (1911); Checkers speech given on television by vice presidential candidate Richard Nixon (1952)
LUCKY NUMBER: 5
BIRTHSTONE: Opal
POSITIVE TRAITS: Passionate, pure-hearted, childlike
NEGATIVE TRAITS: Excessive, self-indulgent, stubborn

You take a pure and primal pleasure in everything you do, and it shows. In fact, when something captivates you, your enthusiasm can veer toward the excessive. Your zeal is contagious, firing up colleagues, friends, and children and inspiring everyone to pull together and do their best. The most casual gatherings turn into a party when you arrive—and you love a party. On those rare occasions when your energy flags, you tend to become irritable and discombobulated, mostly because you feel cheated out of what is rightfully yours. In spite of this, you are an easygoing, indulgent, passionate mate—and a faithful one. Though it is true you love a party, you always go home to the one you love.

September 24

ASTROLOGICAL SIGN: Libra

PEOPLE BORN TODAY: Phil Hartman, Linda McCartney, Anthony Newley, Jim McKay, Jim Henson, F. Scott Fitzgerald

FAMOUS EVENTS: First flight in an airship made by Henri Giffard (1852); first tennis grand slam won by Don Budge (1938); first broadcast of *60 Minutes* (1968)

LUCKY NUMBER: 6

BIRTHSTONE: Opal

POSITIVE TRAITS: Observant, wry, skillful

NEGATIVE TRAITS: Aloof, judgmental, excluded

You stand apart from the activity that buzzes around you, the better to observe and digest. Your gimlet eye catches all the absurdities perpetrated by your coworkers and acquaintances, and your equally sharp tongue provides a running commentary for the amusement of bystanders. These descriptive gifts are exceptional, but you have to curb your tendency to use them as a defense or a barrier to closer communication. Though you enjoy people—mostly in crowded gatherings where your chances to witness entertaining tableaux are the greatest—few people get close enough to distill your essence as aptly as you distill theirs. And although you are a lively and amusing romantic partner, you need a mate who can teach you to feel comfortable with intimacy.

September 25

ASTROLOGICAL SIGN: Libra

PEOPLE BORN TODAY: Will Smith, Heather Locklear, Scottie Pippen, Christopher Reeve, Barbara Walters, Phil Rizzuto, Red Smith, William Faulkner

FAMOUS EVENTS: Pacific Ocean sighted by Balboa (1513); world heavyweight crown won by Sonny Liston (1962); Sandra Day O'Connor sworn in as first female Supreme Court justice (1981)

LUCKY NUMBER: 7

BIRTHSTONE: Opal

POSITIVE TRAITS: Industrious, dedicated, charming

NEGATIVE TRAITS: Driven, demanding, strict

You attain success the old-fashioned way: You earn it, and you expect everyone else to do the same. You profit more from hard work than from good luck, and you openly resent those for whom the formula seems to work in reverse. Your standards are high but not impossible, and though you are quick to criticize, you are even quicker to praise. Your friends are people you respect as much as you like; some may even be former rivals who have won your admiration. You can be surprisingly seductive with romantic partners, but you require absolute loyalty and are slow to forgive any falls from grace. Learn to relax; if nothing else, this downtime will revitalize you for the work ahead.

September 26

ASTROLOGICAL SIGN: Libra

PEOPLE BORN TODAY: Linda Hamilton, Carlene Carter, Bryan Ferry, Olivia Newton-John, Jack LaLanne, George Gershwin, T. S. Eliot

FAMOUS EVENTS: Thomas Jefferson named first U.S. secretary of state (1789); *West Side Story* premieres on Broadway (1957); Babe Ruth's season home-run record tied by Roger Maris (1961); cult film *Rocky Horror Picture Show* premieres (1975)

LUCKY NUMBER: 8

BIRTHSTONE: Opal

POSITIVE TRAITS: Smooth, determined, strong

NEGATIVE TRAITS: Deceptive, unyielding, private

Your mild-mannered charms are deceptive—they conceal a core of titanium. Though you normally only flex your muscles when challenged, you occasionally put on a show of strength just to let people know who and what they are dealing with. Socially, you exert yourself at every opportunity, working a room with enviable ease. As a friend you are both entertaining and embracing, enfolding your intimates with a protective attitude. As a romantic partner you are no pushover, resisting your mate's ideas and influence with stubborn determination while at the same time trying to run the show yourself. Face it: You're bossy; if you want your love to last, find a partner as tough as you are, or at least as willing to fight for power.

September 27

ASTROLOGICAL SIGN: Libra

PEOPLE BORN TODAY: Shaun Cassidy, Cheryl Tiegs, Meat Loaf, Mike Schmidt, Jayne Meadows, William Conrad

FAMOUS EVENTS: First public passenger railway inaugurated (1825); first golf grand slam won by Bobby Jones (1930); invention of the telephone answering machine (1950); *Tonight* show debuts, with Steve Allen (1954)

LUCKY NUMBER: 9

BIRTHSTONE: Opal

POSITIVE TRAITS: Amiable, outgoing, entertaining

NEGATIVE TRAITS: Frustrated, unaware, insecure

Friends and lovers find you a joy to be around, not just because you have a knack for drawing people out, but because you show a genuine and deep interest in the lives of others. You take a childlike delight in surprises, and friends and family frequently bring you gifts for no other reason than that they were thinking of you. In fact, though you have difficulty believing it, you make a lasting impression on people—a good one. Why else would so many job offers and social invitations rain down on you? Learn to develop faith in your abilities, which are considerable, and you will never lack for allies willing to help you get to the top—where you belong.

September 28

People born today: Moon Zappa, John Sayles, Brigitte Bardot, Marcello Mastroianni, Ed Sullivan, William S. Paley, Stephen Spender

Famous events: England invaded by William the Conqueror (1066); California discovered by John Cabrillo (1542); home run hit by Ted Williams in final at bat (1960)

Lucky number: 1

Birthstone: Opal

Positive traits: Seductive, charismatic, exciting

Negative traits: Spoiled, manipulative, needy

You possess the enviable ability to turn on the charisma and wrap others around your little finger, but be wary of believing that you can succeed through charm (and a *little* hard work) alone, or that your appealing qualities make you more deserving of good fortune than anyone else. Romantic partners feel the full blast of your seductive warmth, and even friends may fall prey to your flirtatious cajoling and pleading when you set out to get your way. Your mate will be an indulgent partner who gives you the coddling you crave in return for your deeply felt affection. Dealing with others in a forthright manner may be asking too much of you, but keep your manipulations to a minimum and all will be well.

September 29

ASTROLOGICAL SIGN: Libra

PEOPLE BORN TODAY: John Paxson, Bryant Gumbel, Lech Walesa, Madeline Kahn, Jerry Lee Lewis, Greer Garson, Miguel de Cervantes

FAMOUS EVENTS: First dispatch of bobbies to patrol London streets (1829); first heavyweight boxing match refereed by a woman (1977); first space shuttle launch since *Challenger* disaster (1988)

LUCKY NUMBER: 2

BIRTHSTONE: Opal

POSITIVE TRAITS: Bold, reforming, unconventional

NEGATIVE TRAITS: Rebellious, self-destructive, undisciplined

You are a maverick unafraid to buck convention. When you disagree with the rules imposed by friends, family, or society, you work to change them or embark on a path of rebellion. Your winning personality and humanitarian proclivities often garner you followers, even though you make no conscious effort to foment revolt in the ranks. In fact, you are decidedly *not* a team player, preferring to go your own way and use your own methods, which may eventually cause others to resent you. The handful of intimates you do have, however, can claim your loyalty for life; so can your partner, though your insistent need to be on the cutting edge of things can cause a great deal of tension in your relationship.

September 30

ASTROLOGICAL SIGN: Libra

PEOPLE BORN TODAY: Crystal Bernard, Barry Williams, Marilyn McCoo, Johnny Mathis, Angie Dickinson, Truman Capote

FAMOUS EVENTS: *Porgy & Bess* premieres (1935); death of James Dean in car accident (1955); Haitian president Jean-Bertrand Aristide ousted in coup (1991)

LUCKY NUMBER: 3

BIRTHSTONE: Opal

POSITIVE TRAITS: Truthful, open, revealing

NEGATIVE TRAITS: Critical, hurtful, smug

Both at work and in social situations, you are quick to assess a situation and make the critical appraisals that fainter hearts may shrink from. Fortunately, you are able to take criticism yourself, which offsets any resentments that your astute assessments might stir up. If resentments do arise, your general good nature and adroit mediating skills enable you to smooth things over quickly. You have the devotion of a group of loyal friends, who love being with you in spite of your routine dissections of their character and behavior. Part of your appeal, to friends and lovers alike, is your knack for getting them to laugh while you're skewering them. Choose a mate as thick-skinned as you, or spend all your time on your knees—apologizing.

October 1

ASTROLOGICAL SIGN: Libra
PEOPLE BORN TODAY: Randy Quaid, Wallace Stevens, Julie Andrews, William Rehnquist, Jimmy Carter, Walter Matthau, Vladimir Horowitz, Grete Waitz
FAMOUS EVENTS: First World Series begins (1903); Model T Ford introduced by Henry Ford (1908); Rita Dove becomes first female African-American U.S. poet laureate (1993)
LUCKY NUMBER: 2
BIRTHSTONE: Opal
POSITIVE TRAITS: Disciplined, professional, devoted
NEGATIVE TRAITS: Demanding, driven, intimidating

You wear a proud, even stern exterior that can be intimidating, but intimates know that behind the cool front you are capable of being warm and kindhearted—even a bit silly. You are disciplined and driven in professional endeavors, and have high and sometimes overly demanding expectations of yourself. You hold others to the same standards and accept no excuses from those who don't carry their share of the load. You will gladly go out of your way for friends, though you expect them to return the favor. In love you delight your partner with your secretly sensual nature. You are a patient mate and parent, willing to indulge the moods and whims of your loved ones to maintain family harmony.

October 2

ASTROLOGICAL SIGN: Libra

PEOPLE BORN TODAY: Sting, Lorraine Bracco, Graham Greene, Groucho Marx, Bud Abbott, Donna Karan, Richard III, Mahatma Gandhi

FAMOUS EVENTS: First publication of *Peanuts* comic strip (1950); *Twilight Zone* television series premieres (1959); Thurgood Marshall sworn in as first African-American Supreme Court justice (1967)

LUCKY NUMBER: 3

BIRTHSTONE: Opal

POSITIVE TRAITS: Curious, clever, humanitarian

NEGATIVE TRAITS: Undemonstrative, snobbish, dispassionate

You struggle to embrace others wholeheartedly, but you are not always successful. At work and in your personal dealings you try to treat everyone the same, but can't help favoring those who are as quick and clever as yourself. You are a compelling conversationalist with a great curiosity about different cultures, style, and ways of life, which you satisfy by quizzing everyone you meet about their way of life. You tend to be more at ease in the realm of ideas than in the world of feelings, which can frustrate romantic partners who wish you would open up to them emotionally. Your long-term mate will realize that your feelings run deep even though you don't always feel secure expressing them.

October 3

ASTROLOGICAL SIGN: Libra

PEOPLE BORN TODAY: Jack Wagner, Dave Winfield, Lindsey Buckingham, Gore Vidal, Tommy Lee, Steve Reich, Thomas Wolfe, Chubby Checker, Emily Post

FAMOUS EVENTS: Last Thursday in November proclaimed Thanksgiving Day by President Abraham Lincoln (1863); first federal income tax (1 percent) becomes law (1913); *Mickey Mouse Club* television series premieres (1955)

LUCKY NUMBER: 4

BIRTHSTONE: Opal

POSITIVE TRAITS: Open-minded, seeking, stable

NEGATIVE TRAITS: Stodgy, slow-moving, reactionary

You stay on top of all that is new while firmly embracing the old. At home or at work, you eagerly explore new technologies and trends while still maintaining the best of the old. Though you are an intrepid traveler, a stable home base is absolutely essential for your emotional security. You are unfailingly proper in your dress and behavior, but you are no fuddy-duddy. In fact, you can be the life of a party, regaling your friends and family with tales of your adventures. In love, you prefer a partner with a romantic streak and sense of adventure equal to your own, but also want someone who will work with you to make your home an attractive and welcoming base camp.

October 4

ASTROLOGICAL SIGN: Libra

PEOPLE BORN TODAY: Susan Sarandon, Armand Assante, Jackie Collins, Malcolm Baldrige, Damon Runyon, Buster Keaton, Anne Rice, Patti LaBelle, Rutherford B. Hayes

FAMOUS EVENTS: First U.S. women's golf championship won by Beatrice Hoyt (1896); *Sputnik I*, first manmade satellite, launched into orbit (1957); *Leave It to Beaver* television series debuts (1957); death of Janis Joplin, by drug overdose (1970)

LUCKY NUMBER: 5

BIRTHSTONE: Opal

POSITIVE TRAITS: Aesthetic, agreeable, political

NEGATIVE TRAITS: Acquiescent, passive, manipulative

You have a well-developed aesthetic sense that drives you to make your world a more beautiful place. Coworkers seek your stamp of approval and use you as an amateur image consultant. At work and in social settings, you are careful to couch your strong opinions in terms that are inoffensive and politically correct, and you are able to convince people to do things your way by presenting your arguments with humor, deference, and sensitivity. Your desire for harmony makes you the most agreeable partner imaginable, sometimes landing you in sticky situations that could have been prevented by an assertive word or two. Don't let your naturally nonconfrontational nature keep you from having your say—and doing your own thing.

October 5

ASTROLOGICAL SIGN: Libra

PEOPLE BORN TODAY: Bob Geldof, Karen Allen, Elke Summer, Steve Miller, Jeff Conaway, Mario Lemieux, Ray Kroc, Clive Barker, Grant Hill

FAMOUS EVENTS: First nonstop flight across Pacific completed (1931); *Monty Python's Flying Circus* premieres on British TV (1969); Polish Solidarity leader Lech Walesa wins Nobel Peace Prize (1983)

LUCKY NUMBER: 6

BIRTHSTONE: Opal

POSITIVE TRAITS: Altruistic, warmhearted, sensual

NEGATIVE TRAITS: Neglectful, vague, unrealistic

Whether you spend your days doing social work or making cupcakes for the Cub Scout troop, you understand how your labors benefit others and carry out your duties with joy and dedication. You take lusty enjoyment in the company of others, frequently rounding up friends for a night on the town or a lively party at your place. With your close friends, you brood over the world's ills with the intensity others reserve for their own woes, and suffer pangs of guilt when you feel you can't do enough to help. Though your heart is big, your mate can feel neglected if you get too wrapped up in your good deeds. Give your sensual loving nature free reign at home and your partner will be less inclined to complain.

October 6

ASTROLOGICAL SIGN: Libra

PEOPLE BORN TODAY: Britt Ekland, Jerry Grote, Le Corbusier, Ruben Sierra, Thor Heyerdahl, Carole Lombard, Jenny Lind, Lowell Thomas Jr.

FAMOUS EVENTS: First talking picture, *The Jazz Singer,* premieres (1927); Egyptian president Anwar Sadat assassinated (1981); Elizabeth Taylor marries Larry Fortensky, her eighth husband (1991)

LUCKY NUMBER: 7

BIRTHSTONE: Opal

POSITIVE TRAITS: Talented, adventuresome, exciting

NEGATIVE TRAITS: Undependable, egotistical, selfish

Anyone who tries to keep you to a schedule will fail—miserably. Fortunately, your talents and skills make it possible for you to exist outside the world of datebooks and deadlines: You are a highly creative, disciplined, and ambitious self-starter. Working alone or in a very loosely structured environment allows you to proceed at your own formidable pace. To your many friends, you are equal parts frustration and delight: never there when you say you will be, and then showing up unexpectedly with all the makings for a picnic. Children, of course, think you were created just for them, and when you're in love, which you often are, your partners are usually enthralled by your wacky but wonderful way of life.

October 7

ASTROLOGICAL SIGN: Libra

PEOPLE BORN TODAY: Toni Braxton, John Mellencamp, Heinrich Himmler, Oliver North, Bishop Desmond Tutu, June Allyson, Alfred Drake, Yo-Yo Ma

FAMOUS EVENTS: Marian Anderson becomes first African-American signed by Metropolitan Opera (1954); first made-for-TV movie airs (1964); *Cats* opens on Broadway (1982)

LUCKY NUMBER: 8

BIRTHSTONE: Opal

POSITIVE TRAITS: Charismatic, loyal, stable

NEGATIVE TRAITS: Stubborn, blindered, forgetful

You stick to your guns no matter what opposition you encounter. At work and in social affairs, you speak and act with the certainty that comes from a deeply felt set of beliefs. You're the best friend everyone always wanted: loyal, sympathetic, and fun to be with. Children accept you as one of their own, and you are as comfortable with them as you are with adults. While you're no eager people-pleaser, you act with so much grace and charm that romantic partners find you irresistible—which you are. Your mate prizes your strong sense of commitment, but may bemoan the stubbornness that goes hand in hand with it, though this is a small price to pay for your open-ness and warmth—and those fabulous meals!

October 8

ASTROLOGICAL SIGN: Libra
PEOPLE BORN TODAY: Jesse Jackson, Sigourney Weaver, Chevy Chase, Stephanie Zimbalist, Paul Hogan, Rona Barrett
FAMOUS EVENTS: Great Chicago Fire (1871); first World Series no-hitter pitched by Don Larsen (1956); Toni Morrison becomes first African-American to win Nobel Prize for Literature (1993)
LUCKY NUMBER: 9
BIRTHSTONE: Opal
POSITIVE TRAITS: Visionary, facile, articulate
NEGATIVE TRAITS: Glib, egotistical, impatient

You are quick-witted and articulate, getting your points across to colleagues and companions with the greatest style. You rapidly grasp the outlines of a problem and formulate a workable solution, though you sometimes lack the patience to see it through to its conclusion. You are frequently called on to mediate crises between family members or friends, but your natural reluctance to take sides allows you to keep your distance—and to keep your friends. You are no shrinking violet and any potential romantic partner will have to have as strong a sense of self as you do. Though gentle, you have little tolerance for timidity and need a mate who is ready and willing to accompany you into the great big exciting world; don't settle for less.

October 9

ASTROLOGICAL SIGN: Libra
PEOPLE BORN TODAY: Zachery Ty Bryan, John Lennon, Sean Ono Lennon, Jackson Browne, John Entwistle, Jacques Tati, Yusef Lateef
FAMOUS EVENTS: Calliope patented by Joshua Stoddard (1855); first flight across U.S. by a woman completed by Laura Ingalls (1930); Strawberry Fields memorial in Central Park dedicated to John Lennon (1985)
LUCKY NUMBER: 1
BIRTHSTONE: Opal
POSITIVE TRAITS: Imaginative, idealistic, romantic
NEGATIVE TRAITS: Cynical, caustic, negative

You are cynical enough to expect the worst, yet idealistic enough to hope for the best. Rarely, however, does your cynicism get in the way. Your outlook is cheerful and you genuinely enjoy your life. This *joie de vivre* is evident and contributes to your popularity. You have many talents and it may take many tries before you find the kind of work in which you can use them. You're stylish in an understated way, and though you never flout your keen intelligence, it's obvious in everything you undertake. Only your closest friends can really say they know you; your private life is strictly off-limits to casual acquaintances. You are not afraid of intimacy, however. In a loving relationship, your heart and soul are an open book.

October 10

ASTROLOGICAL SIGN: Libra

PEOPLE BORN TODAY: David Lee Roth, Tanya Tucker, John Prine, Ben Vereen, Helen Hayes, Giuseppe Verdi, James Clavell, Keith Hernandez

FAMOUS EVENTS: U.S. Naval Academy opens (1845); the *New York Times Book Review* debuts (1896); resignation of Vice President Spiro Agnew (1973)

LUCKY NUMBER: 2

BIRTHSTONE: Opal

POSITIVE TRAITS: Dramatic, energetic, vivacious

NEGATIVE TRAITS: Excessive, obsessed, melodramatic

You agree with Shakespeare that all the world's a stage, and you act like you've landed a starring role. You effect a splashy style that gets you noticed on the job and in social situations. Your grandstanding wins you lots of fans and more than a few foes, but it makes it hard for anybody to overlook you. Though your behavior can be excessive, your best friends and closest colleagues know you take your responsibilities seriously and carry out your duties with a surprising attention to detail. You lure more than your share of admirers, but the roar of the crowd may mean more to you than the romantic murmurings of your mate. When you've earned enough raves with your exterior assets, start cultivating an inner life.

October 11

ASTROLOGICAL SIGN: Libra

PEOPLE BORN TODAY: Luke Perry, Joan Cusack, Daryl Hall, Elmore Leonard, Jerome Robbins, Eleanor Roosevelt, Art Blakey, Steve Young

FAMOUS EVENTS: Boer War begins (1899); first broadcast of *Saturday Night Live* (1975); Kathy Sullivan becomes first American woman to walk in space (1984)

LUCKY NUMBER: 3

BIRTHSTONE: Opal

POSITIVE TRAITS: Attractive, popular, self-assured

NEGATIVE TRAITS: Superficial, complacent, frivolous

Popularity and position are yours for the asking, though they may leave you yearning for something more. You are attractive, self-assured, and capable enough to advance rapidly up the career ladder or ascend into the highest social circles. When you reach the pinnacle, you are likely to set more meaningful goals for yourself, such as becoming a teacher or innovator in your field, or abandoning your ambitions to serve needier people. Whether you aim for worldly success or social influence, your easy charm and pleasing manners will help advance your cause. Your golden aura draws romantic interest from many, and a devoted long-term mate will encourage your efforts to back up your appealing style with ever-increasing substance.

October 12

ASTROLOGICAL SIGN: Libra

PEOPLE BORN TODAY: Kirk Cameron, Pat Day, Luciano Pavarotti, Susan Anton, Dick Gregory, Jean Nidetch, Adam Rich

FAMOUS EVENTS: America discovered by Christopher Columbus (1492); Little Richard renounces rock and roll (1957); Weight Watchers founded by Jean Nidetch (1963)

LUCKY NUMBER: 4

BIRTHSTONE: Opal

POSITIVE TRAITS: Assertive, effusive, big-hearted

NEGATIVE TRAITS: Outspoken, outrageous, eccentric

You are a larger-than-life personality who firmly resists efforts to cut you down to size. You are determined that your opinions be heard and heeded, even if you must resort to outrageous antics to ensure it. Yet your heart is as big as your head, and your tantrums are often thrown on behalf of others' interests. You stand up for friends who are less confident, earning their gratitude and, sometimes, their deep embarrassment. You are a passionate, expressive romantic partner and do everything short of wagging your tail to display your puppy-dog devotion to your mate. Your loved ones cater to your needs for attention, but may come to resent your self-appointed spot at the top if you don't occasionally cater to theirs.

October 13

ASTROLOGICAL SIGN: Libra

PEOPLE BORN TODAY: Nancy Kerrigan, Tisha Campbell, Kelly Preston, Marie Osmond, Demond Wilson, Margaret Thatcher, Chi Chi Rodriguez, Paul Simon

FAMOUS EVENTS: Cornerstone of White House laid (1792); B'nai B'rith founded (1843); first ABA basketball game played (1967)

LUCKY NUMBER: 5

BIRTHSTONE: Opal

POSITIVE TRAITS: Dutiful, responsible, modest

NEGATIVE TRAITS: Overidealized, pressured, frustrated

Your exemplary behavior on the job and at home may merit you a crown but it might be too tight for comfort. You refrain from preachiness, but others pronounce you perfect and set ever-higher standards for you. Much as you hate to disappoint others, you become deeply dissatisfied when you tune out your inner voice and let yourself be directed from outside. Even when the push comes from within, you drive yourself hard and can be overly critical. You are most comfortable with friends who are focused on their own goals and share a casual camaraderie with you. You are quick to disabuse romantic partners of any illusions about you, sometimes intentionally indulging in unkind or irresponsible behavior to underline your only-human status.

ASTROLOGICAL SIGN: Libra

PEOPLE BORN TODAY: Harry Anderson, Isaac Mizrahi, Ralph Lauren, Roger Moore, C. Everett Koop, Dwight D. Eisenhower, e. e. cummings, John Wooden

FAMOUS EVENTS: Shooting survived by President Theodore Roosevelt (1912); sound barrier broken by test pilot Chuck Yeager (1947); Martin Luther King Jr. wins the Nobel Peace Prize (1964)

LUCKY NUMBER: 6

BIRTHSTONE: Opal

POSITIVE TRAITS: Sensible, centered, calm

NEGATIVE TRAITS: Tame, impassive, unexciting

You are the steady center to which personal and business contacts return after swinging too far in any direction. You counter extreme opinions and out-of-control emotions with calm logic, and can find yourself lifted to a leadership position largely on the strength of your poise and common sense. Friends bounce their wildest schemes off you before making a move, trusting you to pull them back to reality. You attract romantic partners who seek balance and stability in their lives, but you are happiest with a partner who is as centered as you are. Your home is a sea of tranquillity and you are content to spend time there, particularly when it is just you and your mate—alone together.

October 15

ASTROLOGICAL SIGN: Libra

PEOPLE BORN TODAY: Penny Marshall, Tito Jackson, Richard Carpenter, Linda Lavin, Lee Iacocca, Friedrich Nietzsche, Mario Puzo, Jim Palmer

FAMOUS EVENTS: German spy "Mata Hari" shot by French firing squad (1917); first episode of *I Love Lucy* airs (1951); first vice-presidential debate held between Walter Mondale and Robert Dole (1976)

LUCKY NUMBER: 7

BIRTHSTONE: Opal

POSITIVE TRAITS: Patient, practiced, generous

NEGATIVE TRAITS: Frustrated, self-denying, slow

In your profession, sport, or chosen cause you are a patient apprentice. You are content to toil quietly in the background, lending moral support and practical assistance to those in power while gathering a gold mine of expertise. When your moment comes, you are more than prepared but should beware of alienating others by appearing overly confident. Friends treasure your listening skills and thoughtfulness, knowing you'll be there with a kind word, a sympathetic ear, or a dinner invitation when they need it most. You are an unselfish romantic partner who deftly performs the dances of couplehood, deferring to your mate's needs whenever the situation calls for it. Don't overdo the virtue of patience; push yourself forward when the time is right and not a minute later.

October 16

ASTROLOGICAL SIGN: Libra

PEOPLE BORN TODAY: Tim Robbins, Wendy Wilson, Dave DeBusschere, Angela Lansbury, Eugene O'Neill, Oscar Wilde, Noah Webster, Suzanne Somers

FAMOUS EVENTS: Marie Antoinette guillotined (1793); first birth control clinic opened, by Margaret Sanger (1916); toddler Jessica McClure rescued from well in Midland, Texas (1987)

LUCKY NUMBER: 8

BIRTHSTONE: Opal

POSITIVE TRAITS: Honest, determined, just

NEGATIVE TRAITS: Moody, combative, stubborn

Your judgments are always fair but the outlook for your moods can be stormy. Justice is what you value most, and you strive for equity for all on the job and in society. When your wishes are heeded, you are the epitome of graciousness; when they are ignored, you sulk, and then work doubly hard to achieve your victories, accepting neither failure nor compromise. You act as your friends' conscience as well as their ally, and though they may find you a bit trying, your company is always stimulating. You require a partner whom you can respect and be proud of, but even more important, you desire a mate who is ethical, devoted, and crazy about the great outdoors—just like you.

October 17

ASTROLOGICAL SIGN: Libra

PEOPLE BORN TODAY: George Wendt, Howard Rollins, Tom Poston, Jimmy Breslin, Arthur Miller, Rita Hayworth, Margot Kidder, Evel Knievel

FAMOUS EVENTS: Al Capone convicted of tax evasion (1931); Nobel Peace Prize awarded to Mother Teresa (1979); first game of World Series interrupted by major earthquake in California (1989)

LUCKY NUMBER: 9

BIRTHSTONE: Opal

POSITIVE TRAITS: Bold, self-assured, dashing

NEGATIVE TRAITS: Foolhardy, imprudent, self-centered

You have the bold self-assurance needed to take chances and the stamina to face the consequences. Worrywarts and finger-waggers don't phase you at all: You follow your heart. When your efforts end in failure, you pick yourself up and carry on without complaint. Your fearlessness can make you the idol of others less courageous, though your example is not always one they should imitate. You are a raconteur extraordinaire, embellishing your exploits for the entertainment of adoring friends and family. You cut a stylish figure that makes the hearts of romantic partners beat faster. Though your lack of caution can cause your partner many sleepless nights fretting over your future, there won't be any sleepless nights wondering where you are: You're home, where your heart is.

October 18

ASTROLOGICAL SIGN: Libra

PEOPLE BORN TODAY: Wynton Marsalis, Pam Dawber, Jean-Claude van Damme, Martina Navratilova, George C. Scott, Lotte Lenya, Terry McMillan

FAMOUS EVENTS: Nobel Prize awarded to Watson, Crick, and Wilkins for DNA research (1962); first landing on Venus made by Russian spacecraft (1967); three home runs hit in World Series game by Reggie Jackson (1977)

LUCKY NUMBER: 1

BIRTHSTONE: Opal

POSITIVE TRAITS: Creative, dignified, groundbreaking

NEGATIVE TRAITS: Proud, driven, approval-craving

You have all the imagination and fire required to blaze new trails, but even as you do, you are looking to see who's watching. Winning respect for what you do is as important to you as achievement itself. You don't feel a project is a success until it has been applauded by those you look up to. You seldom follow the pattern set by your peers, but you are careful that your individuality doesn't cost you the affections of your cherished friends. Too many evenings spent at home and you're climbing the walls; with your energy, an active and stimulating social life and lots of physical activity are absolutely essential. If your partner can match your stamina, life together should be sweet indeed.

October 19

ASTROLOGICAL SIGN: Libra
PEOPLE BORN TODAY: Jennifer Holliday, Evander Holyfield, John Lithgow, Peter Max, Patricia Ireland, John LeCarre
FAMOUS EVENTS: First wedding performed aloft in a balloon (1874); act ending state of war with Germany signed by President Harry Truman (1951); stock market plunges 508 points (1987)
LUCKY NUMBER: 2
BIRTHSTONE: Opal
POSITIVE TRAITS: Colorful, surprising, impactful
NEGATIVE TRAITS: Challenging, excessive, concealed

You have an emotional and independent streak that you tend to conceal behind a façade of conventionality. When things are proceeding smoothly, you don't make waves. But when a conflict arises, you can become a tidal wave, surprising and even shocking those who don't know you well. Adversity brings out the best in you, stripping away your shyness to reveal your hidden talents and strength of character. Friends are likely to be acquainted with all the colors in your emotional spectrum, since with them you feel secure enough to engage in arguments and lay your more radical convictions on the table. Romantic partners find your personality rousing, your mind intriguing, and your lovemaking electrifying. In fact, you just might be too much of a good thing.

October 20

ASTROLOGICAL SIGN: Libra

PEOPLE BORN TODAY: Tom Petty, Melanie Mayron, Dr. Joyce Brothers, Mickey Mantle, Bela Lugosi, Arthur Rimbaud

FAMOUS EVENTS: General Douglas MacArthur returns to the Philippines (1944); House Committee on Un-American Activities hearings opened (1947); Jacqueline Bouvier Kennedy and Aristotle Onassis wed (1968)

LUCKY NUMBER: 3

BIRTHSTONE: Opal

POSITIVE TRAITS: Dynamic, directing, reasonable

NEGATIVE TRAITS: Bossy, egocentric, dictatorial

You like to think that your focus is other people, but sooner or later your sturdy ego always pushes its way forward and cries "Look at me!" You are the first to sign up for a team project, but the democratic approach rubs you the wrong way and it's just a matter of time before you grab a leadership role. Once in charge, your innate sense of what's right makes you a fair leader. Friends tolerate your take-charge attitude, particularly since you know how to get a good time going—and keep it going. Your spirit of fun also engages would-be romantic partners, but your ideal mate will be the one who can stand up to your forceful personality and give you a run for your money.

October 21

ASTROLOGICAL SIGN: Libra

PEOPLE BORN TODAY: Carrie Fisher, Steve Cropper, Ursula K. LeGuin, Whitey Ford, Sir Georg Solti, Dizzy Gillespie, Samuel Taylor Coleridge

FAMOUS EVENTS: The can-can first performed publicly, in Paris (1858); 170-wpm typing speed record set (1918); opening of the Solomon R. Guggenheim Museum in New York (1959)

LUCKY NUMBER: 4

BIRTHSTONE: Opal

POSITIVE TRAITS: Entertaining, articulate, resilient

NEGATIVE TRAITS: Excessive, verbose, facile

You are as chatty and personable as anyone could wish to be. Every thought, feeling, and impression that passes through your mind instantly pours out of your mouth. Your verbosity can be a social asset, helping make friends out of casual acquaintances or total strangers, but it can blemish your business image if you don't attempt to keep it in check. Indeed, you tend to be impulsive in general, a trait that is at once refreshing and fraught with danger. No one will ever accuse you of being a stick-in-the-mud; you're up for just about anything, anytime. Friends and lovers may have to follow in your wake, if they don't know how to make waves of their own.

October 22

ASTROLOGICAL SIGN: Libra

PEOPLE BORN TODAY: Brian Boitano, Catherine Deneuve, Jeff Goldblum, Annette Funicello, Christopher Lloyd, Sarah Bernhardt, Doris Lessing

FAMOUS EVENTS: First parachute jump, from a balloon (1797); Metropolitan Opera House opens in New York City (1883); photocopying machine invented by Chester Carlson (1938)

LUCKY NUMBER: 5

BIRTHSTONE: Opal

POSITIVE TRAITS: Attractive, charismatic, inspiring

NEGATIVE TRAITS: Temperamental, agitated, disturbing

Anonymity holds no attraction for you, which is fortunate since you couldn't blend into a crowd even if you wanted. Your compelling presence adds impact to your performance on the job and makes it easy for you to dive into new social waters with a resounding splash. Friends bask in your reflected glow and listen patiently to your half-hearted complaints about the difficulties of keeping your glistening image buffed. Potential romantic partners find you extremely seductive, but if a struggle ensues over top billing, watch out. Forced to surrender the spotlight, your tantrums are not pretty. Long-term happiness is most likely with a partner who won't mind being the "best supporting actor" in the exciting movie that is your life.

October 23

ASTROLOGICAL SIGN: Scorpio

PEOPLE BORN TODAY: Dwight Yoakam, Doug Flutie, Michael Crichton, Pele, Johnny Carson, Ned Rorem, Weird Al Yankovic

FAMOUS EVENTS: First-ever solo flight by a woman, Blanche Scott (1910); biggest naval battle of World War II begins in Philippine Sea (1944); Watergate tapes surrendered by President Richard Nixon (1973)

LUCKY NUMBER: 6

BIRTHSTONE: Topaz

POSITIVE TRAITS: Perceptive, versatile, charming

NEGATIVE TRAITS: Moody, quick-tempered, isolated

You are a lively, charming, and entertaining companion and colleague—most of the time. Because you normally run on high-octane energy, you tend to worry when your energy drops, and you find yourself running on regular, like most people. And when you're worried, your moods and emotions take wild swings. This isn't as bad as it could be, however, since you know how to ensure that your energy rarely dips; in fact, you extol the virtues of eating right and exercising regularly. Even when you do get testy, your friends (devoted to you) don't mind much, writing off your moodiness to a behavioral tic, soon to be gone. A supportive mate can provide a vital emotional safety valve—*if* you open up.

October 24

ASTROLOGICAL SIGN: Scorpio

PEOPLE BORN TODAY: Kevin Kline, Bill Wyman, F. Murray Abraham, David Nelson, Dame Sybil Thorndike, Moss Hart, Juan Marichal, Y. A. Tittle

FAMOUS EVENTS: First coast-to-coast telegram transmitted (1861); United Nations officially established (1945); 69.42-carat diamond purchased by Richard Burton for Elizabeth Taylor (1969)

LUCKY NUMBER: 7

BIRTHSTONE: Topaz

POSITIVE TRAITS: Dramatic, masterful, poised

NEGATIVE TRAITS: Calculating, possessive, theatrical

Grand gestures and flowery speeches are your native language, and you tend to play to the gallery even when talking to yourself. You exhibit enviable poise in professional and social situations, seemingly immune to the attacks of nervousness and doubt that assail others. The dramatic flair you bring to everyday activities keeps your friends enthralled, and loved ones understand that your occasional displays of temper and jealousy are mostly for show. In love, your partner will be thrilled by your wholehearted embrace of romantic rituals, your unmitigated love of all things celebratory, and your ability to keep the fires of love burning brightly. Meditation and reflection can keep you in touch with your emotions and prevent you from becoming a caricature of yourself.

October 25

ASTROLOGICAL SIGN: Scorpio

PEOPLE BORN TODAY: Anne Tyler, Brian Kerwin, Bobby Knight, Bobby Thompson, Minnie Pearl, Pablo Picasso, Midori, James Carville

FAMOUS EVENTS: Battle of Agincourt fought by Henry V (1415); charge of the Light Brigade (1854); Grenada invaded by U.S. forces (1983)

LUCKY NUMBER: 8

BIRTHSTONE: Topaz

POSITIVE TRAITS: Steady, focused, reliable

NEGATIVE TRAITS: Self-centered, using, ungenerous

You are a comforting presence in the lives of others, though not through any overt effort on your part. In fact, you can be somewhat indifferent to the needs of others, concentrating instead on your own fulfillment. It's this very steadiness, however, that people find reassuring. You are a role model who demonstrates that focus, organization, and intensity can bring satisfaction and success. You don't, however, completely keep your nose to the grindstone: You open your eyes to other people's qualities mainly when you notice ones that might prove useful to you, and rather than resenting it, your friends clamor to help you out any way they can. Though you can spare little interest for actively courting romantic partners, you attract them through the sheer force of your personality. In a long-term relationship, your self-centeredness tends to lose its charm unless your mate is unusually self-sacrificing or you evolve into a more giving partner.

October 26

ASTROLOGICAL SIGN: Scorpio

PEOPLE BORN TODAY: Hillary Rodham Clinton, Jaclyn Smith, Pat Sajak, Marla Maples, Bob Hoskins, François Mitterand

FAMOUS EVENTS: Erie Canal opens (1825); washing machine invented, by Hamilton Smith (1858); *Doonesbury* comic strip debuts (1970)

LUCKY NUMBER: 9

BIRTHSTONE: Topaz

POSITIVE TRAITS: Shrewd, buoyant, consensus-building

NEGATIVE TRAITS: Opinionated, lenient, pressuring

You are determined to reach your goals, and when you do, you never rest on your laurels; instead, you push on to the next challenge. Whether leading a seminar or directing a bake sale, you are a shrewd judge of people and you know how to mobilize them. Though people find your high ethical standards commendable, they are more drawn to your contagious sense of fun and ability to turn almost any event into a good time. You like to stay busy and frequently overdo it, working or playing too hard for your own good, which worries your loved ones but doesn't worry you. Your love life is usually waxing or waning, which is how you prefer it—at least until you decide you're ready for commitment.

ASTROLOGICAL SIGN: Scorpio

PEOPLE BORN TODAY: Simon LeBon, Fran Lebowitz, John Cleese, Sylvia Plath, Dylan Thomas, Theodore Roosevelt, Ruby Dee

FAMOUS EVENTS: Macy's department store opens (1858); Bruce Springsteen featured simultaneously on covers of *Time* and *Newsweek* (1975); last performance given by Beverly Sills (1980)

LUCKY NUMBER: 1

BIRTHSTONE: Topaz

POSITIVE TRAITS: Perceptive, intellectual, wry

NEGATIVE TRAITS: Sardonic, detached, dark

Your take on life is one of rueful amusement. This perspective serves you well most of the time, though you occasionally become downcast at the more destructive absurdities of your fellow man. You use your humorous detachment to help colleagues and friends gain a better perspective on their problems as well as to charm just about everyone you come in contact with. Your skewed points of view on political and social issues make you a lively and interesting dinner partner and attract romantic partners with a taste for the unconventional. To sustain a relationship with a mate, you must tap into your hidden emotional intensity in a positive way and try not to hide your deeper feelings behind a mask of witty small talk, no matter how sweet.

October 28

ASTROLOGICAL SIGN: Scorpio
PEOPLE BORN TODAY: Julia Roberts, Bill Gates, Dennis Franz, Paul Wylie, Annie Potts, Jane Alexander, Bruce Jenner, Cleo Laine
FAMOUS EVENTS: Statue of Liberty dedicated (1886); Benito Mussolini takes power in Italy (1922); first recorded birth on an airplane (1929)
LUCKY NUMBER: 2
BIRTHSTONE: Topaz
POSITIVE TRAITS: Lively, inquisitive, enthusiastic
NEGATIVE TRAITS: Mercurial, confused, overcommitted

You are powered by an insatiable desire to explore new ideas and get to know new people. When a concept captures your attention, you throw yourself into it wholeheartedly, but when your enthusiasm flags, you often find yourself wondering what you ever saw in it. Unless you are the one in charge, this could earn you a reputation for flightiness or unreliability. Friends are entertained by your parade of passing fancies and occasionally get swept up by your enthusiasm for them—even when they know better. Romantic partners find your high-beam curiosity flattering, and you see long-term potential in every relationship. Though few pan out, you come through each with greater self-knowledge and undiminished hope for that one lasting romance.

October 29

ASTROLOGICAL SIGN: Scorpio

PEOPLE BORN TODAY: Winona Ryder, Randy Jackson, Richard Dreyfuss, Kate Jackson, Denis Potvin, Melba Moore

FAMOUS EVENTS: Sir Walter Raleigh executed for treason (1618); "Black Tuesday," stock market crashes (1929); first peacetime military draft commences (1940)

LUCKY NUMBER: 3

BIRTHSTONE: Topaz

POSITIVE TRAITS: Effective, loyal, honest

NEGATIVE TRAITS: Uncooperative, unyielding, secretive

Following orders goes against your grain: You'd rather be handing out the directives or at least collaborating on the strategy you must carry out. At work and at home, anyone who tries to dictate to you will find you argumentative and uncooperative. You have a wide competitive streak and plot elaborate schemes to outperform your rivals. Though you hatch your plans in secret, your methods are honest and aboveboard. Friends stick close to you, partly because the workings of your mind fascinate them and partly because they would never wish to be your enemy. You are intense in your pursuit of romantic partners and loyal once you make a commitment. However, if a relationship disintegrates, you are likely to hold on to your pain just as firmly.

October 30

ASTROLOGICAL SIGN: Scorpio

PEOPLE BORN TODAY: Henry Winkler, Harry Hamlin, Grace Slick, Louis Malle, Claude Lelouch, Ruth Gordon

FAMOUS EVENTS: First transmission of a moving image televised (1925); panic initiated by *War of the Worlds* radio broadcast (1938); heavyweight crown regained by Muhammad Ali (1974)

LUCKY NUMBER: 4

BIRTHSTONE: Topaz

POSITIVE TRAITS: Probing, active, intent

NEGATIVE TRAITS: Distracted, self-absorbed, distant

You are tuned in to just one channel at a time. Whatever personal or professional project captures your imagination, it monopolizes your time, often causing you to neglect other areas of your life. Romantic partners are thrilled when your attention is focused on them, and much less enchanted when it takes another direction. Because you are warmhearted and without malice, you can usually overcome any rifts in your love life due to your single-mindedness; but for love to last, your chosen one will have to be independent and able to steer his or her own course. Though you have plenty of friends, you tend to go it alone for long periods, which makes you an unintentional recluse. Keep your friends happy: Stay in touch.

October 31

ASTROLOGICAL SIGN: Scorpio
PEOPLE BORN TODAY: Larry Mullen, Deidre Hall, Dan Rather, Jane Pauley, John Candy, Michael Landon, Tom Paxton, John Keats
FAMOUS EVENTS: Martin Luther's ninety-five theses nailed to Wittenberg church door (1517); first hydrogen bomb exploded at Eniwetok Atoll (1956); Indian prime minister Indira Gandhi assassinated (1984)
LUCKY NUMBER: 5
BIRTHSTONE: Topaz
POSITIVE TRAITS: Sympathetic, modest, talented
NEGATIVE TRAITS: Indirect, underhanded, manipulative

You take a backseat though you have the talent necessary to grab the steering wheel. Innately modest, you enjoy extolling the achievements and successes of others, and yours are often the shoulders others stand on to get to the top. You are not completely self-effacing, however, and are pleased to accept any accolades and praise that are genuinely due to you. As a friend, you are supportive and sympathetic, as willing to talk as you are to listen; and you *love* to get in the car and go—anywhere. New sights and new experiences are what energize you. In love, your noncompetitive and openly affectionate nature make real harmony possible. You're no pushover, though, willing to take a tough stand if the situation calls for it.

November 1

ASTROLOGICAL SIGN: Scorpio

PEOPLE BORN TODAY: Fernando Valenzuela, Lyle Lovett, Marcia Wallace, Gary Player, Robert Foxworth, Barbara Bosson, Betsy Palmer, Stephen Crane, Marcel Ophuls

FAMOUS EVENTS: Sistine Chapel ceiling mural unveiled (1512); first medical school for women opens, in Boston (1848); assassination attempt on President Harry Truman, by Puerto Rican nationalists (1950)

LUCKY NUMBER: 3

BIRTHSTONE: Topaz

POSITIVE TRAITS: Energetic, inventive, romantic

NEGATIVE TRAITS: Exacting, scattered, overreaching

Your mind is a hopper of plans and ideas. Sure of your ability to achieve your aims, you dream up ambitious schemes for yourself and any group you are part of. Coworkers and social contacts will be excited by your boundless energy and vital spark, and your willingness to work behind the scenes to make things happen. Though you are not a homebody, your home is extremely important to you as a reflection of your good taste and eye for detail. You are an exciting romantic partner, though a mate who is your spiritual twin may cause your life to spin into happy disarray. A more grounded partner will ensure that you enjoy the pleasures of the body as well as the mind.

November 2

ASTROLOGICAL SIGN: Scorpio
PEOPLE BORN TODAY: Alfre Woodard, Shere Hite, Stefanie Powers, Patrick Buchanan, Ray Walston, Burt Lancaster, Marie Antoinette, k. d. lang, James K. Polk
FAMOUS EVENTS: North Dakota becomes 39th state and South Dakota becomes 40th state (1889); one of only two flights of the Spruce Goose, largest wooden plane ever built, piloted by Howard Hughes (1947); Georgia governor Jimmy Carter elected president (1976)
LUCKY NUMBER: 4
BIRTHSTONE: Topaz
POSITIVE TRAITS: Convincing, persuasive, impactful
NEGATIVE TRAITS: Coercive, power-hungry, pushy

You speak softly and carry a big stick, making your influence felt wherever you go. Though you allow others a certain amount of autonomy, and genuinely respect their talents and contributions, you sometimes can't resist letting them know who's boss. Travel figures prominently in your life. In fact, you are the perfect traveling companion, comfortable in situations others find awkward and genuinely happy to find yourself in unfamiliar surroundings, where you can test your wits and hone your communication skills. Though your taste for the new makes you rather fickle in romance, your short-lived affairs will be fun-filled adventures. Satisfaction in love won't come until the right person sets your heart on fire—and you can't put out the blaze.

November 3

ASTROLOGICAL SIGN: Scorpio
PEOPLE BORN TODAY: Roseanne, Dennis Miller, Phil Simms, Larry Holmes, Tom Shales, Michael Dukakis, Mike Espy, André Malraux
FAMOUS EVENTS: John Adams elected president (1796); Laika becomes first animal launched into space, by the U.S.S.R. (1957); Arkansas governor Bill Clinton elected president (1992)
LUCKY NUMBER: 5
BIRTHSTONE: Topaz
POSITIVE TRAITS: Stimulating, assertive, progressive
NEGATIVE TRAITS: Confrontational, bossy, volatile

You require resistance to gain strength. Dissatisfaction is your natural state, and setting things right on the job, at home, and in society is your mission. Others count on you to be an assertive spokesperson and agent for change, working to better conditions for them as well as yourself. Though you have trouble putting your confrontational ways aside when dealing with loved ones, your basic goodwill can carry the day. You're a great entertainer; friends and family congregate at your place, enjoying your hospitality and the lively ambience of your home. Your ideal mate will be able to match your mental acuity and be as fearless as you are in any verbal showdown. Because you want your love to last, it does.

ASTROLOGICAL SIGN: Scorpio
PEOPLE BORN TODAY: Ralph Macchio, Markie Post, Joe Niekro, Art Carney, Walter Cronkite, Robert Mapplethorpe, Yanni, Sam Shepard, Will Rogers
FAMOUS EVENTS: First fashion show, hosted by *Vogue*, in New York City (1914); Dwight D. Eisenhower elected president (1952); hostages seized by revolutionaries at U.S. Embassy in Iran (1979)
LUCKY NUMBER: 6
BIRTHSTONE: Topaz
POSITIVE TRAITS: Creative, tender, empathetic
NEGATIVE TRAITS: Interfering, overoptimistic, obtuse

Difficult situations that would make others run a mile often prove irresistible for you. You are lured into the tangled webs woven by colleagues and friends, and trust in your magic touch to help unravel their problems. You can indeed be an effective problem solver at home and in the workplace, but you must not overestimate your ability to help or other people's desire to enlist it. An empathetic friend, you experience your companions' emotional highs and lows right along with them and offer all the support you can muster. Your quickness to jump into conversations and social situations maximizes your opportunities for romance, and your tender heart will help you hold on to a mate. Learn to give assistance generously, but wait until it's requested.

November 5

ASTROLOGICAL SIGN: Scorpio

PEOPLE BORN TODAY: Tatum O'Neal, Bryan Adams, Bill Walton, Joel McCrea, Vivien Leigh, Art Garfunkel, Roy Rogers

FAMOUS EVENTS: Susan B. Anthony fined for attempting to vote (1872); Sinclair Lewis becomes first American to win the Nobel Prize for Literature (1930); first FM radio broadcast transmitted (1955)

LUCKY NUMBER: 7

BIRTHSTONE: Topaz

POSITIVE TRAITS: Skillful, innovative, ambitious

NEGATIVE TRAITS: Overaccommodating, self-effacing, reticent

You radiate a bright light, which you are all too often trying to dim. Though you possess the skill, creativity, and poise to be recognized as a star in your own right, you tend to take a backseat to someone you consider—rightly or wrongly—to be your superior. It can take a crisis or change of heart to make you step up to the plate and show your stuff. Friends recognize your special qualities, but you shift the focus to their talents and ambitions, spurring them on to the kind of achievements you dream of yourself. In romance, finding a partner you consider ideal can actually be a setback if you defer too often to his or her wishes. Find a partner who spurs *you* on.

November 6

ASTROLOGICAL SIGN: Scorpio

PEOPLE BORN TODAY: Maria Shriver, Sally Field, Lori Singer, Glenn Frey, Mike Nichols, John Philip Sousa, John Falsey, Lance Kerwin

FAMOUS EVENTS: Abraham Lincoln elected president (1860); suicide by arsenic poisoning of Peter Ilich Tchaikovsky (1893); Ella Grasso of Connecticut becomes first woman elected governor without succeeding husband (1974)

LUCKY NUMBER: 8

BIRTHSTONE: Topaz

POSITIVE TRAITS: Determined, energetic, positive

NEGATIVE TRAITS: Driven, obedient, unsure

You may ride a long way on someone else's steam before getting in the conductor's car. You are an energetic overachiever whose accomplishments suggest a great inner drive, but your impetus to succeed is likely to be the influence of a mentor. You may need to come to a complete stop temporarily to determine what your own goals are; once you do, you'll be back on track, charging forth more forcefully than ever. You are a role model for friends, sharing your positive mental attitude with them as well as constructive advice. Your golden aura of success makes you sought-after by romantic partners who hope some of your winning spirit will rub off. You will thrive with a mate who encourages you to think for yourself.

November 7

ASTROLOGICAL SIGN: Scorpio

PEOPLE BORN TODAY: Joni Mitchell, Joan Sutherland, Al Hirt, Billy Graham, Albert Camus, Marie Curie, Johnny Rivers

FAMOUS EVENTS: Jeannette Rankin first woman elected to Congress (1916); Carl Stokes of Cleveland elected first African-American mayor of major city (1967); announcement of retirement by Magic Johnson following positive test for HIV (1991)

LUCKY NUMBER: 9

BIRTHSTONE: Topaz

POSITIVE TRAITS: Precise, masterful, entertaining

NEGATIVE TRAITS: Preoccupied, excessive, cool

Getting things right matters more to you than making others happy. You don't intentionally ignore people, but your pursuit of excellence at any cost can put off many of your less driven associates. You carry out your responsibilities on the job or at home with precision—and with laudable results. Though friends and family are resigned to your detached and sometimes hermitlike methods, they know and love your flip side: the fun side. When you break loose, you're a hoot. You can be the life of the party, whether you're clowning at a child's birthday party or enchanting adults at a social event. Unfortunately, you don't break loose nearly enough; the right partner can see to it that both sides of your personality are given equal playing time.

November 8

ASTROLOGICAL SIGN: Scorpio

PEOPLE BORN TODAY: Rickie Lee Jones, Christie Hefner, Mary Hart, Bonnie Raitt, Leon Trotsky, Morley Safer, Margaret Mitchell, Alain Delon, Katharine Hepburn

FAMOUS EVENTS: Louvre art museum opens in Paris (1793); Montana becomes 41st state (1889); first X ray, by William Roentgen (1895); John F. Kennedy elected first Catholic president (1960)

LUCKY NUMBER: 1

BIRTHSTONE: Topaz

POSITIVE TRAITS: Reliable, driven, talented

NEGATIVE TRAITS: Needy, repressed, reticent

Glory, rather than material rewards, is what propels you onward and upward. You may effect a quirky or eccentric style as a way to distinguish yourself, but it isn't necessary: Your natural talents will win you the approval and admiration you crave from others. Though you've proven your reliability time and again, you warn your friends not to count on you because you don't want to risk failing them. Romantic partners are drawn to your air of freewheeling independence, yet once enmeshed in a relationship you are likely to put your mate's priorities ahead of your own. Getting in touch with what makes you happy will help you internalize the independent spirit you wear on your sleeve—but not in your heart.

ASTROLOGICAL SIGN: Scorpio

PEOPLE BORN TODAY: Tom Fogerty, Carl Sagan, Spiro Agnew, Hedy Lamarr, Clifton Webb, Stanford White, Anne Sexton

FAMOUS EVENTS: Northeast darkened by major blackout (1965); first issue of *Rolling Stone* published (1967); demolition of Berlin Wall begins (1989)

LUCKY NUMBER: 2

BIRTHSTONE: Topaz

POSITIVE TRAITS: Practical, earthy, generous

NEGATIVE TRAITS: Overcautious, tame, unromantic

You believe in only that which you can see, hear, and touch, disregarding all rumors and speculation, and putting little stock in your intuition. You won't decide any personal or professional matter until all the evidence is in front of you, in neatly labeled exhibits. Practicality wins you respect, although your cautious nature can prevent you from seizing the opportunities that lie directly in your path. Friends turn to you when they need a reality check; you help them keep their feet firmly on the ground. Romantic partners find you reassuringly reliable, if less than romantic. In the security of a long-term love relationship, you reveal your earthy sensuality and provide a stable emotional and financial base for your mate and family.

November 10

ASTROLOGICAL SIGN: Scorpio

PEOPLE BORN TODAY: Sinbad, Jack Scalia, Ann Reinking, Roy Scheider, Richard Burton, Martin Luther

FAMOUS EVENTS: First motorcycle ride, by Paul Daimler (1885); first episode of *Sesame Street* airs (1969); Vincent van Gogh's painting, *Irises*, sells for $53.9 million (1987)

LUCKY NUMBER: 3

BIRTHSTONE: Topaz

POSITIVE TRAITS: Confident, sociable, perceptive

NEGATIVE TRAITS: Self-satisfied, judgmental, limited

You operate with assurance from your personal power base. You use your social skills to cultivate a far-flung network of business and personal contacts and work it like a switchboard for your own benefits and that of your family and friends. Though you attain a measure of success with relative ease, your progress can be limited by your tendency to rest on your laurels. You need stimulation, challenge, and change to spur you toward personal growth and professional accomplishment. You seldom take anything at face value, relying instead on your keen perceptions to get beneath the surface of people and situations. You are a devoted mate, and take a great deal of pleasure in ensuring that your home is a beautiful feast for all the senses.

November 11

ASTROLOGICAL SIGN: Scorpio

PEOPLE BORN TODAY: Leonardo DiCaprio, Demi Moore, Fuzzy Zoeller, Jonathan Winters, Kurt Vonnegut Jr., Gen. George Patton, Fyodor Dostoyevsky

FAMOUS EVENTS: Washington becomes the 42nd state (1889); Armistice signed ending World War I (1918); Tomb of the Unknown Soldier dedicated at Arlington Cemetery (1920)

LUCKY NUMBER: 4

BIRTHSTONE: Topaz

POSITIVE TRAITS: Charismatic, generous, strong

NEGATIVE TRAITS: Bossy, manipulative, unaware

Your compelling personality inspires cooperation, but if you underestimate your natural charisma, you may resort to unnecessary forcefulness. Veiling your naked ambition may be the smartest strategy for winning others to your point of view. You are slow to welcome acquaintances into your circle of intimates, but develop an almost proprietary attitude toward them once you do. Though you can't resist enlisting your friends to help you with work or home projects, you pay them back in kind—and more. You're generous (too generous, sometimes) with money and few people are as open to new experiences as you are. Friends find your company stimulating; you're the first one consulted when a celebration is in the works. You may take some tumbles in love, but the bruises won't last.

November 12

ASTROLOGICAL SIGN: Scorpio

PEOPLE BORN TODAY: Tevin Campbell, Tonya Harding, Nadia Comaneci, Neil Young, Booker T. Jones, Princess Grace of Monaco

FAMOUS EVENTS: Judge Kenesaw Landis elected first commissioner of baseball (1920); first sighting of Nessie, the Loch Ness monster (1933); first space shuttle, *Columbia*, launched (1981)

LUCKY NUMBER: 5

BIRTHSTONE: Topaz

POSITIVE TRAITS: Daring, sassy, fun

NEGATIVE TRAITS: Amoral, uncommitted, troubling

You have a strong sense of entitlement that makes you feel whatever you want is right simply because it is you who wants it. You are tempted to flaunt convention, believing that the ends justify the means. Success may depend on how far you go in your rebellion and how discreetly you bend the rules. While you risk censure from some, friends and family admire your boldness and imagination and provide plenty of moral support. Your personal magnetism and outlaw sensibility are irresistible to romantic partners, though you may find it hard to commit yourself irrevocably to a mate, closing your eyes to other attractive possibilities. Conserve your energy and avoid unnecessary trouble by writing off past injustices and focusing on future opportunities.

November 13

ASTROLOGICAL SIGN: Scorpio

PEOPLE BORN TODAY: Whoopi Goldberg, Joe Mantegna, Vinny Testaverde, Garry Marshall, Madeleine Sherwood, Jean Seberg, Robert Louis Stevenson

FAMOUS EVENTS: Holland Tunnel, first underwater tunnel for auto traffic, opens, in New York City (1927); Walt Disney's *Fantasia* premieres (1940); Vietnam Veterans Memorial dedicated, in Washington, D.C. (1982)

LUCKY NUMBER: 6

BIRTHSTONE: Topaz

POSITIVE TRAITS: Interested, curious, engaged

NEGATIVE TRAITS: Scattered, interfering, frustrated

You overflow with enthusiasm for everything and everyone that crosses your path. If you focus your efforts, your insatiable curiosity and keen intelligence can make you an effective leader. If you scatter your energies and get left out of the loop, however, you're likely to become frustrated, and overlook even the most obvious opportunities. You make friends easily and eagerly offer them help and advice, which they soon learn to value and depend on. Casual acquaintances may consider you a busybody, but close companions know the worth of your friendship. Romantic partners take an immediate liking to you, though they may wish to claim more of your attention and affection than you are used to concentrating on any one person. Try harder; you can't lose.

November 14

ASTROLOGICAL SIGN: Scorpio

PEOPLE BORN TODAY: Charles, Prince of Wales, Boutros Boutros-Ghali, Brian Keith, McLean Stevenson, Aaron Copland, Claude Monet

FAMOUS EVENTS: Streetcar debuts, in New York City (1832); *Moby Dick* published, by Harper & Brothers (1851); Atlanta burns (1864)

LUCKY NUMBER: 7

BIRTHSTONE: Topaz

POSITIVE TRAITS: Kind, understanding, sensual

NEGATIVE TRAITS: Detached, hurtful, restless

You regard your fellow human beings with the affectionate detachment of an entomologist spotting a favorite insect. You make a broad study of human nature and relate to everyone on an almost entirely intellectual level. Though you are capable of genuine kindness, you play down your emotions and have been known to lack sensitivity to the feelings of others. You like life on the go; new people and new experiences fuel your imagination and provide you with an endless repertoire of stories, which you relate with the wit and charm of a born raconteur. Romantic partners find you amusing, sophisticated, and satisfyingly sensual, which, in the short run, compensates for your emotional reticence. For the long run, you'll have to get in touch with your feelings.

November 15

ASTROLOGICAL SIGN: Scorpio
PEOPLE BORN TODAY: Kevin Eubanks, Beverly D'Angelo, Sam Waterston, Petula Clark, Edward Asner, Georgia O'Keeffe, Marianne Moore
FAMOUS EVENTS: Free postal delivery begins (1869); first radio broadcast by National Broadcasting Company (1926); cornerstone of Jefferson Memorial laid by President Franklin D. Roosevelt (1939)
LUCKY NUMBER: 8
BIRTHSTONE: Topaz
POSITIVE TRAITS: Protective, courageous, loving
NEGATIVE TRAITS: Smothering, wary, contentious

You have an incendiary temper that is most often inflamed by injustices done to others. You respond to personal slights with the merest grumble or snarl, but act aggressively to defend coworkers, friends, or family members who are under attack. You are willing to put your own security on the line for the interests of others. Friends may protest that your efforts are unnecessary, but they enjoy your protectiveness, if only because it indicates how deeply you care. Though you affirm that romantic partners are on the side of the angels before you entrust them with your affections, you demonstrate unshakable loyalty to a treasured mate. Reserve the full force of your fury for situations that warrant it; don't break out the big guns when a flyswatter will do.

November 16

ASTROLOGICAL SIGN: Scorpio

PEOPLE BORN TODAY: Martha Plimpton, Lisa Bonet, Dwight Gooden, Zina Garrison, Burgess Meredith, W. C. Handy, Bo Derek, George S. Kaufman

FAMOUS EVENTS: Oklahoma becomes the 45th state (1907); NBA rebound record set by Bill Russell (1957); construction of Alaska oil pipeline authorized by President Richard Nixon (1969)

LUCKY NUMBER: 9

BIRTHSTONE: Topaz

POSITIVE TRAITS: Challenging, seeking, truthful

NEGATIVE TRAITS: Tactless, judgmental, jumpy

You are quick to criticize standard operating procedures and eager to institute new and better ways of doing things. Though you often find upholders of convention narrow in their thinking, your scope can be equally limited if it takes in only the most radical possibilities. Nevertheless, your reforming spirit has its roots in a genuine desire to do good, and change for its own sake holds little allure for you. You socialize with a forward-thinking group of friends, and as you get older you may lean toward the company of younger, or at least young-thinking, companions. You draw romantic partners from the same progressive pool, though you may benefit from a long-term relationship with a mate who is slightly slower-moving without being stodgy.

November 17

ASTROLOGICAL SIGN: Scorpio

PEOPLE BORN TODAY: Mary Elizabeth Mastrantonio, Martin Scorsese, Danny DeVito, Lauren Hutton, Tom Seaver, Peter Cook, Rock Hudson

FAMOUS EVENTS: Lyndon Baines Johnson and Claudia "Lady Bird" Taylor wed (1934); NBC broadcast of Jets-Raiders game cut off by movie *Heidi*, creating fan uproar (1968); President Richard Nixon proclaims his innocence in Watergate affair (1973)

LUCKY NUMBER: 1

BIRTHSTONE: Topaz

POSITIVE TRAITS: Charming, effective, capable

NEGATIVE TRAITS: Sober, strict, controlling

Your breezy charm and lighthearted humor are your most apparent assets, but you have much more substantial qualities to offer. If given the chance to set the agenda at work or at home, you demonstrate how responsible and efficient you can be, impressing those who thought your only skills were social ones. Coworkers and friends don't mind looking to you as a leader, but you can turn them off by becoming too strict and controlling when you wear your all-business hat. Aim for balance by being pleasant without being a pushover. Letting your sunny side shine can bring romantic partners flocking to your warmth; and you can pleasantly surprise a mate with your level-headed ability to organize social gatherings and plan for your shared future.

November 18

ASTROLOGICAL SIGN: Scorpio

PEOPLE BORN TODAY: Kevin Nealon, Warren Moon, Linda Evans, Alan B. Shepard, Johnny Mercer, W. S. Gilbert, Margaret Atwood

FAMOUS EVENTS: Antarctica discovered by Capt. Nathaniel Palmer (1820); first drawing of Mickey Mouse executed (1928); film *Ben Hur* premieres (1959)

LUCKY NUMBER: 2

BIRTHSTONE: Topaz

POSITIVE TRAITS: Distinctive, entertaining, sparkling

NEGATIVE TRAITS: Needy, overshadowing, competitive

You are most at home in a group, not blending seamlessly into the picture but counting on others to frame you to best advantage. True ensemble efforts at work or in social situations fail to gratify your need for star treatment. You seek out crowds in which you are likely to stand out, though you would rather not bear the burdens of a leadership role. Your constant grab for the spotlight would alienate your friends if you weren't so vivacious and fun to be with. You can be an exceptionally responsive, sexy, and romantic partner, as long as your mate makes you feel cherished and coddled. Cultivate a giving mindset: There is enough attention and affection for everyone and your emotional generosity can only add to the supply.

November 19

ASTROLOGICAL SIGN: Scorpio

PEOPLE BORN TODAY: Jodie Foster, Meg Ryan, Sharon Olds, Dick Cavett, Indira Gandhi, Ahmad Rashad, Calvin Klein, Ted Turner, Larry King, Roy Campanella

FAMOUS EVENTS: Gettysburg Address delivered by President Abraham Lincoln (1863); second manned Moon landing made by *Apollo XII* (1969); mass suicide in Guyana, by cult followers of Rev. Jim Jones (1978)

LUCKY NUMBER: 3

BIRTHSTONE: Topaz

POSITIVE TRAITS: Worldly, ambitious, secure

NEGATIVE TRAITS: Overworked, preoccupied, difficult

Home may be where your heart is, but your energies are focused out in the world. Your natural confidence and clarity of vision make you well suited to take or share the lead, and your independent temperament gives you little enthusiasm for working toward goals set by others. Your friends are likely to be fellow achievers whose verve and wit are a match for your own formidable physical and mental energy. Your focused lifestyle leaves little room for casual relationships, so you like to set aside time to cultivate a romantic union that will require little ongoing attention once it takes root. Though your outside endeavors are the source of your greatest satisfaction, a stable domestic situation and a loving, but independent, mate round out your happiness.

ASTROLOGICAL SIGN: Scorpio

PEOPLE BORN TODAY: Sean Young, Veronica Hamel, Dick Smothers, Richard Dawson, Alistair Cooke, Robert F. Kennedy, Duane Allman, Gene Tierney, Nadine Gordimer

FAMOUS EVENTS: Peregrine White, first child of Plymouth colony, born aboard the *Mayflower* (1620); Princess Elizabeth and Philip Mountbatten wed (1947); Windsor Castle damaged by fire (1992)

LUCKY NUMBER: 4

BIRTHSTONE: Topaz

POSITIVE TRAITS: Assertive, articulate, fun-loving

NEGATIVE TRAITS: Blunt, tough, naive

You're a born fighter who's not afraid to stand up for what's right, even if you stand alone. You present your case forcefully yet articulately to the people in charge and openly thumb your nose at those in authority if you deem them unworthy of your respect, which can decidedly slow your ascent to the top and curtail your effectiveness. Your bluntness can cost you casual acquaintances, but the companions who can withstand your candid appraisal find it a reasonable price for an unfailingly honest and devoted friend. And besides, you are not all fight: you're fun too. Romantic partners don't impress you easily, and you'd rather go it alone than settle for a mate who is any less solid and honorable than yourself.

November 21

ASTROLOGICAL SIGN: Scorpio

PEOPLE BORN TODAY: Mariel Hemingway, Ken Griffey Jr., Goldie Hawn, Tina Brown, Marlo Thomas, Marilyn French, Stan Musial, Voltaire, Troy Aikman, Rene Magritte

FAMOUS EVENTS: First free-flight balloon trip made (1783); phonograph invented by Thomas Edison (1877); Mick Jagger and Jerry Hall wed (1990)

LUCKY NUMBER: 5

BIRTHSTONE: Topaz

POSITIVE TRAITS: Discriminating, attractive, imaginative

NEGATIVE TRAITS: Workaholic, unaware, clumsy

You're an innovator blessed with infinite patience and determination. Around the house, you're a miracle worker, creating a stylish and comfortable abode from even the most meager materials. In the workplace, you're a dynamo, knowing exactly the right moment to introduce a new idea and successfully organizing others to carry it out. Even when someone else is in the driver's seat, you manage to steer everyone in your desired direction. People want to please you, not just because your ideas appeal to them but because your enthusiasm is catching and your motivation is evident: You want everyone to share in your success. True love can be yours for the taking: Just be sure you're not so busy giving that you miss your opportunity.

November 22

ASTROLOGICAL SIGN: Scorpio

PEOPLE BORN TODAY: Jamie Lee Curtis, Tina Weymouth, Billie Jean King, Terry Gilliam, Ruth Breed Stark, Hoagy Carmichael, Mary Ann Evans (George Eliot), Boris Becker, Charles de Gaulle

FAMOUS EVENTS: National Hockey League established (1917); Elijah Muhammad founds the Nation of Islam, in Detroit (1930); President John F. Kennedy assassinated in Dallas (1963)

LUCKY NUMBER: 6

BIRTHSTONE: Topaz

POSITIVE TRAITS: Refreshing, exciting, innovative

NEGATIVE TRAITS: Rebellious, perverse, excessive

You're more than a breath of fresh air—you're a gust of wind strong enough to knock others off their feet. You have difficulty taking orders and tend to challenge authority or limited thinking whenever you encounter it. Your rebellious spirit can get you labeled a troublemaker in highly structured environments; you work best independently, with lots of room for creative choice. Your friends can claim in you a surefire antidote to boredom, though the more complacent types may resist your pressuring them to imitate your footloose ways. You're an exciting romantic partner who doesn't mind committing to a mate as long as you get to dictate the terms. Do whatever you must to keep life fresh, but don't toss anything out before you're sure it's stale.

November 23

ASTROLOGICAL SIGN: Sagittarius

PEOPLE BORN TODAY: Bruce Hornsby, Maxwell Caulfield, Billy the Kid, Steve Landesberg, Franklin Pierce, Luis Tiant, Boris Karloff, Harpo Marx

FAMOUS EVENTS: First jukebox installed, in San Francisco (1899); Metropolitan Opera debut of Enrico Caruso (1903); first issue of *Life* magazine published (1936)

LUCKY NUMBER: 7

BIRTHSTONE: Turquoise

POSITIVE TRAITS: Amusing, independent, discerning

NEGATIVE TRAITS: Critical, detached, unconscious

Whether you are leading a seminar or writing a letter, you get it right: Words are your favored medium, your weapon, your olive branch, and your love line. You know how to think on your feet, and your wit and grace in the workplace and at social events makes you a valued employee and sought-after guest. Usually, however, it is you who does the inviting: You have a knack for making people comfortable in your house and an RSVP in the negative is almost unheard of. Children take to you immediately, intuitively recognizing a seriously playful cohort. Romantic partners may feel under siege if your sweet talk isn't backed up by deeper, more substantial communication, but not to worry—it will be.

ASTROLOGICAL SIGN: Sagittarius

PEOPLE BORN TODAY: Steve Yeager, Pete Best, Oscar Robertson, William F. Buckley Jr., Scott Joplin, Lucky Luciano, Toulouse-Lautrec, Carry Nation

FAMOUS EVENTS: First edition (1,250 copies) of Charles Darwin's *Origin of Species* sells out in one day (1859); barbed wire patented by Joseph Glidden (1874); Kennedy assassin Lee Harvey Oswald shot dead by Jack Ruby (1963)

LUCKY NUMBER: 8

BIRTHSTONE: Turquoise

POSITIVE TRAITS: Lively, deep, social

NEGATIVE TRAITS: Restless, contentious, challenging

Whether conducting a civilized debate or engaging in a spirited argument, you relish the opportunity to influence other people's thinking. Currents of popular opinion wash over you with little effect; you formulate your positions based on a thorough examination of all the information at your disposal and once your mind is made up, it stays that way. You find issues more compelling than personalities, but you have a knack for reading the emotional signals sent out to you by friends and loved ones. You enjoy circulating at social events and making conversation with stimulating people, and your lively intellectual curiosity can be exciting to romantic partners. A mate who wishes to settle into a mindlessly comfortable routine will be thwarted by your insistence on living a thoroughly examined life.

November 25

ASTROLOGICAL SIGN: Sagittarius

PEOPLE BORN TODAY: John F. Kennedy Jr., Christina Applegate, Virgil Thomson, Bucky Dent, John Larroquette, Joe DiMaggio, Andrew Carnegie, Zachary Taylor

FAMOUS EVENTS: Dynamite patented by Alfred Nobel (1867); *Christian Science Monitor* debuts (1908); King Tutankhamen's tomb opened (1922)

LUCKY NUMBER: 9

BIRTHSTONE: Turquoise

POSITIVE TRAITS: Intense, even, masterful

NEGATIVE TRAITS: Demanding, intense, judgmental

You make it your business to learn every single aspect of anything important to you. When you turn your attention to an important task, no detail escapes your notice and you are willing to take all the time necessary to complete your project perfectly. Striking a balance is crucial to you: You scrutinize your emotions with the same intensity that you bring to your intellectual endeavors. Friends can find you intimidatingly fierce about the most trivial matters, but your ability to laugh at yourself wins them over every time. Your masterful air impresses romantic partners, but your mate will need steady nerves not to be rattled by your steady scrutiny. Struggle for excellence, but keep in mind that sometimes good really is good enough.

November 26

ASTROLOGICAL SIGN: Sagittarius

PEOPLE BORN TODAY: John McVie, Wendy Turnbull, Tina Turner, Rich Little, Robert Goulet, Charles M. Schulz, Eugene Ionesco, Eric Sevareid

FAMOUS EVENTS: First national Thanksgiving Day celebrated (1789); film classic *Casablanca* premieres (1942); first TV dinner marketed (1954)

LUCKY NUMBER: 1

BIRTHSTONE: Turquoise

POSITIVE TRAITS: Companionable, iconoclastic, intuitive

NEGATIVE TRAITS: Vague, undirected, argumentative

You know intuitively what you don't want; what you do want is less obvious to you. Multiple abilities and talents could be part of the problem: Many paths are open to you. Because you are project oriented, you tend to find yourself at loose ends if you are not working toward a goal. You're creative and good with your hands, and your home reflects these talents. Though you have a wide circle of friends with whom you socialize regularly, you are on an intimate basis with only one or two. You don't reveal yourself easily and it takes you a long time to trust; and an even longer time to recover from a broken trust. Nevertheless, when cupid strikes, you succumb.

November 27

ASTROLOGICAL SIGN: Sagittarius
PEOPLE BORN TODAY: Jaleel White, Caroline Kennedy, Eddie Rabbitt, Robin Givens, Buffalo Bob Smith, Jimi Hendrix, James Agee, Bruce Lee
FAMOUS EVENTS: First permit to drive a car in Central Park granted (1889); Joe DiMaggio voted MVP for third time (1947); San Francisco mayor George Moscone and supervisor Harvey Milk murdered at City Hall (1978)
LUCKY NUMBER: 2
BIRTHSTONE: Turquoise
POSITIVE TRAITS: Enthusiastic, affectionate, high-spirited
NEGATIVE TRAITS: Unrealistic, hasty, naive

You greet every new idea with the enthusiasm of a puppy, and sometimes end up with your tail between your legs when your enthusiasm overrules your common sense. You trust your instincts and they frequently pay off; just as frequently, however, they don't. No matter what setbacks result from your failed ventures, they fail to make a dent in the armor you wear against cynicism. Your buoyant spirits make you the life of every party, and your trusting, affectionate nature earns you plenty of friends. You idealize love partners and may rush into relationships too hastily for your own good. A mate whose sterling qualities are still evident when the romantic haze clears will provide the steady support you can rely on when your dreams go poof.

November 28

ASTROLOGICAL SIGN: Sagittarius

PEOPLE BORN TODAY: Ed Harris, Paul Shaffer, Randy Newman, Gary Hart, Hope Lange, Berry Gordy Jr., William Blake, Rita Mae Brown

FAMOUS EVENTS: First American auto race begins (1895); Grand Ole Opry debuts on radio (1925); meeting to plan Allied assault in Europe begun by Roosevelt, Churchill, and Stalin (1943)

LUCKY NUMBER: 3

BIRTHSTONE: Turquoise

POSITIVE TRAITS: Caring, deep, sensitive

NEGATIVE TRAITS: Vacillating, distant, insecure

You vacillate between earnestly pursuing your ambitions and mocking them, constantly adjusting your emotional distance in order to fend off the pain and disappointment you might encounter should you fail to achieve them. This approach can leave people guessing what you really want, and even though they recognize your formidable talents, they will be stymied in helping you toward your goals. Friends consider you an entertaining enigma, though your true intimates recognize your defense mechanisms and do their best to build up your confidence in your abilities. Your distancing act can keep romantic partners at arm's length, but in a committed relationship you succumb to your passionate nature and indulge in your love for all things romantic. Like your friends say, you're a winner.

November 29

ASTROLOGICAL SIGN: Sagittarius

PEOPLE BORN TODAY: Andrew McCarthy, Cathy Moriarty, Howie Mandel, Louisa May Alcott, Garry Shandling, Suzy Chaffee, Chuck Mangione, C. S. Lewis, Adam Clayton Powell Jr., Diane Ladd

FAMOUS EVENTS: Invisible ink first used, by Silas Deane (1775); first flight over South Pole completed, by Richard Byrd (1929); Warren Commission established to investigate JFK assassination (1963)

LUCKY NUMBER: 4

BIRTHSTONE: Turquoise

POSITIVE TRAITS: Brave, daring, uncompromising

NEGATIVE TRAITS: Shocking, controversial, agitating

Sometimes it seems as though your mere presence is enough to stir up controversy. Your opinions tend to be controversial and you have never been good at keeping them to yourself. Going your own way is not for you; you thrive on interacting with others and are equally content with positive or negative reactions; what matters is that people do react. Conversely, you enjoy solitude, in which you read, write, or do nothing. Because your abundant energy keeps you fired up, exercise is *de rigueur* for your overall well-being. In love, you will be happiest with a partner who can appreciate your need for a lively and animated relationship and at the same time lead you through the pleasures of heightened intimacy, emotional as well as sensual.

November 30

ASTROLOGICAL SIGN: Sagittarius

PEOPLE BORN TODAY: Bo Jackson, Mandy Patinkin, David Mamet, Abbie Hoffman, Dick Clark, Sir Winston Churchill, Mark Twain, Jonathan Swift,

FAMOUS EVENTS: First international soccer match (1872); engagement of Julie Nixon and David Eisenhower announced (1967); RJR Nabisco obtained by Kohlberg Kravis Roberts in record $24 billion takeover (1988)

LUCKY NUMBER: 5

BIRTHSTONE: Turquoise

POSITIVE TRAITS: Versatile, humorous, youthful

NEGATIVE TRAITS: Touchy, proud, oversensitive

You have so many ambitions and abilities that it would take several lifetimes for you to fulfill your potential. This time around, you content yourself with pursuing your passions, either simultaneously or in succession. Your sense of responsibility ensures that you finish one task, giving it your complete energy and concentration, before moving on to the next. Your wide range of interests and impish sense of humor make you a delightful friend, though your intimates learn that they must sometimes tiptoe around your ego, which is more fragile than it appears to be. Your ever-growing list of accomplishments, and even longer list of plans, impresses potential partners, but if you want a lasting love, you will have to concentrate some of that formidable energy on your intended.

December 1

ASTROLOGICAL SIGN: Sagittarius

PEOPLE BORN TODAY: Carol Alt, Bette Midler, Richard Pryor, Lee Trevino, Woody Allen, Mary Martin

FAMOUS EVENTS: First service station opens, in Pittsburgh (1913); Boys' Town founded by Father Flanagan (1917); Monopoly board game introduced (1935); Rosa Parks arrested for refusing to sit in back of Montgomery, Alabama, bus (1955)

LUCKY NUMBER: 4

BIRTHSTONE: Turquoise

POSITIVE TRAITS: Dynamic, colorful, outgoing

NEGATIVE TRAITS: Confused, outrageous, excessive

You are an irrepressible bundle of energy who delights in raising eyebrows. Others are drawn to your outrageous wit and charm, and they often count on you to be the life of the party, but although you radiate self-esteem, privately you crave reassurances from friends and family. Your natural vitality attracts many romantic partners, but proceed slowly and be truthful to yourself about what you really want in a love relationship. Looking for stability and discipline in your life, you are likely to choose a mate who plays a parental role in your life. Set aside time for quiet reflection: A life in the spotlight may seem exciting and limitless, but true fulfillment requires a clear focus on personal goals.

ASTROLOGICAL SIGN: Sagittarius

PEOPLE BORN TODAY: Monica Seles, Stone Phillips, William Wegman, Julie Harris, Maria Callas, Alexander Haig Jr., Gianni Versace

FAMOUS EVENTS: Napoleon Bonaparte crowned emperor of France (1804); abolitionist John Brown hanged (1859); first successful artificial heart implant performed (1982)

LUCKY NUMBER: 5

BIRTHSTONE: Turquoise

POSITIVE TRAITS: Intense, passionate, demonstrative

NEGATIVE TRAITS: Intimidating, uncontrolled, hot-headed

You tend to wear your thoughts and emotions on your sleeve: While others equivocate, you say what you mean, and usually get results. This honesty can be refreshing, but be careful not to trample on the feelings of those around you. Your energy and drive make you an excellent leader and an inspiration to friends and coworkers, especially if you learn to balance your outspokenness with some tact and delicacy. Making a good first impression comes easily to you: Follow up initial contacts with solid action for the best results. You are a hotly passionate mate who argues and reconciles with equal fervor. To safeguard your domestic bliss, practice taking a few deep breaths whenever you feel like blowing your top.

December 3

ASTROLOGICAL SIGN: Sagittarius

PEOPLE BORN TODAY: Anna Chlumsky, Katarina Witt, Ozzy Osbourne, Rick Mears, Jean-Luc Godard, Ferlin Husky,

FAMOUS EVENTS: First marriage annulment granted (1639); first coed college opens, Oberlin (1833); first Technicolor film premieres (1922); first successful heart transplant performed (1967)

LUCKY NUMBER: 6

BIRTHSTONE: Turquoise

POSITIVE TRAITS: Dedicated, driven, intense

NEGATIVE TRAITS: Difficult, unorthodox, distracted

Face it: When you set your mind to accomplishing an objective, you're unstoppable. You tend to seek out others with similar passions and consequently have little time for pure socializing. Meeting your own high standards usually means more to you than winning points with the higher-ups, but don't forget how to be a team player. Though your unorthodox methods may startle others at first, your perseverance will usually win them over to your side. Romantic partners are fascinated by your intensity and will practically stand on their heads to get you to focus it on them. Be choosy: Your long-term mate should be that rare individual who respects your independence but lends you moral support when you need it.

December 4

ASTROLOGICAL SIGN: Sagittarius

PEOPLE BORN TODAY: Marisa Tomei, Bernard King, Patricia Wettig, Jeff Bridges, Wink Martindale, Lillian Russell, Rainer Maria Rilke

FAMOUS EVENTS: Elvis Presley, Carl Perkins, Johnny Cash, and Jerry Lee Lewis record at Sun Records (1956); world's longest airplane flight embarked upon (1958); U.S. Army and Marine forces dispatched to Somalia by President George Bush (1992)

LUCKY NUMBER: 7

BIRTHSTONE: Turquoise

POSITIVE TRAITS: Disciplined, gregarious, spunky

NEGATIVE TRAITS: Pushy, overexcited, undirected

You display tremendous self-control in both professional and social settings, successfully mastering your emotions without losing your thirst for adventure. Your eagerness to share the secrets of your success with everyone around you is commendable, but don't strain your vocal chords: Actions speak more loudly than words. Friends and coworkers admire your perpetual optimism, and it's bound to rub off on them eventually. In both your work and your personal affairs, you boldly forge ahead with new projects, and yet you have the guts to admit your mistakes when your gambles don't pay off. Focus on give-and-take in love matters: You can be an exciting romantic partner, as long as your energy level doesn't overwhelm that of your mate.

December 5

ASTROLOGICAL SIGN: Sagittarius

PEOPLE BORN TODAY: Jose Carreras, Jim Messina, Calvin Trillin, Joan Didion, Little Richard, Walt Disney, Christina Rossetti, Fritz Lang, Art Monk

FAMOUS EVENTS: Death of Wolfgang Amadeus Mozart (1791); reports of California gold strike confirmed by President James Polk, prompting gold rush (1848); Prohibition repealed (1933)

LUCKY NUMBER: 8

BIRTHSTONE: Turquoise

POSITIVE TRAITS: Visionary, energetic, self-assured

NEGATIVE TRAITS: Inflated, unreasonable, conceited

You dare to tackle projects most people wouldn't even consider. In work and in your personal life, you seem to set impossible goals, but with a little extra stretch you usually nab what you're after. As the star of your own show, you prefer to work alone rather than with a team. This solo performance lets you shine in the spotlight, but it may also leave you exhausted. Treat yourself now and then: Let friends or coworkers take the reins periodically so you can rest up for the next big challenge. Your stubborn but endearing belief in happy endings makes you a passionate romantic partner: Don't lose that dream! Constant striving for a better way of life keeps you youthful and energized.

December 6

ASTROLOGICAL SIGN: Sagittarius

PEOPLE BORN TODAY: Janine Turner, Peter Buck, Steven Wright, Tom Hulce, Agnes Moorehead, Ira Gershwin

FAMOUS EVENTS: First sound recording made by Thomas Edison (1877); first presidential address broadcast on radio, by President Calvin Coolidge (1923); murder at Altamont speedway concert, during Rolling Stones performance (1969)

LUCKY NUMBER: 9

BIRTHSTONE: Turquoise

POSITIVE TRAITS: Guiding, realistic, down-to-earth

NEGATIVE TRAITS: Dictating, insistent, unimaginative

You are clear-eyed and practical, able to see the forest and the trees. Your no-nonsense approach to everyday roadblocks makes you an invaluable team player. Friends and coworkers seek out your sage advice when they're in trouble, even when you insist they face facts, waving the evidence in their faces! Enjoy their thanks, but at the same time be careful not to meddle too much in others' personal lives. You are a caring and steady partner who takes relationships one step at a time, choosing long-term commitment over one-night stands. Your ideal mate is a creative and romantic lover who appreciates your down-to-earth qualities. Cultivate this contrast: Your complementary natures will surely keep the romance alive.

December 7

ASTROLOGICAL SIGN: Sagittarius

PEOPLE BORN TODAY: Larry Bird, Tom Waits, Ellen Burstyn, Johnny Bench, Noam Chomsky, Ted Knight, Willa Cather, Harry Chapin, Roy Cameron

FAMOUS EVENTS: James Madison elected president (1803); Pearl Harbor, Hawaii, attacked by Japan (1941); last American moon mission, *Apollo XVII*, launched (1972)

LUCKY NUMBER: 1

BIRTHSTONE: Turquoise

POSITIVE TRAITS: Independent, original, distinctive

NEGATIVE TRAITS: Quirky, isolated, rejecting

You are a true trendsetter, writing your own rule book as you go. A free thinker in the workplace or on the social scene, you may startle others by your pioneering style, but a long history of successes is your best ally. You tend to be a loner, but at parties and other social gatherings your uniquely colorful personality keeps you from blending into the woodwork. Loyal friends are usually content to ride along on your daring coattails; don't forget to thank them for their steadiness and support. Romance seems to find you even though you don't seek it out, and you can forge a powerful partnership with a mate who respects your independence and refuses to cramp your style.

December 8

ASTROLOGICAL SIGN: Sagittarius

PEOPLE BORN TODAY: Sinead O'Connor, Teri Hatcher, Kim Basinger, John Rubinstein, Jim Morrison, Sammy Davis Jr., James Thurber, David Carradine

FAMOUS EVENTS: First Shakespearean role played by an actress (1660); war on Japan declared by U.S., Great Britain, and Australia (1941); John Lennon shot to death in front of his New York City apartment building (1980)

LUCKY NUMBER: 2

BIRTHSTONE: Turquoise

POSITIVE TRAITS: Attractive, charismatic, stirring

NEGATIVE TRAITS: Misguided, muddled, mercurial

You sparkle with energy and appeal, turning heads and making a definite impact wherever you go. Your naturally sunny disposition draws many friends; it's up to you to separate the kindred spirits from the social butterflies. When an opportunity crops up, you jump on it, but though you're usually the first one out of the starting blocks, you sometimes lose your wind rounding the first turn. Build up your long-distance stamina: Select new projects carefully and then practice following through. You'll win more points for dependability than for mere enthusiasm. True romance may find you almost by accident: Pay close attention to the shy ones. Squeaky wheels may get the grease, but are they worth all that pain and heartache?

December 9

ASTROLOGICAL SIGN: Sagittarius
PEOPLE BORN TODAY: John Malkovich, Joan Armatrading, Beau Bridges, Dick Butkus, Kirk Douglas, Redd Foxx, John Milton, World B Free, Buck Henry
FAMOUS EVENTS: First Christmas cards sent (1843); Lynda Johnson wed to Charles Robb at White House (1967); separation of Prince Charles and Princess Diana announced by Prime Minister John Major (1992)
LUCKY NUMBER: 3
BIRTHSTONE: Turquoise
POSITIVE TRAITS: Intense, ardent, compelling
NEGATIVE TRAITS: Disdainful, insulting, self-satisfied

You burn brightly with the fervor of your convictions; even the rough road of progress doesn't faze you. As a born leader, your biggest challenge is patience: Cultivate the listener in yourself. Learn when to push forward with new ideas and suggestions, and when to step aside and merely observe. You'll be amazed at the response from friends and coworkers when they know you are giving them equal time and attention. Your emotional intensity can be fascinating to romantic partners, although your ideal mate may be one who tempers your fire and shows you the quieter, private side of life. Stay in touch with old friends and family members: The bonds you share can smooth your ride on the roller coaster of life.

December 10

PEOPLE BORN TODAY: Kenneth Branagh, Susan Dey, Gloria Loring, Harold Gould, Chet Huntley, Emily Dickinson

FAMOUS EVENTS: President Theodore Roosevelt given first Nobel Peace Prize awarded to an American (1906); Ralph Bunche given first Nobel Peace Prize awarded to an African-American (1950); Otis Redding killed in plane crash (1967)

LUCKY NUMBER: 4

BIRTHSTONE: Turquoise

POSITIVE TRAITS: Introspective, secure, devoted

NEGATIVE TRAITS: Elusive, unrevealing, guarded

You have a remarkable strength of spirit that shields you from the vicissitudes of fortune. Cautious to the core, you can be slow to make friends, but when you do discover a kindred spirit, your innate warmth removes all roadblocks to friendship. You share your most heartfelt wishes and dreams with a close circle of friends and loved ones who appreciate your earnestness and your distaste for gossip. With romantic partners you are attentive and affectionate, but you sometimes put potential mates through a battery of emotional tests before opening your heart to them. You're only as old as you feel: Kick off your shoes and toss your hat into the air. A little craziness can be good for the soul.

ASTROLOGICAL SIGN: Sagittarius

PEOPLE BORN TODAY: Jermaine Jackson, Bess Armstrong, Teri Garr, Jean-Louis Trintignant, Grace Paley, Alexander Solzhenitsyn, Christina Onassis

FAMOUS EVENTS: Indiana becomes the 19th state (1816); first dental procedure performed with anesthesia (1844); first public basketball game played (1892); British throne abdicated by Edward VIII (1936)

LUCKY NUMBER: 5

BIRTHSTONE: Turquoise

POSITIVE TRAITS: Influential, charming, persuasive

NEGATIVE TRAITS: Needy, manipulative, social-climbing

You combine persistence with charm, making sure your voice is heard and your vote is counted. Being in the spotlight makes you purr like a contented cat: You excel in social situations and are happiest with all eyes turned in your direction. Your proven strategy for advancing your agenda—whether personal or professional—is to cultivate influential contacts, the movers and shakers in your world. This works well in most cases, but don't ignore the smaller voices around you: When the chips are down you may find that the best help comes from unlikely sources. You are an inveterate charmer, but don't sacrifice honesty to get results: Double-check yourself in romantic situations to be sure you're saying exactly what you feel.

December 12

PEOPLE BORN TODAY: Mayim Bialik, Tracy Austin, Grover Washington Jr., Dionne Warwick, Joe Williams, Frank Sinatra, Gustave Flaubert

FAMOUS EVENTS: First transatlantic radio transmission received by Guglielmo Marconi (1901); land for United Nations headquarters donated by John D. Rockefeller (1946); Jerry Lee Lewis and thirteen-year-old cousin Myra wed (1957)

LUCKY NUMBER: 6

BIRTHSTONE: Turquoise

POSITIVE TRAITS: Vital, loyal, committed

NEGATIVE TRAITS: Stubborn, temperamental, grudging

You throw yourself body and soul into projects and relationships. Such total commitment requires that you maintain the mental and physical fitness to perform at peak level. Colleagues and friends may envy your ability to focus and even try to match you at it: Take the time to encourage them and you'll likely earn their everlasting loyalty. Romance pursues you even if you aren't looking for it: Don't let your close attention to projects blind you to the possibilities of love. Once settled with a mate, however, you're likely to give the relationship your all, taking full responsibility for success, or full blame for failure. Don't be too hard on yourself: Learn to shrug your shoulders and move on with your life.

December 13

PEOPLE BORN TODAY: John Davidson, Christopher Plummer, Dick Van Dyke, Archie Moore, Carlos Montoya, Mary Todd Lincoln

FAMOUS EVENTS: First savings bank opens (1816); first presidential visit to Europe made by President Woodrow Wilson (1918); U.S.–Mexico border redefined by President Lyndon Johnson and President Gustavo Diaz Ordaz (1964); first Susan B. Anthony dollar coins minted (1978)

LUCKY NUMBER: 7

BIRTHSTONE: Turquoise

POSITIVE TRAITS: Precise, knowledgeable, enlightening

NEGATIVE TRAITS: Exacting, picayune, unyielding

You set high standards and demand perfection, both for yourself and for others. As a boss or leader, your demands can seem almost impossible, but subordinates give 100 percent or more in hopes of winning your approval and coming a little closer to your example. Friends appreciate your succinct advice on business and finance as well as personal matters, though they sometimes wish they could escape your exacting eye. In the first flush of romance, your partner can do no wrong, but as time goes on, resist the natural urge to criticize; patience and understanding will build a more enduring relationship. If loved ones measure up in the most important ways, lay aside your yardstick for judging their day-to-day behavior.

December 14

ASTROLOGICAL SIGN: Sagittarius
PEOPLE BORN TODAY: Patty Duke, Michael Ovitz, Stan Smith, George Furth, Morey Amsterdam, Lee Remick, Spike Jones, Charlie Rich
FAMOUS EVENTS: Screw patented (1798); Alabama becomes 22nd state (1819); expedition led by Roald Amundsen reaches South Pole (1911); Jack Johnson becomes first African-American world heavyweight boxing champion (1915)
LUCKY NUMBER: 8
BIRTHSTONE: Turquoise
POSITIVE TRAITS: Creative, original, stylish
NEGATIVE TRAITS: Lonely, depressed, unsociable

You possess unique tastes and objectives that set you apart from the crowd. Seek out organizations and groups that give you leave to express yourself without interference or censorship. Entertaining friends at home in your own high style will probably be more satisfying than learning to mingle at big parties. Your customary cheerfulness, while seemingly invincible, may be quickly dampened by sharp criticism, so take steps to strengthen your self-esteem: It's the most loyal friend you can have. Romantic partners rely on you to support their impulsive ideas, and you always manage to make them feel special. Remember to get out and share your gifts; the appreciation you receive will remind you that you're an original, not an oddball.

December 15

ASTROLOGICAL SIGN: Sagittarius
PEOPLE BORN TODAY: Helen Slater, Edna O'Brien, Don Johnson, Tim Conway, John Hammond, Alan Freed, J. Paul Getty
FAMOUS EVENTS: *Gone with the Wind* premieres in Atlanta (1939); disappearance of bandleader Glenn Miller over the English Channel (1944); first sex-change operation, on Christine Jorgenson (1952)
LUCKY NUMBER: 9
BIRTHSTONE: Turquoise
POSITIVE TRAITS: Popular, broad-minded, optimistic
NEGATIVE TRAITS: Changeable, irresolute, dominating

You delight in expanding your own horizons and broadening the outlook of others. Your pioneering curiosity looks at objects and ideas from all sides, and when you unearth new sources of enlightenment, you excitedly point them out to colleagues and friends. The zeal you bring to learning and sharing these treasures makes you an effective teacher, whether you're training coworkers or talking to children. Although others are inspired by your infectious optimism, don't let their expectations overpower your own sense of self: Keep tabs on your personal needs. Your ideal partner is one who shares your zest for life and appreciates your independence. Be sure to focus extra attention on your loved ones, letting them know they rank highest on your list.

December 16

ASTROLOGICAL SIGN: Sagittarius

PEOPLE BORN TODAY: Alison LaPlaca, Ben Cross, Lesley Stahl, Liv Ullman, Noel Coward, Ludwig van Beethoven, Jane Austen, Margaret Mead

FAMOUS EVENTS: Boston Tea Party (1775); Missouri struck by major earthquake (1811); first issue of *Variety* published (1905)

LUCKY NUMBER: 1

BIRTHSTONE: Turquoise

POSITIVE TRAITS: Perceptive, compassionate, creative

NEGATIVE TRAITS: Detached, cynical, isolated

You observe those around you with the fascinated detachment of an anthropologist. Coworkers, friends, and strangers all come under your sharp-eyed scrutiny, yet you manage to balance your analytical side with genuine compassion for your fellow human beings. Working within the structure of a team suits you better than laboring solo, but at social gatherings, you are more comfortable entertaining a small group with funny stories than mingling out on the floor. You are probably much too pragmatic to lose your head at the first sign of romance, but your perceptive nature makes you a fair and forgiving mate. Remember that life is not a research laboratory: In love as well as friendship, some things are best left unexamined.

December 17

Just the facts, ma'am" could be your personal motto. You are dependable and literal-minded, saying exactly what you mean and insisting that others do the same. You thrive in a structured environment, and if your home or workplace is in temporary disarray you can be counted on to put it in apple-pie order. This organizational talent is good for keeping in touch with old friends, although usually you end up doing all of the scheduling and legwork. Your innate sincerity and steady temperament hold the interest of romantic partners, but don't let a comfortable relationship become a grind: Vary the routine now and then by taking an impulsive trip or treating yourself to a night on the town.

December 18

ASTROLOGICAL SIGN: Sagittarius

PEOPLE BORN TODAY: Brad Pitt, Ray Liotta, Charles Oakley, Steven Spielberg, Leonard Maltin, Betty Grable, Kiefer Sutherland, Ozzie Davis

FAMOUS EVENTS: Mother Goose stories first published in English (1719); golf tee patented (1899); death of Marcel Proust (1922); Keith Richards and Patti Hansen wed (1983)

LUCKY NUMBER: 3

BIRTHSTONE: Turquoise

POSITIVE TRAITS: Quick-witted, curious, versatile

NEGATIVE TRAITS: Fickle, unsure, unfocused

You are a sponge for information and impressions. You learn quickly, soaking up facts and mastering skills in record time. Although the ideas that spill from your lips may not always linger in your brain, your skill in verbalizing new concepts makes you invaluable as a member of a team. If you sometimes feel you are getting nowhere in work and life, look to your steadier, slower-moving pals to throw you an anchor and shore up your self-esteem. Your social calendar is always full, but romance can be elusive due to your ever-evolving concept of the ideal partner. Don't demand perfection in a relationship: Your mate should be able to offer you emotional fulfillment without cramping your personal style.

December 19

ASTROLOGICAL SIGN: Sagittarius
PEOPLE BORN TODAY: Alyssa Milano, Jennifer Beals, Tim Reid, Maurice White, Cicely Tyson, Edith Piaf, Jean Genet, Reggie White
FAMOUS EVENTS: First issue of *Poor Richard's Almanac* published by Benjamin Franklin (1732); Charles Dickens's *A Christmas Carol* published (1843); Donald Trump and Marla Maples wed (1993)
LUCKY NUMBER: 4
BIRTHSTONE: Turquoise
POSITIVE TRAITS: Strong, persistent, sensitive
NEGATIVE TRAITS: Overemotional, easily hurt, depressive

Your great sensitivity conceals even greater inner strength. When criticism from associates or friends stings you sharply, you don't bother to hide your feelings. While others may mistake your tears for weakness, however, you actually thrive on this outpouring of emotion, emerging even stronger than before. In the professional world your revealing honesty may work against you: Learn to step back and reassess before "losing it." Close friends serve as a vital support network for you, and you return their caring with unswerving loyalty. You are a flirtatious romantic partner and a sensitive mate, though lovers' quarrels can send you into week-long funks. Save your Richter-scale responses for major quakes and try to take the tremors in stride.

December 20

ASTROLOGICAL SIGN: Sagittarius
PEOPLE BORN TODAY: Peter Criss, Uri Geller, Nadine Gordimer, George Roy Hill, Irene Dunne, Branch Rickey, Hazel Hotchkiss Wightman
FAMOUS EVENTS: Pilgrims set sail from England for America (1606); U.S. purchases Louisiana Territory from France (1803); incandescent lamp demonstrated by Thomas Edison (1879)
LUCKY NUMBER: 5
BIRTHSTONE: Turquoise
POSITIVE TRAITS: Efficient, result-oriented, direct
NEGATIVE TRAITS: Impatient, short-tempered, sloppy

You are quick to seize opportunities or act on inspirations; you are just as likely, however, to fly off the handle at criticism. Your strong suit is understanding the "big picture": When you know you're on track, don't let the naysayers shut you down. Although your results-oriented approach may draw criticism as well as praise, you are an effective organizer at work and in personal affairs, especially with a support staff to dot your i's and cross your t's. Potential mates are enchanted by your directness and snappy style, but your short fuse may threaten a long-running union. Curb your customary impatience when it comes to love and friendship: Learn to appreciate the slow burn as well as the fireworks.

December 21

ASTROLOGICAL SIGN: Sagittarius

PEOPLE BORN TODAY: Florence Griffith Joyner, Chris Evert, Jane Fonda, Phil Donahue, Paul Winchell, Frank Zappa

FAMOUS EVENTS: First feature-length silent movie released (1914); first animated feature, *Snow White and the Seven Dwarfs*, premieres (1937); first Moon shot launched into orbit, *Apollo VIII* (1968)

LUCKY NUMBER: 6

BIRTHSTONE: Turquoise

POSITIVE TRAITS: Determined, competitive, motivated

NEGATIVE TRAITS: Domineering, egotistical, unrelenting

You are highly motivated, going to great lengths to prove yourself or get your point across. Competitive by nature, you usually prefer a no-holds-barred battle to a pleasant chat. This makes you a terrific persuader, but a sometimes difficult companion. Pick your fights carefully: Although loved ones may enjoy engaging in issue-oriented discussions, don't ruin a friendship by pushing too hard. In romance you may swing wildly from like-minded partners to direct opposites, but either one can probably fill the bill. A feisty mate will keep you on your toes; a quieter one will temper your fire with a devoted steadiness. Focus on ultimate goals, but don't forget to thank those who gave you help along the way.

December 22

ASTROLOGICAL SIGN: Capricorn

PEOPLE BORN TODAY: Lauralee Bell, Jan Stephenson, twins Maurice and Robin Gibb, Diane Sawyer, Steve Carlton, Claudia "Lady Bird" Johnson, Steve Garvey

FAMOUS EVENTS: First electric Christmas tree lights used (1882); official mourning period for President Kennedy ends (1963); crew of USS *Pueblo* released from captivity by North Korea (1968)

LUCKY NUMBER: 7

BIRTHSTONE: Garnet

POSITIVE TRAITS: Poised, sophisticated, capable

NEGATIVE TRAITS: Self-righteous, complacent, superior

You are accustomed to being in the winner's circle and sometimes feel that this is your birthright. You carry yourself with well-earned poise and self-assurance, accustomed to success and comfortable as a role model for others. Complacency can be a trap, however, and difficult challenges may leave you dismayed. Now is the time to review the high standards you set for yourself: Don't be afraid to suggest teamwork on a tricky project. True friendship depends on mutual trust, so let down your guard now and then to show loved ones that you're only human. You attract romantic prospects as accomplished as yourself, and together you may build a relationship that offers refuge from the pressures of the outside world.

December 23

ASTROLOGICAL SIGN: Capricorn

PEOPLE BORN TODAY: Corey Haim, Slash, Susan Lucci, Harry Shearer, Robert Bly, Harry Guardino

FAMOUS EVENTS: Clement Clarke Moore poem *A Visit from St. Nicholas* first published (1823); Vincent van Gogh cuts off his ear (1888); former Japanese prime minister Tojo hanged for war crimes (1948)

LUCKY NUMBER: 8

BIRTHSTONE: Garnet

POSITIVE TRAITS: Hardworking, resilient, inner-directed

NEGATIVE TRAITS: Controlling, rigid, overworked

You often feel that the pursuit of excellence is its own reward, plugging away relentlessly whether or not your efforts are noticed. If you're passed over for a project or promotion, you hardly miss a beat, more attuned to personal satisfaction than to public adulation. Your efforts to help friends achieve similar success are usually well-received, but some may resist, feeling pushed toward your goals rather than their own. Cultivate a tolerance for individuality: Using a shoehorn to fit others to your own program may lead to painful blisters. Your inner security is a great asset in romance: By being true to yourself you attract the right mate, and with patience and flexibility you'll keep the fires of love burning brightly.

December 24

ASTROLOGICAL SIGN: Capricorn

PEOPLE BORN TODAY: Bill Rogers, Mary Higgins Clark, Ava Gardner, Robert Joffrey, Howard Hughes, Nostradamus

FAMOUS EVENTS: Treaty of Ghent signed, ending War of 1812 (1814); fire at the Library of Congress in Washington, D.C., destroys two-thirds of the collection (1852); Enrico Caruso gives his last performance, at the Metropolitan Opera (1920)

LUCKY NUMBER: 9

BIRTHSTONE: Garnet

POSITIVE TRAITS: Farsighted, ambitious, innovative

NEGATIVE TRAITS: Premature, discouraged, withdrawn

You have a gift for seeing far into the future, and a talent for living today by tomorrow's methods. If projects near and dear to your heart fall flat, leaving you depressed and discouraged, pick yourself up, brush yourself off, and start again. You may ultimately be applauded as a visionary. Staying connected to a wide network of forward-looking friends is vital for keeping your spirits up and your expectations at a realistic level. Romantic partners find you thrilling and adventurous, if slightly eccentric. In a long-term partnership, you crave emotional support from your mate as well as occasional spells of solitude to cook up new schemes. Leave the couch potatoes in your dust: "Dynamic" is your middle name.

December 25

ASTROLOGICAL SIGN: Capricorn

PEOPLE BORN TODAY: Anwar Sadat, Carlos Castaneda, Jimmy Buffett, Annie Lennox, Clara Barton, Ken Stabler, Humphrey Bogart

FAMOUS EVENTS: First recorded celebration of Christmas on this date (A.D. 336); General Washington and troops cross the Delaware (1776); Hirohito crowned emperor of Japan (1926)

LUCKY NUMBER: 1

BIRTHSTONE: Garnet

POSITIVE TRAITS: Idealistic, visionary, sublime

NEGATIVE TRAITS: Weird, unrealistic, demanding

You dare to envision a perfect world and you do your utmost to make it real. Naysayers may label your high-minded view naive, but you would rather prove them wrong than waste your breath arguing. At work and at home, learn to temper your demands on others with a clear understanding of human nature; unreasonable expectations can make for a lonely road. You gravitate toward companions who believe in you and support your goals, but even those who question your idealism find it intriguing. In romance you are happiest with a mate who shares your visionary outlook and places spiritual aspirations above material ones. The key is balance: Enjoy the clouds, but keep your feet firmly on the ground.

ASTROLOGICAL SIGN: Capricorn

PEOPLE BORN TODAY: Phil Spector, Carlton Fisk, Alan King, Steve Allen, Henry Miller, Mao Ze Dong, Ozzie Smith, Glenn David

FAMOUS EVENTS: Percolating coffee pot invented by James Nason (1865); Clare Booth Luce's drama *The Women* opens on Broadway and runs for 657 performances (1936)

LUCKY NUMBER: 2

BIRTHSTONE: Garnet

POSITIVE TRAITS: Strong, courageous, patient

NEGATIVE TRAITS: Bossy, domineering, rigid

You push yourself forward with plenty of oomph, but once you reach a destination you plant yourself and refuse to budge. You may drive nonstop to a top position in business or society, then devote your energies to sustaining this vantage for the rest of your days. Perseverance is your strong point; security your constant goal. Practice the art of compromise: Often the greatest forward progress requires giving up some ground. Friends rely on you for moral support and transfusions of your abundant courage; your momentum alone inspires them more than you know. Romantic partners find you dynamic, though their appreciation of you may waver if they feel you're trying to change them. Remember that flexibility is as important as fortitude.

December 27

ASTROLOGICAL SIGN: Capricorn

PEOPLE BORN TODAY: Tovah Feldshuh, Cokie Roberts, Gérard Depardieu, Marlene Dietrich, Anna Russell, Louis Pasteur

FAMOUS EVENTS: First public train with steam locomotive makes trip (1825); first performance of *Show Boat* (1927); first show at Radio City Music Hall (1932).

LUCKY NUMBER: 3

BIRTHSTONE: Garnet

POSITIVE TRAITS: Clever, witty, generous

NEGATIVE TRAITS: Repressed, frustrated, self-blaming

Your natural wit and charm win the hearts of many, though privately you may be dogged by self-doubt. You set—and meet—ambitious standards for yourself in professional and personal dealings, so when praise is offered, accept it graciously as well-deserved. If a rainstorm of insecurity threatens your parade, don't be afraid to seek reassurance and encouragement from a mentor. You are a dependable friend with a delightfully wry sense of humor, able to evoke laughter amid a cloud of complaints. In romance, your passion for the unconventional may attract some wild characters at first, but you are happiest in the long term with a mate who projects poise and respectability while remaining supportive of all your emotional colors.

December 28

ASTROLOGICAL SIGN: Capricorn

PEOPLE BORN TODAY: Denzel Washington, Hubie Green, Edgar Winter, Dame Maggie Smith, Earl "Fatha" Hines, Woodrow Wilson, Lew Ayres, Ray Knight

FAMOUS EVENTS: Iowa becomes 29th state (1846); William Semple patents chewing gum (1869); Muriel Siebert becomes the first woman to own a seat on the New York Stock Exchange (1967)

LUCKY NUMBER: 4

BIRTHSTONE: Garnet

POSITIVE TRAITS: Purposeful, confident, crisp

NEGATIVE TRAITS: Unemotional, solitary, serious

You impress others with your no-nonsense approach and clear sense of direction. Capable in a crisis, you'll take the helm at a moment's notice, even in the roughest of seas. This decisiveness serves you well in private as well as professional matters, but be careful that your independent streak doesn't alienate loved ones or coworkers. Leave ample room for teamwork: You never know when you may need an ally. You rarely indulge in idle flirtation, but you wisely try to balance your own serious nature by seeking spice and adventure in romance. Friendship may sometimes seem an option rather than a necessity, but true kindred spirits won't let you hibernate: They spy the warmth and kindness beneath your cool-headed exterior.

December 29

ASTROLOGICAL SIGN: Capricorn

PEOPLE BORN TODAY: Gelsey Kirkland, Marianne Faithfull, Ted Danson, Mary Tyler Moore, Tom Jarriel, Pablo Casals, Andrew Johnson, Jon Voight

FAMOUS EVENTS: Texas becomes 28th state (1845); first YMCA founded in America (1851); massacre at Wounded Knee (1890); Fred Newton swims Mississippi River (1930); Princess Caroline of Monaco and Stefano Casiraghi wed (1983)

LUCKY NUMBER: 5

BIRTHSTONE: Garnet

POSITIVE TRAITS: Industrious, optimistic, romantic

NEGATIVE TRAITS: Unrealistic, overambitious, workaholic

You're a true romantic, seeking your ultimate happiness from personal relationships, even though projects and enterprises are your most constant companions. You're in great demand because of your competence and adaptability, and since you find it hard to say no, be careful you don't overload yourself. Friends and family appreciate your always sympathetic ear; if one of their wild schemes piques your interest, indulge yourself by joining in—you deserve it. Your professional demeanor attracts earnest suitors who prefer sunshine to a stormy relationship, and your ability to keep personal and professional spheres separate enables you to work side-by-side with your partner. Safeguard your need for solitude, however, and seek out ways to stoke the passion that brought you together.

December 30

ASTROLOGICAL SIGN: Capricorn

PEOPLE BORN TODAY: Tracey Ullman, Jeff Lynne, Davy Jones, Mike Nesmith, Sandy Koufax, Bo Diddley, Rudyard Kipling, Paul Bowles

FAMOUS EVENTS: First California freeway opens (1940); minting of Kennedy half-dollar authorized by Congress (1963); bombing of Hanoi in Vietnam War halted by President Richard Nixon (1972)

LUCKY NUMBER: 6

BIRTHSTONE: Garnet

POSITIVE TRAITS: Incisive, funny, prudent

NEGATIVE TRAITS: Laconic, reserved, misunderstood

You are a person of few words, but when you do express yourself you're likely to stun listeners with your perceptiveness and incisive humor. In social or professional settings, you prefer to take in the scenery, holding your tongue until you can comment intelligently and with impact. Casual acquaintances may misjudge you as disinterested, but intimates consider you one of their most charming friends. In romance, your laid-back demeanor means you usually set your line and wait for a bite, rather than casting or trolling. Don't let the big fish get away: Complacency could spell heartbreak. You may not be demonstrative in public, but you are sensuous and responsive in private. Reserve ample time for passion and communication in your relationship.

December 31

ASTROLOGICAL SIGN: Capricorn

PEOPLE BORN TODAY: Val Kilmer, Donna Summer, Patti Smith, Diane von Furstenberg, Sir Anthony Hopkins, Henri Matisse

FAMOUS EVENTS: First New Year's Eve broadcast by Guy Lombardo and the Royal Canadians (1929); end of World War II officially proclaimed by President Harry Truman (1946); John Lennon, George Harrison, and Ringo Starr sued by Paul McCartney to legally dissolve Beatles partnership (1970)

LUCKY NUMBER: 7

BIRTHSTONE: Garnet

POSITIVE TRAITS: Individualistic, assured, rational

NEGATIVE TRAITS: Isolated, reluctant, limiting

Your impeccable taste and confident opinions attract admirers wherever you go. Others may choose you to be their spokesperson: Accept the honor, though it may occasionally hamper your ability to tackle the projects at hand. The epitome of modesty, you never grab for more than you feel you deserve: Even a life in the spotlight won't tarnish this innate honesty. Loved ones look to you for guidance as well as companionship, and though you may resent this extra responsibility, you maintain intimate friendships even while taking the reins of leadership. Your individualism can give romantic suitors a mistaken image of you as a free spirit, but long-term mates will discover that you hold some surprisingly traditional values and aspirations.